AMERICAN ZEUS

AMERICAN ZEUS

*The Life of
Alexander Pantages,
Theater Mogul*

Taso G. Lagos

McFarland & Company, Inc., Publishers
Jefferson, North Carolina

LIBRARY OF CONGRESS CATALOGUING-IN-PUBLICATION DATA

Names: Lagos, Anastasios George author.
Title: American zeus : the life of Alexander Pantages, theater mogul / Taso G. Lagos.
Description: Jefferson, North Carolina : McFarland & Company, Inc., Publishers, 2018. | Includes bibliographical references and index.
Identifiers: LCCN 2017052161 | ISBN 9781476668383 (softcover : acid free paper) ∞
Subjects: LCSH: Pantages, Alexander, 1867–1936. | Motion picture theater owners—United States—Biography. | Theatrical producers and directors—United States—Biography. | Businessmen—United States—Biography.
Classification: LCC PN1998.3.P3537 L34 2017 | DDC 792.02/32092 [B] —dc23
LC record available at https://lccn.loc.gov/2017052161

BRITISH LIBRARY CATALOGUING DATA ARE AVAILABLE

ISBN (print) 978-1-4766-6838-3
ISBN (ebook) 978-1-4766-3037-3

© 2018 Taso G. Lagos. All rights reserved

No part of this book may be reproduced or transmitted in any form or by any means, electronic or mechanical, including photocopying or recording, or by any information storage and retrieval system, without permission in writing from the publisher.

Front cover photograph: Alexander Pantages, 1910 (University of Washington Libraries, Special Collections, UW2242)

Printed in the United States of America

McFarland & Company, Inc., Publishers
  Box 611, Jefferson, North Carolina 28640
  www.mcfarlandpub.com

To Nektaria and Elisabeth

Contents

Acknowledgments ix
Preface 1
Introduction 7

1. Beginnings   17
2. Apprenticeship   35
3. Mogulhood   56
4. Mt. Olympus   78
5. 1929   101
6. Mogul's Trial   129
7. Aftermath   153
8. Wrap-Up   170

Chapter Notes 179
Bibliography 203
Index 209

Acknowledgments

The inspiration to write this biography of Alexander Pantages came from a Greek-American friend, Nick Arkhon: On a working trip in Alaska and a sightseeing tour of Denali Park and its museum, he came across a photo of Alexander Pantages and wondered what a Greek was doing in Alaska during its Gold Rush. Nick asked me that very question, suggesting I do research on the man. I dismissed the idea; I was in graduate school then and there were not enough hours in the day for another project. But when doing research on my Master's thesis on early motion picture history in Seattle, Pantages appeared on numerous occasions and I became interested.

I dug more into Pantages—how at the age of nine he suddenly and shockingly left his father on a business trip in Cairo, Egypt, hopped on a cargo ship and never returned to his native Greece. By the mid–1920s, he commanded one of the great theater circuits in America, and was a millionaire many times over. I also came across his famous 1929 rape trial where he was accused of molesting a 17-year-old dancer. It was an extraordinary story, with apparently little written about him, despite his enormous contribution to the development of motion picture theaters.

What followed were years of research, writing, more research, more writing. Yet the more material I gathered, the more enigmatic he became. Since I am not a forensics expert, I had to put aside determining his guilt or innocence of the assault charges; I focused instead on the myths and distortions that flew around the case. The story is not about one man and his sensational trial, but rather a snapshot of a momentous moment in a nation struggling to come to terms with its immigrants that still echoes today.

Many folks helped to bring the Pantages research to fruition. I am indebted to the University of Washington and its extraordinary Suzzallo/Allen Library staff for their thoughtful and always cheerful assistance, in particular, Glenda Pearson (now retired), Terry Kato and Jessica Albano of Newspaper Archives who were a key part of my research and whose encouragement still warms my heart. Professor and Executive Provost of the UW, Dr. Jerry Baldasty, provided thoughtful suggestions in shaping the original research. Without the assistance of the staff of UW Special Collections, this book would still be a hope. Several UW undergraduate students also assisted in the research, and I am grateful to Ashley Whitlatch, Karin Wagner, Grace MacMillan, Kimberly Evans, Jerimiah Keller and Sue Ellen White. If I missed any student from this pool, my deepest apologies.

I am thankful for the encouragement I received from the Modern Greek Studies Association, including the editors and blind reviewers of its *Journal of Modern Greek Studies*, particularly Professor Maria Koundoura of Emerson College who edited my first published piece on Pantages for the *Journal*. Professor Yiorgios Anagnostou of Ohio State University was another important supporter, not only in conversations about the Pantages research but also in the immense intellectual debt I owe to his work on "white ethnicity." Professor Alexander Kitroeff of Haverford College is another influence whose work on Greek-America studies helped to shape my work and who was kind enough to read my manuscript. Much thanks also goes to Dan Georgakas, a stellar light in the work and knowledge he has contributed about Greek-America diaspora history, who also read the manuscript. My sister and distinguished professor at California State University, Sacramento, Dr. Katerina Lagos, gave me advice early on in my path towards publication. My brother, Demetre Lagos, as well as my parents, George Lagos and Helen Lagos, were staunch enthusiasts of my work.

My mentor and graduate school advisor, and who I can perhaps now call a friend, W. Lance Bennett, distinguished professor at the University of Washington, stands as my inspiration, both academically and spiritually, for my approach to academic research, publication and general life. He was, and remains, a teacher of wisdom, integrity and discernment, as well as a guiding light for other scholars—young and old—who undertake the perilous path towards serious academic work, and all the challenges and triumphs this entails.

For my longest-running friend, Mark Rosman, I treasure both his companionship as well as his suggestion to begin the story on the night of the grand opening of the Hollywood Pantages theater. It was the inspiration needed to make sense of the story.

S.T. Joshi was an early and steadfast supporter of the project; his enthusiasm for it sustained me through many a difficult moment. Thanks also to Philip Haldeman, writer, classic-car enthusiast, and publisher who graciously offered to publish the manuscript if "no one else would."

Lastly, I am indebted to Dr. Nektaria G. Klapaki and our daughter Elisabeth for providing me the inspiration and courage to continue working on the project when prudence would have told me to give up. Without their presence and sustaining love, the journey towards publication (if not my life) would have been a lonely and empty exercise. Dreams come true, but they are better and richer when you are not alone.

There are many other anonymous folks in the journey to final publication who gave me encouragement and succor, both small and timely, and to them I am deeply grateful.

And highest thanks of all, to you the reader, for imbibing in this work. All great dreams need witnesses, and now you are mine!

Preface

The constellation of movie stars rivaled the Academy Awards. The "sparklers of cinema," as the *Los Angeles Times* called them, arrived in their stretch limousines at the corner of Hollywood and Argyle for the grand opening of the Hollywood Pantages Theatre on June 4, 1930.¹ "The recent absence of such premieres," the *Times* noted, reflecting the nation's growing economic woes, "caused it to be an event and the maximum of resplendence therefore attended."² Resplendence indeed: Mary Pickford and Douglas Fairbanks, Greta Garbo, Buster Keaton, Maurice Chevalier, Louis B. Mayer, Irving Thalberg, Howard Hughes, Irving Berlin, Carl Laemmle and Eddie Cantor as master of ceremonies.

The Hollywood Pantages "will be a new and magnetic goal for the seeker of entertainment," the *Times* promised.³ The magnet already revealed itself that night—all 2703 seats were filled. If the United States headed into "economic nihilism," as the Great Depression promised, the gala opening was an act of courage and defiance.⁴ Movie ticket sales plunged in the early 1930s, and Hollywood studios, those wondrous factories producing hope and cheer, experienced serious gloom for the first time in their brief history.

Meanwhile, the man who envisioned, financed and built the "first great Art Deco movie palace" (designed by longtime Pantages associate and brilliant architect, B. Marcus Priteca), the one who for many was the epitome of theatrical showmanship and the very embodiment of the rags-to-riches American Dream, lay on a hard bed in the hospital wing of Los Angeles County Jail as a convicted felon suffering from chest pains.⁵

Only seven months earlier, on October 27, 1929, two days before Wall Street famously laid its rotten egg, Alexander Pantages was tried, convicted and sentenced to 50 years in San Quentin for sexually assaulting a 17-year-old dancer, Eunice Alice Pringle. It was a stunning outcome for

The grand opening of the Hollywood Pantages Theater on June 4, 1930 (*Marc Wanamaker, Bison Archives*).

one of America's most powerful theater magnates and a true motion picture theater pioneer. He started with one tiny storefront theater in Seattle in 1902, and by the 1920s had fashioned a great North American theater chain that stretched from the West Coast to New Jersey and into Canada. Yet he could not read or write English.

His Greek immigrant background ("that illiterate Greek peasant" as one Hollywood chronicler put it) likely played a role in his conviction, although few at the time admitted it.[6] Others saw a morality tale of the comeuppance of a man who left a trail of broken hearts and unhappy business associates. Pantages claimed he was framed, although he refused to name names. That was left to Hollywood wags, who filled in the blank with none other than Joseph P. Kennedy, doyen of an emerging American "royal" family and father of a future American president, who wanted Pantages' theaters for his own RKO movie studios.

It was convincing. "Hollywood," film star Joan Crawford tartly observed, "[that place] where gossip flourishes like fungus in a swamp."[7] Whatever the rumor's veracity, it gave Pantages some solace since at least within the movie colony (certainly not in public opinion), he was the victim and not the sexual predator that Pringle claimed. Pringle's daughter today insists that her mother was raped.[8]

This is a cultural biography of Alexander Pantages' unique life and extraordinary career in the motion picture and vaudeville theater business. His journey encompasses several lives squeezed into one: from growing up on the small Greek island of Andros, to running away from home at nine, to back-stressing low-skill jobs, to his first taste of theater management during the Alaska Gold Rush, and to growing his theatrical empire. Cultural in that it contextualizes his extraordinary journey from obscurity to the height of business prowess, and focuses on that part of the American experience in the early twentieth century that saw immigrants like him transform the once marginalized art-form of movies into an important industry.

Cultural also in that it examines the unique if not distorted lenses of the nation's presses; more specifically, the realm of "narratives," or the storylines that journalists employ to make sense of daily events. There has always been a tension between factual, "objective" reporting on the one hand and capturing the reader's attention and imagination on the other. Partisanship in newspapers is not unique; the nation's first newspaper, *Publick Occurrences* in 1690, accused the French king of sexual impropriety.[9]

Not for the first time did immigrants fashion a new business out of thin air; it happened, for example, in the explosion of coffee houses in Europe two centuries earlier.[10] While developing the new film industry these immigrants unwittingly waded into the culture wars that pitted traditionalists and nativists against urbanists who celebrated a more diverse, secular, liberal and, unconvincingly, gender-equal society.

These cultural battles played out in the nation's newspapers, and few shaped this war zone better than press baron William Randolph Hearst. He was both a traditionalist (preferring old-fashioned roles for women and men in society) and nativist (a nationalist, or "Americanist," to the point of obsession) whose peculiar politics—at once progressive and reactionary—molded much public thinking around both Hollywood and its immigrants. Pantages came into the crosshairs of Hearst's bromides against immorality. Such campaigns satisfied Hearst's longing for power, while also entertaining his readers and providing huge revenues to his press empire. No one monetized scandal quite as profoundly and successfully as William Randolph Hearst.[11]

It is easy to criticize traditionalists and nativists for their lack of compassion, petty-mindedness, prejudice and isolationism, yet in a society riven by extraordinary change in every arena of national life, it was a natural if distorted reaction. The challenge facing Americans in the early twentieth century was coping with the headwinds of an increasingly diverse, technologized and mass-oriented society that was painfully if not fundamentally altering the nation's very social fabric and the psychological stresses that went along with it.

Many suffered from the culture wars, including Pantages, but they were not always immigrants. In 1921, popular movie comedian Roscoe "Fatty" Arbuckle faced assault and manslaughter charges for the death of a young movie starlet. Known for childish pranks and "inhuman escapades," Arbuckle became "famous for throwing lavish, drunken parties that lasted for days with exclusive guest lists of those more immature actors."[12] During one such party in San Francisco in 1921, young Virginia Rappe fell ill and died a few days later. Under the relentless attack by Hearst during the three trials, and despite final acquittal, Arbuckle's career was completely ruined.

While immigrants who came to the U.S. survived and even thrived within a deeply exploitative and discriminatory system, leading lives of quiet, unassuming dignity, Pantages' path was more circuitous and noteworthy than most. Hanging uneasily throughout Pantages' unique path is his "immigrantness." His thick accent, Levantine manners, dark complexion and sputtering, broken English testified to his alien roots. These exclusionary factors fall under the label of *white ethnicity*—the social stratification process that marginalized immigrants in racialized America at the turn of the twentieth century.[13] "An ethnic," one historian offered, "is a proximate but subordinate other, too close to be foreign, too different to be the self. According to the twentieth-century sensory regime of Americanism, an ethnic looks different, sounds different, and prefers different food."[14]

Mediterranean immigrants like Pantages were shoved into social purgatory—"dark" by virtue of their ethnicity and their supposedly "olive complexion," yet "white" when contrasted against Asian, African and Native Americans. When showing off their cultural attributes such as food and religious rites, they could be considered "model ethnics"; but when immigrants protested appalling working or social conditions (or, as in the case of Pantages, were accused of a felony), public condemnation was swift and brutal. "Classified within the underbelly of whiteness," the cultural ethnographer Yiorgos Anagnostou wrote, "the undesirable immigrant is subjected to the disciplinary gaze of the dominant."[15]

As the Arbuckle case showed, the nation didn't need any more reminders of Hollywood's moral depravity. The public was used to the film colony's sordid tales of alcohol and drug abuse, pornography, sexual escapades of one kind or another, and even murder. The Pantages case was simply one more tale of the twisted ethical universe of the film industry and its un–Christian (code for Jewish) ways. "Movies are schools of vice and crime," one traditionalist concluded, "offering trips to hell for [a] nickel."[16]

Of particular concern to many was the tawdry impact of films on impressionable youth. Traditionalists had long fought Hollywood over its corrupting vulnerable youth, but it wasn't until 1933 that the Payne Fund studies ("the first large-scale investigation into the effects of media"[17]) finally offered supposed evidence of the deleterious effects of movies on the young, who made up over a third of the film audience and went to the movies weekly.[18] While some social commentators saw through the studies' bogus science, others did not: the studies' one-volume summary highlighted Hollywood movies' unending emphasis on drinking, intoxication, murder, assault and various mayhem that caused children to lose sleep, quicken their heart rate, and even criminalize them. "In a study of 110 young men in prison, the movies were blamed by 49 percent of them for instructing them on how to pull off a caper."[19] It was said of producer William Fox, but true of all movie studio heads, that he "could manipulate the public's will."[20] A trial that focused on whether Pantages committed an act of violence on an underage female turned into a broader adjudication of Hollywood itself.[21]

Pantages should have been aware of the anti-immigrant sentiment reaching a climax by the 1920s, but his intense focus on his business blinded him from reality. He paraded himself as the embodiment of the American Dream, the man who rose literally from nothing to a vast fortune—and his relentless focus on the customer, long before it became a religion in our digital era, set him apart from many of his competitors and gave his theater circuit a reputation for outstanding service and value. For many working families, being attended by white-gloved ushers amidst ornate chandeliers and stately decorations had a touch of idyllic consumerism.[22]

The Pantages circuit was the last and the greatest independent chain still standing. Theater pioneers like the Balaban Brothers and Sid Grauman of Grauman's Chinese, just a few blocks from the Hollywood Pantages, had sold out to the major studios in a period of great industry consolidation (Grauman claimed the arrival of "talkies" led him to get out of exhibition and into production).[23] As with John D. Rockefeller's earlier efforts with oil production, the goal was to bring efficiency to filmmaking.[24] Studios made, distributed and exhibited their films under one business umbrella and benefited from economies of scale and guaranteed screening of their films.²⁵ This vertical integration also gave Hollywood studios complete control over what Americans moviegoers watched. This form of vertical integration was ruled monopolistic in 1948 by the Supreme Court.

Prior to the gala opening, Pantages' lawyer frantically tried to get him temporarily released so that he could join the evening's activities, but the chief deputy prosecuting attorney of Los Angeles flatly refused, saying that his office had no jurisdiction in such motions.²⁶ Pantages had lost his theatrical empire, his reputation and his standing among free people; now at the moment of the unveiling of his greatest creation, he was not there to witness it.

The grand opening was broadcast not on one but two radio stations, KMTR and KFVD, starting at 8:30 p.m. Benjamin Blank, the jail hospital physician, took pity on Pantages and let him listen to a radio next to his bed. "All the music, songs and all the applause of the audience were heard by Pantages and a number of other prisoners in the jail's hospital."²⁷

Pantages was at the gala in mind and spirit. He felt the event's pulsating energy and joy flowing through the airwaves. He knew what a theater opening felt, sounded, even smelled like. He'd done it before dozens of times. He could do it in his sleep; he may have felt as if he had, 78 times. But none of his theaters matched the glory of the Hollywood operation. It was one of the greatest theaters ever built in America, for many years home of the Academy Awards, and still a working theater today.

On stage, Eddie Cantor introduced Lloyd Pantages, who along with his brother Rodney was slated to manage the theater. Lloyd thanked the audience in a "natural and unaffected speech."²⁸ The young man promised to "carry forward the ideals of this theater" that his father had established over a long and illustrious career.²⁹ Then Lloyd paid tribute to his absent father, speaking of the "inspiring influence" of the man who built "this shrine of amusement" for the benefit of all. There was no mention of his prisoner status. Pantages listened to his son's words in bed, a welter of emotions running through his exhausted body.

Two days later, on Friday, June 6, 1930, he was released from prison. His appeal to the California State Supreme Court for a new trial succeeded. He was free to start the long climb back to rehabilitation. But did he have the fight to do so?

Introduction

Theodore Saloutos, historian of the Greeks in America, called Alexander Pantages an "exceptionally gifted Greek immigrant who rose from obscurity to become the head of the largest independently owned circuit of motion pictures houses in the United States." By the mid–1920s, Pantages was reportedly worth between 24 and 32 million (540 to 720 million in today's dollars).[1] There were other successful Greek-American film exhibitors, among them Spyros Skouras, "King Greek," who started out with nickelodeons and eventually became head of 20th Century-Fox. There was also Gus Kerasotes, who opened his first storefront movie theater in Spring, Illinois, in 1909 and went on to found a major movie theater chain. But no one came close to the extraordinary feats, fame and notoriety of Alexander T. Pantages.

Pantages went from operating one Seattle nickelodeon ("nick" colloquially) in 1902 to owning and operating 78 movie and vaudeville theaters by the end of the 1920s—a colossal theater chain that spread across much of English-speaking North America.[2] While Skouras feared mixing vaudeville with motion pictures, Pantages thrived on it.[3] He blended the two to insure a steady diet of popular shows that also provided him some flexibility: If there was a dearth of good movies, he could rely on vaudeville, and vice versa.

Pantages' extraordinarily beautiful movie palaces set standards for opulence and customer comfort, even as he followed customary yet no less excusable discriminatory seating practices against African Americans. His work with architect B. Marcus Priteca, a Jewish immigrant from Scotland, left a huge imprint on the national obsession with elegant movie theaters.

Pantages exhibited a strong sense of economic efficiency. He opened many acts in outlying theaters such as those in Winnipeg and Edmonton, Canada, before taking them to larger markets like San Francisco and Los

Angeles. He opened up booking offices in New York and Chicago to expedite the operation.[4] He would book acts for 32 weeks, but his contracts read "'14 weeks or more,' keeping his options open if the acts did not work out or if they demanded more money."[5] Often he booked acts in Chicago and New York for an agreed amount, but when the performers came to the West Coast he immediately cut their salaries by 25 percent.[6] Actors could continue or quit; usually they chose to continue. They consoled themselves with the knowledge that at least they had a job.

His illiteracy contributed to his success. Rather than relying on critics or gossip columnists, Pantages watched acts with audiences to test their drawing power. He never took anyone's word about performers and in the process developed a unique "ability to foresee what his customers wanted in the way of entertainment and then [to] give it to them."[7]

Pantages' life has that enigmatic mystery that haunts so many immigrants. Not only are different dates offered for his year of birth, some

The entrance to the Hollywood Pantages, like the theater itself, was an Art Deco masterpiece. For many years it hosted the annual Academy Awards and today it's a showcase for popular Broadway musicals (*Marc Wanamaker, Bison Archives*).

reports claim he was born in Athens, not Andros, and that his real name was Pericles before changing it when he heard about Alexander the Great. There is one indisputable fact: He changed his last name from Pantazis to Pantages.[8]

Pantages' spectacular rise in the exhibition industry came at a time of growing national hysteria surrounding the huge influx of immigrants. In the four decades after 1880, more than 20 million foreigners entered the U.S.[9] In 1910, over 14 percent of the total population was foreign-born.[10] That number included about 450,000 Greeks.[11] "Old Immigrants," or those from northern and western Europe who were more able to assimilate into mainstream American society, could now be separated from darker "New Immigrants" from south and southeastern Europe whose ability to integrate into society was severely challenged. In 1896 "immigrants from the latter area for the first time in history composed a majority of newcomers, 57 percent of all immigrants in that year."[12]

"Immigration created the American nation and defined its role in world history," as Reed Ueda asserted in *Postwar Immigrant America*, but there has always been an unease about new arrivals in the U.S., and for one overriding reason: With each successive wave of new immigrants, the supposed "civic and social foundations of American nationhood shifted accordingly."[13] The "garlic eaters" from southeastern Europe, who lacked an education as well as "Western" attributes, disturbed the American peace. Such rapid social dislocation would be difficult for any nation to bear, let alone one as insular (and often isolationist) as the U.S.[14] "[A]nti-immigrant prejudice has for centuries played an important role in shaping the experience of an American immigrant and the history of the United States."[15] By the 1920s, it became a clarion call to maintain social tradition and cohesion.

The rapid urbanization of a growing industrial society had its consequences.[16] The heterogeneity of older cities was also being replaced by segregation according to ethnicities; hence the rise of Chinatowns, Greek towns, Little Italies, etc., or what historian Maria Christina Chatziioannou termed "introvert communities."[17] This demarcation served as the basis for the rise of movies, which catered to immigrants.

Because the movie colony included many immigrants (read Jews), Hollywood came under special attention. Questions arose about the value and impact of movies on the nation's psyche. "Ministers, social workers, civic reformers, police, politicians, women's clubs and civic organizations accused movies of inciting young boys to crime by glorifying criminals and corrupting young women by romanticizing 'illicit' love affairs."[18]

"Vamp" film star Theda Bara, with her sultry, lascivious characters, provided a stark contrast against what for many women were the traps of traditional and therefore dead-end roles as housewives. This new woman, already well defined by alarmed elders, was joined by an even more troubling version in the 1920s: the flapper. "Restless, excited, noisy, they trot like foxes, limp like lame ducks, one-step like cripples, and all to the barbaric yawp of strange instruments which transform the whole scene into a moving-picture of a fancy ball in bedlam."[19] Sexual liberation added to new cultural opportunities available to women, in the process changing the American leisure landscape.[20] "New sex magazines and movies depicted the sexual revolution, one movie ad promising Neckers, petters, white kisses, red kisses, pleasure-mad daughters, sensation-craving mothers, the truth bold, naked, sensational."[21]

The tremendous changes wrought by the industrial revolution were so diffuse yet fundamental, it was hard to pinpoint one source as the culprit. So traditionalists had to channel their ire somewhere. "In their frustrations, rural old-stock America found scapegoats: it must be the Reds; it must be the Catholics; it must be the Jews; it must be the immigrants."[22] Eventually they settled on Hollywood as the catchall warehouse holding all the nation's social ills, particularly since Jews and immigrants dominated America's dream factories.[23]

Conservative forces made life hell for film exhibitors. "Blue laws, insistence on clean movies, the Scopes trial, the flow of nostalgic writing celebrating village life, the success of fundamentalist preachers like Aimée Semple McPherson all marked the effort to retain familiar American values."[24] Certainly by the 1920s, the outsized role that movies played in the lives of Americans was apparent. Films not only helped "shape their attitudes and social values," but "offered a private refuge from the pressures of the outside world."[25] For millions, "the theater was a dark cavern into which no parent, boss, spouse or anyone else could intrude and in which the mind was free to roam wherever the picture took it."[26]

Blue laws shut down theaters on Sunday, decency leagues tried to determine what films could be shown, and the Payne Fund studies declared war on the movie industry. At every turn, movie exhibitors like Pantages were confronted with forces that stood ready to run their businesses out of town. These tectonic social upheavals came to an explosive climax in the Pantages rape trial that began on the morning of October 4, 1929, in Superior Court in downtown Los Angeles. Uncannily paralleling the country's own financial meltdown, the case proved an economic disaster for Pantages. His assumption that his wealth insulated him from society's headwinds was about to be severely and damagingly tested.

Once the story of his arrest broke on August 10, 1929, the headlines were relentless, particularly on the West Coast where the Pantages theatrical circuit was based. In the *Los Angeles Times*, readers were hit with, "Alexander Pantages Placed in Jail When Young Girl Accuses Him of Statutory Offense," accompanied by a photo of the haggard and clearly shocked girl, Eunice Alice Pringle.[27] The front page of the *Seattle Times* showcased the event, completely with Pringle's wrong age: "A. Pantages in jail on complaint of girl, 16."[28] In the *San Francisco Chronicle*, the headline read "Girl Accuses A.T. Pantages" and the article went on to say that according to Pantages, the young dancer had been coming to see him for two days, begging him to revive her failed act.[29] On the East Coast, the coverage of the case was subdued. The event appeared deep inside the *New York Times* with less drama: The simple headline read "Pantages Accused by Girl."[30]

None of the newspaper accounts damaged him more than William Randolph Hearst's *Los Angeles Examiner*, which fashioned the narrative as the assault of innocent youth by the corrupt, immigrant Hollywood mogul. It didn't help Pantages' cause that he first appeared in the newspaper's photos of the case with particularly enigmatic, European coolness—legs crossed, smoking a cigarette in the manner of an insufferable Continental artist, and listening to the proceedings with dismissive indifference. Meanwhile, Pringle was the very picture of inflicted trauma: sick and sallow, utterly dejected, and in a state of catatonic stupor. It was classic Hearst.

The passage of time helps make sense of the Pantages case. Issues of "who narrates the past and who is excluded—and for what purpose" are addressed.[31] This is not merely an academic issue, since cultural memory and historical consciousness speak directly to our national capacity to learn and to grow as a society. Had Pantages been native-born rather than an immigrant, would the press coverage of the trial been different? What was the *meaning* of Pantages' ethnic background as disseminated in the coverage, and did that contribute to how he is remembered (or not) today? Are financially successful immigrants recalled less in our society than their successful non-immigrant counterparts? Had he not been accused of rape, would history think better and more of him today? When cultural memory is involved, such questions take on an intense hue, since the capacity for understanding the past and its meaning speaks directly to the ability to remember and to reflect morally and ethically as a society.

Pantages was a tireless, manipulative, scheming, brilliant if unsavory visionary who fell victim to two other tireless, manipulative, scheming, brilliant if unsavory visionaries—not just William Randolph Hearst, but according to legend also Joseph P. Kennedy, great patriarch and incubator of America's sole princely family.

Kennedy wanted Pantages' movie theaters as part of his growing movie empire, so he approached the theater impresario. Pantages refused to sell. Kennedy tried again, and again was rebuffed. Determined to have his way, Kennedy gave $10,000 to Pringle to set up Pantages, and in doing so bring down the Greek immigrant's empire. This she did, in the process forcing Pantages to sell out to Kennedy at a fraction of the original price. Later, out of guilt, when Pringle decided to go public with the scheme, she suddenly died under mysterious circumstances.

Such combustible mythmaking appeared in Hollywood Babylon–type accounts of the rape trial. While Kennedy had meetings with Pantages over purchasing some of his theaters, by the summer of 1929 Kennedy had grown weary of Pantages' negotiating tactics and, in fact, had made plans to get out of the movie business altogether. Since truth in most events is difficult to establish, narratives provide an acceptable but exaggerated substitute. Truth can never step on a good narrative.

The tabloidization of news spread the power of narratives. Although tabloids, or "compact daily newspapers," with their emphasis on "the lurid, shocking and emotive," had existed a few decades prior to their popularization in the U.S. after 1919, their explosive growth in the 1920s forced mainstream newspapers to regard news more for its commercial exploitation than its informational value.[32] The spread and commercial possibilities of news gave papers an oversized cultural impact. "Extensive circulation and diversified content gave the press a position of particular influence," wrote one newspaper historian, "and journalists and social commentators recognized this power."[33] And none more influential than Hearst, who upon his death was said to have presided over "the mightiest publishing venture the world has known."[34] For American press barons at the time, this social power translated into "government by newspaper."[35] In the 1920s, one in five Americans read a Hearst newspaper, which gave Hearst extraordinary social, cultural and political reach. Pantages was tried in two courts: in Los Angeles County Superior Court and the court of public opinion as expressed by the nation's presses.

Hearst started in the newspaper business in 1887 with the *San Fran-*

cisco Examiner as a modernizer and social crusader for the underprivileged. "Hearst learned early that a newspaper with bold type, simple ideas and passionate appeals for social justice could command the pennies and the votes of the immigrant working class."[36] When it came to foreign-born Americans, he followed the prevalent social prejudice in California against Chinese and Japanese, while he often had kind things [to say] for Germans, Italians and Jews.[37] Meanwhile, the competing *San Francisco Chronicle* offered its own version of anti-immigrant hysteria with headlines such as "JAPANESE A MENACE TO AMERICAN WOMEN" and "BROWN ARTISANS STEAL BRAINS OF WHITES."[38] Hearst admonished one of his editors to "deplore any race prejudice and to promote good feelings among all creeds and classes and protect the interests of every worthy cause."[39] It's the kind of cosmopolitanism that exemplifies a certain magnanimous spirit, but it was always wrapped under a virulent nationalism.[40] World War I hardened attitudes towards immigration (as exemplified by the Immigration Act of 1917, passed by Congress to limit the number of foreigners coming into the U.S.).[41]

Hearst's papers had a strong identification "with national purpose and chauvinistic impulses."[42] They fetishized "America" and "American," along with "patriotism," "nationalism" and "destiny." He led anti-immigrant crusades because imported labor was "robbing 'white' workers of their livelihood and destroying San Francisco by promoting gambling, lotteries and houses of ill fame."[43] He became an American Firster, proudly wearing "his nativist's credentials on his sleeves as well as the masthead of his newspapers that displayed the American eagle along with the words: 'America First—An American Paper for the American People!'"[44] That presumably did not include loyal immigrants like Alexander Pantages.

Hearst "loved the words 'cosmopolitan' and 'international,'" which for him "stood for huge, all-embracing [American] power" on the global stage.[45] He spoke of the world as an abstraction, embracing a kind of intellectual racism, as when he warned in a letter about the rising Japanese power: "Who shall say that the stupidities and jealousies of the white peoples shall not some day create a situation which will arouse the yellow races to succeed?"[46] If politics stood at the center of white ethnicity, so did its commercial exploitation. In Pantages, the press lord had a twofer: a Hollywood mogul revealed as a sexual predator with an immigrant background.

Hearst offered up to eight extra editions of his newspapers a day if the news stories demanded it. Tall and imposing, with penetrating eyes, he never let facts get in the way of a great story, and in Pantages' case it came with large, bold banners with capital letters attached. Hearst long knew stories with clearly delineated antagonists, protagonists and plots provided readers with simple, easy-to-follow modern drama that kept them coming back for more. He reasoned that it was better to have an interesting, compelling, even controversial paper that millions of Americans wanted to read than one that offered more important and significant news but had limited circulation.

Pantages was only one part of the explosive narrative; the other was the young dancer, Eunice Alice Pringle. Every protagonist needs an antagonist in a calibrated plot. Hearst transformed an ambitious, determined young female into the nation's sweetheart. While the *Los Angeles Examiner* showed photos of Pantages either surrounded by a phalanx of expensive lawyers or in grim-faced aloofness, Pringle's pictures had family members or obliging city officials present. Despite her parents being separated, her photos revealed a family united by tragedy. The thousands of words the photos spoke all condemned Pantages.

The portrayal of Pringle also represented Hearst's own personal crusade in regard to women's proper roles in society. In Hearst's world, women came in two varieties: flaming beauties often displayed in his newspapers in cheesy swimsuit contests, or the domestic type that exemplified the hearth of America. Hearst had perfected the use of cheesecake exhibition of women in his newspapers' pages. His tendency was to glamorize women—not out of any sense of emancipatory celebration or gender respect for their status as equals of men, but instead out of a clear reductionist desire to spread sexual attraction and guileful femininity, presumably as a way to grab men's attention. The message was clear: Women could agitate for equality, but it had to be on terms established and operated by men. It was, according to social historian Alice Kessler-Harris, all part of the "gendered imagination."[47]

There was also an unmistakable undercurrent of feminine "weakness" to the *Examiner* accounts of the trial, as if the female victim in the Pantages case needed the protection of the male-dominated *Examiner* to maintain the sanctity and virtue of womanhood. Today such a primitive attitude flies against a gender-sensitive society, but in the 1920s it served notice that women needed male champions to protect them from sexual beasts like Pantages, and none more vociferously and chivalrously than Hearst's *Examiner*.

Hearst himself openly lived with his mistress, Marion Davies, and unfailingly promoted her career even as he remained married and turned her life into a jewel-encrusted cage. "It was like Svengali, or Pygmalion and Galatea," Davies later wrote.[48] They met when she was 16 and he 58. Hearst refused to divorce his wife out of fear of an expensive settlement and what it might do to his reputation. With Hearst, it was fruitful to always recall Oscar Wilde's adage: "Every saint has a past and every sinner a future."[49] Meanwhile, life went on swimmingly for the press lord. He named an elephant in his private zoo after Marion and she felt insulted.[50] Davies' own niece was an avowed lesbian, and he was infuriated by the niece's "refusal to adhere to what he believed was moral and decent."[51]

The moving picture machines that came out of the labs of grand tinkerers like Thomas Alva Edison in the 1890s rendered spectacle and amusement into mass arts, "the ultimate form of mass consumption."[52] The third dimension (movies) was projected onto the second dimension (screen), which in the dark theater resembles the mind's dreams.[53] Films provided audiences with escape as well as "ready-made, prepackaged recreation that provided instant gratification for every nickel and dime."[54] Particularly for women and men of the labor force who spent 12 hours per day on the job, "punching in at six or sometimes seven, checking out again at six, in winter never seeing sunlight off the job."[55] Their wages usually meant less than $4 per week, which priced them out of more expensive leisure activities, but which for a family of four at the local nickelodeon fit their budget.[56] Not only were movie shows cheaper, they were shorter than traditional stage performances, thus saving the working class both time and money. The genius of exhibitors like Pantages was to fashion an entirely new industry from these working stiffs with nickels in their pockets. Storefronts movie theaters became movie cathedrals, on par with some of the finest buildings in the country. Now the admission price to a movie theater came with attendants and lush interior designs once the reserve of the upper classes.

Pantages built some of the country's leading theaters, yet the stench of the assault trial insured that his life would always be associated with notoriety. Has history been unkind to Pantages? It's difficult to say, since the circumstances that led him to be alone in a tiny room in his theater complex in downtown Los Angeles on a hot August afternoon in 1929 were not entirely out of his control. A more circumspect individual might not have let down his guard or refused to meet alone with Pringle in a less commonly used room.

About the book's title. I chose "Zeus" to establish Pantages' powerful role as a theater magnate. Zeus was the king of all the gods on Mt. Olympus and ruled over them with sometimes judicious but capricious ways, a little like Pantages himself. He had a wife but also many consorts, some of whom mythology indicates he raped (some interpreters prefer seduced, but this is obfuscation). This does not imply any conclusion on my part about Pantages' actions on that fateful Friday afternoon, August 1929; only the participants knew and both are long dead. On the symbolic level, Zeus' myths bear no relation to the life and times of Pantages. But I chose the title because Zeus leads the pantheon of anthromorphic, all too-human deities whose messy lives Pantages could relate to. And "American" since Pantages' story could only have been fashioned within the rich but sometimes bitter American experience.

Approaching Pantages' former home island of Andros in the Aegean, the observer is startled by its desolated, sunbaked beauty. It rises defiantly out of the Aegean Sea, a lump of crusted, dusty, gravity-defying rock. Strewn all around this magnificent speck in the deep dark sea are shipwrecks that, over thousands of years, failed to navigate its treacherous waters. They lie as piles of broken heaps, testaments to our mortality. We may be gods for a while, but in the end we all perish as humans.

1. Beginnings

According to a 1927 theater management book, "Modern theaters, large or small, cannot be run on chance or guesswork."[1] Sound business practices and stringent methods must be "combined with acute personal intelligence."[2] The exhibition career of Alexander Pantages provides an abundance of the second, less so of the first—at least, for the first part of his career in theater exhibition. He used his considerable knowledge to grow his business and ward off competitors, ones better financed and more established than he, yet his illiteracy meant that he ran the empire entirely by memory and relied on others to handle his correspondence. He was not the first illiterate to run a company, but he was probably the wealthiest and most prominent.

Pantages left few personal or business papers behind; much of the information on his life's trajectory must be gleaned from newspaper, magazine and trade journal accounts, leaving a lot to speculation and mystery. His son, Rodney A. Pantages, wrote that "none of us ever considered the future historical value of keeping an accurate record" of the operations.[3] Even some basic life facts are controversial: was he born on the tiny, seahorse-shaped Greek island of Andros or in Athens?[4] Which of the various birth years between 1864 and 1875 that are offered is correct? And was he really born Alexander and not Pericles, which he later changed when reading about Alexander the Great?

At the time of his trial in 1929, he gave his age as 54, putting his birth in 1875. The mausoleum erected by his family at Forest Hills in Glendale, California, lists 1867. No birth certificates were issued at the time in Greece, yet simple math helps narrow the range. Since he was reputedly 11 when he landed at the Panama Canal under French control (1881–1889), he could not have been born before 1870.[5]

Besides confusion over his birth year and birthplace, there is dispute whether he was really christened Pericles instead of Alexander. Rodney claims his father was christened Alexander from the start.⁶ What is certain is that his surname was Pantazis; when he altered it to Pantages is not known, although it was already in evidence by the time he lived in San Francisco in the 1890s.

The world that Pantages saw in Andros can be described as rustic. The perennially wind-addled island, like most other Aegean islands, is a heap of craggy, rocky mountains tossed errantly into the Aegean, which guaranteed its inhabitants a life of harsh toil, hot summers and conditions that had changed little from previous centuries. A person on Andros in 1870 had more in common with someone from two centuries earlier than an Athenian at the same time.⁷ The island is 36 nautical miles away from the mainland (Athens and the peninsula of Attica), but in culture, politics and economy, the distance is considerable. Its 137 square miles contain a few rich valleys but mostly dust and crusted desolation. Those valleys supported its modest population (19,674) spread across villages with names like Vitalli, Gides, Aidonia, Batsi and (the main town) Hora, where the Pantages family resided.⁸

The seasons and the Greek Orthodox Church regulated existence on the island. An ambitious young man would be struck by its severe limitations; there was birth and death, and some peaks in between—marriage, children, and endless labor. This static, stable but ultimately harsh reality was anathema to an ambitious type like Pantages who demanded more of life than Andros could provide. Few means of climbing social ladders existed on the island; any realistic professional career could be pursued in Athens, but even there it required circulation amongst the elite classes that controlled most of the economy. "Government institutions were used by the elite to further their careers and those of their children."⁹

In one historical account describing the Pantages family, his father was a constable, or honorary police officer, and also ran a general store.¹⁰ In that capacity, he often traveled to Cairo, Egypt, to buy goods, taking young Alexander with him. For Pantages, Cairo was a window into the wider world: Then a cosmopolitan city of over 700,000, it was also a great stew of humanity, including many Europeans brought in to modernize Egypt.¹¹ Wandering around the city, Pantages might have been dazzled by the opulent Cairo Opera House, the Citadel or spacious parks such as Tahrir Square. A country still nominally under the rule of the Ottoman sultan in Istanbul, it gained international trade with the 1869 completion of the Suez Canal that connected the Mediterranean to the Red Sea. This was a monumental feat of French engineering, ably supervised by French diplomat Ferdinand de Lesseps, whose future path intersected with Pantages'. Underneath the modernization efforts, and the Western organizers that came along, brewed Pan-Islam nationalism uneasy about the growing European influence; it urged followers to resist Western culture, even by violence. The young Pantages was ignorant of this gathering storm, but he did realize that the wondrous sights and sounds of the city made returning to the backwater of Andros difficult. Pantages, Greek-America historian Theodore Saloutos wrote, was an "unhappy boy without any emotional attachment to the mother country and her traditions."[12]

In another version, young Alexander joined his father in Cairo not to buy goods for the general store back home but as a father-son team working as busboy and waiter in a restaurant in the city. In this second, more pedestrian version, the father was a "menial storekeeper [on Andros] and the family lived in bitter poverty, something that Alexander never forgot and that spurred his feverish drive to extreme wealth."[13] In a third version, he is apprenticed to his older brother John at a tobacconist shop in Cairo.[14] Wherever the truth may lie—and with Pantages, this is an open question for his whole life—what is not in dispute is that at the age of nine he made his first bold move: He ran off and left his family behind. Traveling aboard a ship from the "Cairo hovel" he shared with his family, young Alexander "slipped overboard and swam to a French tramp steamer where he hired on as a cabin boy."[15]

What led young Alexander to suddenly abandon his family for unchartered waters? According to one version, Alexander grew "unimpressed with the bickering and the traffic in goods ... [and] he wandered away from his father to Cairo's center of amusement."[17] Whether he had thought about running away from his family prior to the trip or simply acted on an impulse, he didn't say. When asked about this bold move in the 1920 interview, he was evasive: "Everybody was born on the sea. It was natural that I should go to the sea."[18]

In 1920, speaking of his early childhood, Pantages proudly told a newspaper reporter that he was a showman from the start. "I was born that way," he crowed, adding that his father ran a circus on the island.[16] How a small island of struggling farmers, sheepherders and fishermen with little time for leisure could support a circus, he did not say. His father may have arranged for small circus acts on special occasions to a population starved for outside entertainment, but a permanent operation on Andros is unlikely. But it's a great story, as if fate had blessed him to be an entertainer from the very beginning of his life.

"Being near the warmth and gaiety of people amusing themselves [in Cairo] helped him overcome some of the remorse that had seized him for leaving his father."[19] The remorse was not great enough, however, to prevent him from heading to the city's port and getting on a tramp steamer heading for France, never to return home and leaving his father behind. He would never see his family again. "Did I run away from home?" he facetiously asked. "No, and yes. We all had to make our way."[20]

The way he did so was by means of a two-year stint on trips around the world working as a cabin boy on various cargo ships. It was a formative period; the lad witnessed worlds he could scarcely imagine back on Andros, and it filled him with wonder. He enjoyed his freedom and independence from his family, and even found time to "visit music halls," where he "saw people 'eating and drinking, trying to be happy.'"[21] These visits made a deep impression. "With keen insight, he saw from firsthand observations, and very early in life, that people paid handsomely for chances at happiness."[22] He kept those thoughts to himself; any dreams of entertaining the masses would have to wait. Yet he was not in a hurry to get there; the cargo boats gave him an education in real life. He was missing his elementary schooling back home, but he was getting an education in the ways of the world that would serve him well. And he kept his own schedule, which meant he was his own master. "When I was tired of one place, I would ask for a new job on a ship, and travel some more."[23]

Pantages soon enough grew weary of the nomadic life and, possibly on a whim, disembarked while his boat was in Panama. Perhaps it was the prospect of good wages that attracted him to the Panama Canal being built by the prodigious French; perhaps it was that he got tired of being on the water for weeks on end; perhaps he wanted a new adventure to continue to learn in his school of the real world.

The same wily personality that successfully built the Suez was now running the construction of another fantastic canal, this one in the Isthmus. Pantages never met Ferdinand de Lesseps, nor knew (or cared) anything about his extraordinary exploits. Pantages came to Panama to work. "[H]e stayed on the isthmus two years, swinging a pick and running a donkey engine in the ill-starred French attempt to dig a canal," one account described.[24] The decision nearly cost him his life.

Lesseps had performed a miracle in Egypt but he faced special challenges in Central America. He had come from a family of diplomats who regarded public service as an act of devotion to France. Known to some as "The Great Engineer," and to others as "an unprincipled entrepreneur," he tackled the Suez project with thunderous effort, attention to detail, charm, wit and not a little bravado.[25] Other great project makers of the time, including the Roebling brothers with the Brooklyn Bridge in New

York, also worked tirelessly to complete their work, but not with the joy, manners and sophistication of Lesseps. "He traveled in style—his own private tent, mahogany furniture, quilted silk bedding, ice for his drinking water."[26]

"The [Suez] Canal was to be for all nations, "the French hoped, and indeed it was but more so for the glory of France and Lesseps personally.[27] It was a parting of the desert, as one chronicler called it.[28] It took 15 years from the time he first proposed the Suez to its completion on November 17, 1869. An opera house had been built for the occasion and an opera by Verdi, *Aida*, was commissioned for the grand opening, although it would be performed two years later. By any measurement (cultural, diplomatic, financial), the Suez was a stunning success. Leaders back in Paris considered the Canal and the company that founded it "two of France's greatest achievements and Lesseps as a national treasure."[29] Lesseps married his 20-year-old second wife and promptly set about producing 12 children, "which in some circles was considered a more notable accomplishment than the [Panama] canal."[30]

Other mortals might have taken the glory and rested on their laurels, but not Lesseps. Feeling overconfident after the Suez Canal's success, he looked around for another gargantuan project that had long fired up European imaginations but that was considered economically and technologically impossible. On top of the list was a canal through the Isthmus of Panama, first proposed in the early sixteenth century, which would end the arduous sailing journey around the dangerous tip of South America. Settling on a 48-mile route in Panama suggested by an Irish physician in 1850, Lesseps also made the fateful decision to repeat the same sea-level waterway without locks of the Suez. It was the first of many fatal mistakes that ruined his reputation and put him in the middle of two sensational trials in France after the project was abandoned in 1889. The syndicate of 270 wealthy and influential friends Lesseps persuaded to fund the ditch in Panama had no clue what they were getting into.[31] "I maintain that Panama will be easier to make, easier to complete, and easier to keep up than Suez," Lesseps proudly boasted to his supporters.[32]

The Sinai is no Panama. It is no match for the devouring jungle of the Isthmus where "nature declared total war against the white."[33] Heat and dust in the Sinai were replaced in Panama by a primeval earth "filled with strange forms and elusive shadows."[34] "The soil, the branches, and the streams are constantly traversed by armies of reptiles, insects and lower vertebrates in a state of perpetual hostility to the intruder. The earth bitterly resents the tools that open its wounds."[35] For Pantages and the thousands of other workers, it was not just the construction of the project that presented difficulties, but also simply living in this nightmarish environment. "If the night catches you in the jungle, not even a bonfire will drive away the curious tenants of the forest whose rights you have violated with your trespass. No dose of tranquilizer or alcohol can shut out the nocturnal choir of the animal kingdom."[36]

While they carefully considered many possible locations for the canal, the organizers grossly underestimated the costs of completing the work, and never bothered to go to Panama to inspect the conditions there more closely. The Panamanian soil was quite unlike the European dirt in which they conducted their preliminary tests. These flaws existed during the building of the Suez, but the severe conditions in the desert were not enough to derail the project. The jungle of Panama was different. "The creation of the Panama Canal was far more than a vast, unprecedented feat of engineering," wrote one historian. "It was a profoundly important historic event and a sweeping human drama not unlike that of war."[37]

There were also management problems. Corruption and graft were common, with "expenses of all sorts … systematically 'padded'" and contractors who "received millions of francs for services never rendered."[38] Also, squeezing together tens of thousands of workers from a variety of nations and backgrounds into a cutthroat environment was a call to disaster. The conditions produced results that included suicides, murders and political intrigues, or some combination of all three, "where *liberals* and *conservadores* awaited a signal to butcher each other, protected by the shadows of the night."[39] Weather conditions caused untold damage and stopped the work. With eight months out of the year in torrential rain, the Chagres River that ran alongside the waterway regularly flooded, burying human beings and equipment in the process.[40] The French didn't help themselves or their employees by creating near semi-slavery working conditions that, despite the decent pay, exacerbated the ill effects of the disease-infested topography. "Many times I met death at the door," recalled one laborer.[41] The canal company running the project "had to save itself by calling on the United States to end mob rule in the isthmus."[42] The French who saw the Panama Canal as a way to slow American dominance of the Western Hemisphere now turned to that very country for help.

Better planning, execution and luck might have overcome these setbacks, but unbeknownst to the French the greatest enemy of the project was a tiny six-legged creature buzzing around the jungle by the millions. As early as 1836, suggestions of a connection between malaria and mosquitos were made, an idea that became more widespread after 1881, when excavation on the canal had begun. But the French chose either to ignore it or to dismiss these reports altogether.[43] French doctors at the hospital set up for canal workers still believed that malaria was a result of bad air ("mal aria"). This ignorance, willful or accidental, cost the lives of tens of thousands.

The *Anopheles* mosquito (from the Greek word that ironically means "no profit," given the eventual bankruptcy of the company behind the canal) did its malaria-carrying work silently. "[I]n the swamps and puddles, fever-carrying mosquitoes bred in their millions to launch themselves on the toiling laborers."[44] The diseases came with colorful names: "paludism, yellow fever, blackwater fever, tick paralysis, equine encephalitis, dysentery and beriberi."[45] It didn't help that work on the canal began in January 1881, the month of the mosquitos' mating season.

Small and serene these mosquitoes were, but they lethally ruled Panama. Crockery rings used to protect plants around on the French hospital grounds became perfect breeding grounds for the yellow-fever mosquito.[46] A famous American weekly asked if Lesseps was a "Canal Digger or a Grave Digger."[47] Although well-trained French engineers also died within "three months of arriving on Panama's 'Fever Coast,'" the vast majority of the victims were ordinary, anonymous workers.[48] The "most conservative estimate of the death toll is 25,000 [or] 500 lives for every mile of the canal."[49] This compares to the total of 5000 who died under the direction of the Americans when the Canal was completed in 1914. Many more contracted the disease without dying, including Pantages himself. Seeking medical advice, he was told by a doctor "he would die if he did not leave."[50] At 13, Pantages was pushed into the next part of his journey. He had been in the Isthmus for two years. Where to go next?

The four years away from home offered Pantages worldly experiences that few other teenagers possessed. Alone, without family, and seemingly devoid of friends, he knew firsthand the various facets of human existence that prepared him—for good or ill—for the rigors and marathon of adulthood. This hardscrabble life even offered wisdom, but the question he might have asked himself was: What to do with this knowledge? Being alone of the kind that Pantages practiced then and later did not always produce reflection, but it did provide him the kind of inner strength needed to succeed in a highly competitive career. He was not by nature a reflective person; dogged is more appropriate, given his willful determination to complete the task, work diligently and with conviction, and never back down in the face of obstacles. He never bared his inner core to anyone, preferring to let his actions speak for themselves. Neither was he a voluble man given to glibness; he could be charming when it suited him and necessary, but he generally preferred his own company.

The task at hand now was where to go after Panama. He had no grand plan and moved to where the wind blew him next, in this case a schooner heading for North America. As the boat sailed toward Seattle along the Pacific, he might have been reminded of his cargo ship days. Perhaps, too, memories of his home on Andros, and the life he had abandoned. Was it worth the pain and suffering his running away inflicted on his family to be a stranger in a strange land, alone and suffering from malaria?

As the vessel sailed into picturesque, wooded Puget Sound and neared Seattle, "he fell off the yard-arm into the chill water, a shock treatment that he later claimed cured his malaria."[51] While spending a few days in the city, Pantages was taken in by the chaotic lumber town with its vice dens and brothels on display, made possible by political corruption and secret payoffs to the Seattle police. This "free and easy atmosphere" caught his attention, as did the many stage shows that provided visual titillation for the tough, gritty working class who lacked female companionship.[52] It was a raw place, but also exciting and vibrant in its moral excess and decadence, and this attracted him. It reminded him of his days on the cargo boats. He was ready to settle in Seattle, but "a companion persuaded him it would be better to go on the beach in San Francisco."[53]

California, "perhaps the most desirable region on the face of the earth for the abode of man," had its own appeal, and none more so at the time than its crown jewel, San Francisco.[54] The city grew considerably from mineral discoveries in the late 1840s and rapidly developed an odd if complex reputation. It swelled from 34,780 residents in 1850 to over 234,000 in 1880, and with it came a stark rise in corruption and unruliness.[55] "San Francisco, a city like none other in the world," one historian wrote, "had a faculty for producing citizens of marked ability, eccentricity or villainy, but who were seldom merely commonplace."[56] Surrounded on three sides by water, with a remarkably even-tempered climate, San Francisco also buzzed with intense immigrant energy and favorable working conditions for laborers. "The unique environment of the city," a labor historian wrote, "characterized by its isolation from other major population centers, [and] a heritage of high wages bequeathed by the gold rush and silver boom," provided relatively decent working conditions compared to other cities.[57]

As inviting as the "queen of the Pacific" was, political conditions were less than majestic, "a rough-and-tumble Punch and Judy show … where politics and entertainment were deftly mixed and political violence shared the stage with sexual bawdiness."[58] The great disparities between rich and poor were glaring and telling: tony French eateries on the one end and slums in Chinatown on the other; theaters and libraries for the literate-minded, and 2000 saloons, or one for every 117 people in the city, for the working classes.[59] Coupled with the fact that 40 percent of the population was born outside the United States and that racism was accordingly institutionalized, the mixture of under-privilege and discrimination was toxic and bloody.[60] In 1877, an Irish populist, Dennis Kearney, stirred violence against the Chinese immigrants while holding a noose in his hands.[61] It was a different human pressure cooker from the one Pantages knew in Panama, but no less dysfunctional. "Violence, vice and harlotry throve so that San Francisco became known as the wickedest city in the world."[62] "[D]ramatic duels seem to have been an annual event."[63] A popular stanza at the time offered this observation about the city:

> The miners came in forty-nine,
> The whores in fifty-one,
> And when they got together,
> They produced the native son.[64]

Citizen of no one country, denizen of all, Pantages was in his element.[65] He found his first employment as a dishwasher at a German beer restaurant on the waterfront, soon rising to server. Apparently the owner liked him "because he could always find a language in which to communicate with a sailor."[66] Pantages would later claim that the owner, Walter Meyer, "didn't speak any more English than me. And I spoke none."[67] The young man's lack of education did not concern Meyer. Pantages was like many other Greek immigrants at the time who arrived with only a few years in a village school.[68] "Though multilingual, [Pantages] could read 'very little much more than my very own name.'"[69] He may have spoken half a dozen languages, but it was his extraordinary work ethic and meticulous way with figures that mattered most to Meyer.[70] When Meyer decided to visit the German homeland, he left Pantages in charge of his operation. "Pantages seems to have run it efficiently" in his absence.[71] Without realizing it, Pantages got valuable training in running a small business. "The job," one historian suggested, "opened up other vistas for Pantages. He was near music and food, and he could watch the slapstick comedians and the dancing girls." Once more he regarded the power of entertainment and it made a deep impression. "As he heard the proprietor's till clatter with coins, the idea kept running through his mind that people will pay well for momentary happiness."[72]

But starting his own stage theater required a sizable investment; even a low-rent version of his dream required space, talent, publicity and paying customers, and he needed more than just an attractive face. He could cut corners on one or two of these elements, but not all. And his prodigious doggedness could only get him so far. His acquaintances (hard to say friends, since he appears to have had few) were not habitués of bank offices or corporate boardrooms. Pantages "had trained in the tough school; many of his friends were mugs and pimps; the most legitimate people he knew were gamblers."[73] He could ask Meyer, and it is possible that he tried, but the German émigré may have been in no financial position to bankroll the young upstart. Pantages could seek a bank loan, but aside from a lack of collateral, his illiteracy would arouse the suspicion of any serious banker. All avenues to the necessary funding were closed.

Pantages could only play a peripheral role. To "get his first taste of the theater business, [he] became a theater utility man, passed out programs, worked as an usher and became acquainted with Eddie Foy, June McCree, David Belasco and others."[74] He "staged shows in old barns around the Mission and in the firehouses, where the men were always good to the kids," he later recalled.[75] Foy, McCree and Belasco are not household names today, but in theater and vaudeville circles at the time they represented the major leagues in acting and playwriting. Belasco was a highly successful California-born writer and theater producer most often associated with early twentieth-century popular melodrama. Pantages could look at them as idols and mentors, but he could never follow in their paths. He had no acting talent, and writing was out of the question. Once more he confronted the limitations of his theatrical ambitions: He could own or run a theater and hire the talent, but could never become the talent himself. He was back at the beginning: no funding.

Pantages settled on another scheme for the quick payoff. His Panama days wielding a pickaxe had padded his short frame with muscle, and he decided to try his hand in boxing for an instant payoff. It was disastrous. He didn't particularly care for physical work, and the hours needed in the gym must have given him pause; but boxing was wildly popular at the time (it captured the polemic ethos of the era) and offered the possibility of large winnings. He practiced for two years before taking on his first opponent. Short (about five feet, six inches) but stocky, he fought as a natural welterweight, 144 pounds.[76]

"Mysterious" Billy Smith was Canadian-born, stood five feet, eight-and-a-half inches and was considered "one of the dirtiest fighters who ever fought," having been schooled in the hard-knocks docks of eastern seaboard cities like Halifax and Boston.[77] He became welterweight champion of the World in 1892 and held the title until mid–1894.[78]

The day of the match between Pantages and the savage Smith proved prophetic for the Greek refugee. "The ringside experts soon decided that Mysterious Billy Smith, reigning welter champion, had nothing to fear from Pantages."[79] "[T]hough it took [Pantages] longer to make up his mind, he came to the same conclusion and hung up his gloves."[80] He lost the fight in a sustained bloody effort. He would have to find another way to wealth.

Another quick-money scheme was less savory. On November 23, 1896, Pantages and Greek fisherman Sam Brown were arrested for trying to dispose of 185 tins of opium in downtown San Francisco.[81] The *San Francisco Examiner*, first writing of the case on December 3, called Pantages an owner of a restaurant at 121 Fifth Street. At the county jail, Pantages asked to be in the same cell as Brown, but his request was flatly denied. As if suggesting an alibi for Pantages, the article notes that he had placed a $500 bet on boxer Bob Fitzsimmons against challenger Tom Sharkey in a heavyweight match that took place on December 2, 1896 (Sharkey won the match under controversial circumstances).[82] On December 8, 1896, the *Examiner* has *Pericles* Pantages being freed on $1500 bail and then on December 22, 1896, the start of the trial of Sam Brown and "Aleck" Pantages in the United States District Court.[83] It lasted until the following day. In what came to represent the Hearstian style already on exhibit, the article focused not on Pantages but on an argument between the prosecution and the defense involving Pantages' landlady, Mrs. Koster. At Pantages' arrest, she denied she knew him, but at the trial "she sat alone in court weeping while the jury was out."[84] When the verdict that gave Pantages his freedom was read, "the woman dried her eyes and smiled a happy smile."[85] He squeezed through the ordeal, and his alibi about the boxing match bet worked, but it revealed a foolish risk-taking that would come back to bite him.

At the same time that Pantages desperately searched for new and evocative ways to make money, William Randolph Hearst in 1887 was busy in another part of town resuscitating his father George Hearst's failing *San Francisco Examiner*. George, a self-made, semi-literate mining millionaire and U.S. Senator, "had purchased the paper after staking it to several loans."[86] In some historical accounts, the father hoped his son would take over the family's extensive ranch interests instead of the paper, but in a letter from George to his wife Phoebe, the old man is clear about his intentions: "I hope the Boy will be able, as I think he will, to take charge of the paper soon after he leaves college."[87] His son soon expressed his desire to do exactly that. "When he wants cake," the father said of his and wife Phoebe's only child, "he wants cake, and he wants it now. I have noticed that, after a while, he gets the cake."[88]

Hearst's takeover of the *Examiner* was not without a history, and it started at Harvard University after he enrolled in 1882. He did well academically in his first year, but soon he turned his attention toward the college's titillating social scene. He had a flair for the theatrical, a quality he shared with Pantages.[89] "He was a showman," his widow Millicent Hearst later told a biographer.[90] Not content with the joyous frivolities of Harvard's social elites, he stood out within the intensely hierarchical and status-driven school by investing considerable mental, physical and sometimes monetary resources in childish pranks that became legendary. He and his cronies pelted actors with custard pies at a performance in Boston, and threw oranges at police officers on a trip back from the city.[91] More memorable was walking his pet alligator "Champagne Charlie" (named for the copious amounts of alcohol Hearst shoved down its throat) around the campus.[92] To celebrate the victory of Hearst's preferred candidate in the presidential election in 1884 (the Democratic nominee, Grover Cleveland), he released roosters in the early morning into Harvard Yard.[93] College officials were not amused. Then in 1885, as a junior, he sent chamber pots to all his professors with their names written on the bottom of each.[94] He was expelled, and attempts to test out his subjects so he could at least receive his degree were refused.

Despite dismissal, Harvard piqued Hearst's interest in newspaper publishing through his involvement with the satirical *Harvard Lampoon*; it also embellished his lifelong love for theater with acting at the Hasty Pudding Club theatrical productions (he donned blackface in one play).[95] The latter expressed itself in an intense interest in vaudeville and musical theater, where he found his mistresses and his wife. He followed his triumph resurrecting the financial fortunes of "The *Lampy*" by being hired as a reporter at Joseph Pulitzer's *New York World*, a paper he would later torment and surpass. He was "attracted by Pulitzer's odd combination of idealism and circulation-raising stunts."[96] The man with the "girlish" lisp would copy and later outdo Pulitzer in their titanic and often bizarre circulation wars.[97]

The budding new press mogul transformed the *San Francisco Examiner* into a formidable publication—adding more graphics, doubling the size of the paper to eight pages, reducing the number of columns from nine to seven, splashing bigger headlines, hiring top talent (Mark Twain, Jack London and Ambrose Bierce among them), and emphasizing sex and scandal.[98] "HUNGRY, FRANTIC FLAMES," one of his headlines blared, using adjectives more suited to a crime novel than a major American newspaper, but it got readers' attention.[99] "Editors of the other San Francisco papers, sitting back and smirking, waited for the blond young man to crash, soon found very little to amuse them," noted his obituary.[100]

Photographs also grabbed the readers' eyes. For Hearst, photos were the great development of the day, and he used them to powerful effect.[101] "News pictures are what people want," he wrote.[102] A high-level employee who worked for him for 22 years stated that Hearst was "always acutely concerned [with] clearness the eyes encountered."[103] "He was a picture man," a biographer noted. For Hearst, illustrations "were of equal or greater value in a newspaper than words."[104]

"The *Examiner* should blaze with news," Hearst demanded. "Every industry, every laboratory, every romance should give the *Examiner* news."[105] And many did, or he squeezed news out of them at the expense of actual evidence. "Hearst has never had scruples against printing dubious statements as facts."[106] There was restless haste to his reporting whose purpose was to scoop the competition and wrench from his customers emotional attention rather than intellectual reflection. Hearst dismissed concerns about his "carnival brand of journalism."[107] "The modern editor of the popular journal," he once derisively opined, "does not care for the facts."[108]

For Hearst, vibrant journalism required good stories to compete with other forms of entertainment, both old and new emerging ones like movies and radio. "If there are no discernible heroes or villains, no mysteries to uncover, no climaxes, denouements, triumphs or failures, if no one wins or loses in the end, there is no story to tell," a Hearst biographer summed up.[109] Film historian Marc Norman put it this way: "News stories of the period were massaged, the facts sculpted, emphasized or overlooked, given a point of view...."[110] Hearst expected readers to say "Gee whiz!" reading the first page of one of his papers, "Holy Moses!" the second, and "God Almighty!" the third.[111] Hearst not only transformed a sleepy, staid newspaper into a journalistic giant, at least in readership, but in the process he injected press publishing with a vitality, vibrancy and hucksterism that it had never really known before.[112]

The overriding goal for Hearst, then and always, was to increase circulation. While the *Examiner* became an extension of his political self-interests, ambitions and prejudices, these were not yet reflected in moves against the immigrant. Like many Californians, he considered imported Chinese workers a problem, but his family was the biggest employer of cheap Chinese labor in its various and extensive businesses.[113] This was Hearstian racism couched in the aphorisms of hewing close to public opinion. Of course, public opinion could always be used as a smokescreen to hide any number of racial grievances, and Hearst was a master of double-dealing—at once a progressive but also deeply traditional and, increasingly in his later years, reactionary. It was no wonder that by the 1920s he had a reputation as a political radical, seeing the publicity value of hiring Benito Mussolini and Adolf Hitler as columnists in his papers but blind to the cruelty both fascists represented.

Hearst was a man who read the public's mood, and at the turn of the century national anti-immigrationism had not yet coalesced into the stark, sinister political force it became in the 1920s. With 40 percent of San Francisco's population foreign-born, some of them his very own readers, it seemed financial suicide to antagonize immigrants. He was too ambitious and anxious to build his publishing career to allow this form of discrimination to prevail. That would wait until for the heightened racism of the Twenties.[114]

His *Examiner* was a journalistic version of Hearst's Cambridge pranks, but grander and more consequential, all to boost publicity and readership. When a prostitute unexpectedly produced a baby, the *Examiner*, "its heart bleeding with pity, started a fund for the infant, fortunate enough to be born when Hearst needed publicity."[115] Another stunt involved sending a reporter to "faint" in a public street and be taken to City Receiving Hospital; it turned out to be a ruse to produce a scathing exposé on the medical attention she received. On still another occasion, when famed actress Sarah Bernhardt was in town, *Examiner* reporters were on hand to give her a tour of the city as well as the illegal opium dens in Chinatown.[116] It made for good press copy and fun reading for many. That this contributed to the rising sense of moral turpitude on the part of the acting business escaped Hearst's attention.

"News is like wool, or cotton, or raw material," Hearst once maintained. "How much you can sell it for is what you manufacture out of it."[117] As his colorful pranks unfolded, so did another cause: "[H]e attacked abuses and privilege and called for a broad-based movement to secure 'radical democracy.'"[118] Although many of his campaigns were meant to arouse publicity as much as political passions, they arguably made him a pioneer in muckraking journalism and a hero to the downtrodden. His attacks on the corrupt Southern Pacific Railroad in California angered many of his wealthy friends, who called him a traitor to his class, but they upended California politics and, as always, sold newspapers. But they didn't come without costs, not just financial in the size of his reporting staff, but also personal in the amount of effort he put into his work. "I don't suppose that I shall live more than three or four years if this strain keeps up," he lamented to his mother.[119]

His style of journalism was a "frothy blend of exaggeration, distortion, excess and fakery."[120] It's an old argument in the press: how to mix entertainment with objective journalism in a paper that readers are willing to buy on a daily basis. As early as the 1830s, when the nation's first popular newspapers discovered the efficacy of sex, crime and scandal to attract readers, the issue has occupied editors' minds.

Hearst's efforts to transform the *Examiner* paid off. It became popular and profitable, the most important paper not just in the city but on the West Coast, and the kickoff to his publishing empire, the first major newspaper chain to appear in the U.S. Within a few months of his takeover, circulation more than doubled, and in two years the *Examiner* was in the black. In five years, it became the second most profitable paper in the country.[121] Unfulfilled political longings and gamesmanship, personal scandals, circulation wars, business rollercoasters and a huge media empire were all in the future. For the moment, the college dropout had turned a failing, second-rate newspaper into a heady instrument of news of varying quality and personal glory, a megaphone of causes, both sincere and outlandish, and a chronicler of events that he saw fit to publish. Even as Hearst extolled the virtues of a "free press" to "preserve a free people," an important paper had to have "dominant circulation."[122] "It's easy to circulate the best paper," he told a gathering of newspaper publishers and editors. "It's easy to sell what the public wants to buy."[123] If anyone knew what the public wanted, it was Hearst. "Newspapers," one historian wrote, "are in the business of providing news and advertisements to their readers, and the development of truthful, objective news has always been at loggerheads with the most partisan aspects of the press."[124]

That dominant circulation brought Hearst status and great social power. A question remained unanswered in his half-century of journalism: To what end was this power used? He sought to help the underprivileged, and those exploited by the nation's political and financial elites—never mind that he was both himself.[125] He took on the mantle of moral judge and jury when it suited him, his media properties and even the general public's best interests, but this same scion of ethics recoiled when attention turned to his own reckless behavior. He hid behind his carefully constructed, barricaded world, whether it was San Simeon, his newspapers, love affairs or Hollywood productions, while enjoying the fantastic, spoiled trappings of wealth and extraordinary privilege. Genius and naïveté commingled in his actions; a man of boundless passion and enthusiasm was surprisingly blind to the complex realities of human existence. Compromise was difficult for Hearst and he lacked a true inner compass to wisely and judiciously direct his immense flow of energy. He built and destroyed—lives, careers, dreams and hopes—and while a force of nature as an upstart publisher, he ended his days accused of being a fascist. "I always feel that it is not as important to be consistent as it is to be correct," he once said. "A man who is completely consistent never learns anything."[126]

The nation's (and the world's) first true great media mogul, who near the end of his long life lost his voice so that he was barely audible, made life hell for others. When asked by the silent movie star Douglas Fairbanks why he remained in newspapers instead of diving deeper into the movie industry, which offered worldwide audiences, Hearst replied, "Because ... you can crush a man with journalism and you can't with motion pictures."[127]

Pantages' career plans had stalled and he needed a new direction. The jobs he had undertaken until now were physically hard, promised few financial rewards, and came with very little job security. At any moment he could lose out to newly arrived immigrants who showed more industry and determination for less pay. Without an adequate social safety net at the time, sickness or injury meant instant penury, even homelessness. The grim reality of his station in life grated on him. If he remained in the beer garden, he faced long hours standing on his feet, dealing with rude customers, and the ever-present threat of violence that accompanied such joints. He escaped living in squalor and washing dishes in Cairo to come to San Francisco for this?

The answer to his problems literally sailed into San Francisco Harbor in mid–July 1987. "She was short and stubby with a lone black smokestack and two masts. Her superstructure was smudged and grimy and stained with rust marks."[128] But it was less the appearance of the steamer *Excelsior* than what it contained: Several dozen passengers in ragged clothing, sun-blackened faces, and unkempt whiskers stood along the ship's railings. "They were gaunt and they were weary, but their eyes burned with a peculiar fire."[129] With them was an estimated $400,000 worth of Klondike gold. "Miners from the Yukon with Hundreds of Pounds of Gold Dust," the single column announced on page seven of the *San Francisco Examiner* the day after the ship's arrival.[130] It was an unusually muted response from Hearst's *Examiner*, given the gravity of the gold discoveries. The wife of one of the miners claimed no hardships in the Yukon. "I did not mind the intense cold of the long winters," she claimed, "but the sudden changes when summer sets in is trying."[131] Her husband returned with $43,000 in gold dust. There were others with $50,000 worth of gold, others with $35,000, and a once struggling laundryman now walked down the gangplank with $15,000 at a time when a four-bedroom apartment rented for $5 per month, a serge wool suit went for $4 and a good meal for 25 cents.[132]

The next day's *Examiner* made up for the previous day's weak coverage. The story dominated the front page, with four columns and a photo illustration of one of the passes leading to the gold mines. "EL DORADO IN THE ICY YUKON FIELDS," it trumpeted.[133] It listed the names of the miners and their gold values, along with a thorough description of food prices in Dawson City and testimonials of the miners themselves.[134] It was as complete a guide to the boons and dangers of the journey to the north as the paper could muster, suggesting the *Examiner*'s editors were mixed in their appraisal of the discoveries. It warned readers that only the "very courageous" should undertake the journey. "Food is scarce, distances to be traversed are great, and the country is inhospitable."[135] And as a final warning, it indicated that "wealth from mining in that region as a rule is more accidental than otherwise."[136] Yet wrapped in the admonitions were glaring encomiums about "some of the most wonderful gold strikes in all the world's history" and the "richest gold strike the world has ever known" made in the Yukon.[137] "I have been mining in the West for the last 30 years," one lucky miner on the *Excelsior* claimed, "but I never saw any country so rich in gold as Alaska."[138]

There had been other great, desperate waves of humans in a mad scramble for fortune before, but nothing on the scale as the Alaska-Yukon Gold Rush. Certainly not one involving temperatures dropping to minus 70°. "Klondicitis," that peculiar condition that struck ordinary men and women and disrupted daily routines for a foolish chance at wealth and social status, left many impoverished, some dead, and many disillusioned with existence. For the lucky few, it opened up new social arenas. For others, the stampede to the Klondike was perhaps one last attempt at fulfilling the dream long bubbling in the American consciousness: the chance to achieve financial independence. The same yearning burning inside Pantages.

The gold rush touched both personal and national nerves. There had been news of other gold discoveries from the north for perhaps 20 years previous, but what emerged from the fields and slopes and crevices near and around the Klondike River in 1896 was an unwitting answer to populist presidential candidate William Jennings Bryan's demand to "not crucify mankind upon a cross of gold."[139] The crucifixion was to American monetary policy that failed to account for production of gold in the country keeping pace with its growing population and economic activity, thus raising the value of the shiny metal. A paper dollar was worth half as much as a gold dollar, which resulted in gold hoarding. With wealth inequalities growing, "moneymaking was the most prized career."[140]

The Great Panic of 1893 set off a national and global economic depression. Millions were thrown out of work, and Washington, D.C., witnessed the astonishing site of Coxey's Army of the hungry and homeless marching on the capital. Greece defaulted on its loans. Commodity prices plunged. There were riots and protests. It was a financial malaise wide, severe and enduring.[141] When the *Excelsior* and the *Portland* made their fateful port calls in 1897, they arrived as economic miracles and sirens to a financial call of the wild.

Miners coming to shore from the *Portland* in Seattle faced reporters and huge gatherings. They threw nuggets to the crowd. "The country and the world were soon delirious with the news of the Klondike."[142] Mass hysteria followed. "The Klondike stampede did not start slowly and build up to a climax, as did so many earlier gold rushes."[143] If one believed reports from the Klondike, yellow metal spewed freely out of small rivers and washed up ashore on beaches. The *Excelsior* docked not far from Meyers' operation, and Pantages needed no further proof that his ship had truly come in. "Pantages felt that fate had nudged him."[144] According to another account, "It sounded the answer to everything."[145]

He was not the type to fall prey to hysteria, but he knew Alaska would be a big change of scenery. The worst that could happen would be that he would fail and return to another dead-end job. But if he succeeded, life would start anew. He could scarcely imagine what lay in store for him in his journey northward. Pantages, from a tiny island in the Aegean, who had already tasted hard labor on the high seas, the Isthmus of Panama and the docks of San Francisco, was about to put his life on the line. Yet he not only managed to get out of it alive and even prosper, but his time in the Yukon gave him the experience needed to start his theatrical career. He found no gold, didn't even attempt to, but he found wealth in an unexpected way that brought him closer to his dream of participating in the theater business.

And then there was Kate Rockwell.

2. *Apprenticeship*

The gold that was loaded onto the *Excelsior* was first put aboard onto two workhorse riverboats in Dawson City, Northwest Canada, and made a 1700-mile journey to the port of St. Michael, Alaska. Along the way, sub-arctic spring rapidly gave way to resplendent, blooming summer. The riverbanks, as romanticized by one historian, "were ablaze with crimson drifts of fireweed, accented by the blues of lupins and the yellows of arnicas and daisies."[1] The only sounds came from the ship's black stacks, and those from the robins, woodpeckers, moosebirds and chicken hawks that swooped and dove in sharp but smooth patterns above the leaden river.[2] The gold was leaving paradise, at least, in that narrow window before the harsh reality of the frozen north set in autumn.

Several of the 80 *Excelsior* passengers were owners of the three tons of yellow metal parked below the deck in suitcases, leather grips, boxes, belts, pokes of caribou hides, jam jars, medicine bottles, tomato cans and even in blankets that required two to lift. The miners marched aboard the ship, oblivious to the hysteria they would unleash. One gold owner was formerly a prisoner in the Yukon Territory for two years, surviving on half-cooked salmon and seriously contemplating suicide just a few days before discovering gold. Klondicitis enflamed imaginations in the United States and around the globe.[3] Gold, that bane and luster of civilization, was about to cast its addictive, greedy spell and temporarily turn the Yukon into a veritable Shangri-La. Seattle firefighters and police officers quit their jobs and headed north. The 1849 California Gold Rush similarly set off a headlong rush for fortune. "[Many] of those attracted by the prospect of instant wealth were middle class, respectable, hardworking people intent on seizing a chance to improve themselves,"[4] as during the Alaska Gold Rush.

At St. Michael, the precious cargo and humans were divided between the *Portland* destined for Seattle and the *Excelsior* for San Francisco. The

Portland left first, so it took on the most passengers; it took a few weeks to reach Puget Sound. Passengers celebrated the Fourth of July aboard the former *Haitian Republic* and landed in Seattle early on the morning of July 17, 1897.[5] Newspaper headlines followed. The *Excelsior* raced ahead and landed in San Francisco earlier. Pantages felt the excitement and caught the fever when the boat landed in California. "He withdrew all his savings—more than a thousand dollars, for though his pay [at the beer garden] was not large he was frugal—and started north."[6] He had no idea where his ambition was leading him, but his short life was already a testament to taking risks with little forethought or planning on his part. Perhaps that "stubborn sense of personal pride that plagues both educated and uneducated Greeks" got the best of Pantages, or he simply saw no other viable option.[7] What no one told Pantages, and what rarely made it to newspaper headlines, were the hazards of making the journey to the Yukon. He knew the body-sogging heat of the Panamanian jungle; the numbing cold of the north was another matter.

The mad stampede that lasted roughly three years is more popularly known as the Alaska Gold Rush, despite the fact that it took place in Yukon territory, Canada. Some distinctions need to be made. The Klondike refers to the area around the river of the same name where large amounts of gold were found in 1896. It feeds into the Yukon River. Yukon is also the name of the Canadian province that contains the Klondike. There were three main routes to get to the gold fields of the Klondike, and two of them involved going through Alaska; that is why it came to be associated with what was then American-owned land purchased from the Russians in 1867 (it became a territory in 1912 and the forty-ninth state in 1959). The most common route was a boat ride from Seattle to the ports of Skagway or Dyea just north of Juneau in the Alaska panhandle. From there, a long hike commenced up treacherous passes and eventually a boat ride down the Yukon River to Dawson City and (hopefully but rarely) gold. "[The] Yukon was not a river, not a country or territory; it was a romantic pulse beat, a myth come true."[8]

In the first six months of the gold rush, tens of thousands arrived in Alaska for the passage to the Klondike, but many would never make it. It got the better of humans and animals alike; of the 3000 pack-horses used in the mountainous journey, only a handful survived.[9] So many horses died on the White Pass Trail that it became known as "Dead Horse Trail."[10] As is common with hysterias, it didn't last long; the human stampede that was a testament to spirited individuality and mad fortune-seeking reached a crescendo in 1898; a year later, it fell to a trickle.[11] By 1902, five years after the madness began, it was a memory. This "headlong, heedless, mass movement of men like frightened cattle thundering before a rising storm" was by then consigned to history's shelves.[12] Men had an easier time booking passage to Alaska and getting the necessary mining permits. Women got the gold fever too, but had to work harder to make their way to the Yukon. "All that anyone hears at present is 'Klondyke [sic],'" the *Seattle Times* wrote on July 24, 1897. "It is impossible to escape it."[13]

The lust for gold sucked up Americans and foreigners alike. Important gold finds in the region were made by Russians, Scandinavians and Italians, and one even "resulted from the combined effort of a German, a Frenchman and an Irishman."[14] Arabs were also part of the stampede north, though their history in the region is less publicized. Every continent was represented: "professional miners fresh from diggings in Australia and South America, hopeful amateurs from all over the world, Americans from every state."[15] As a mass migration, it was unique in its singular, reckless push, driven by greed and sheer human will, aided by the loudspeaker cheers of newspapers. "Before long," one historian exuded, "the towns of Skagway, Dyea and Dawson City became household words."[16] The only ones who consistently made money in the venture were not the miners, but those that supplied them.

There were guidebooks to help prospective miners, some by well-known scribblers, now long forgotten; they added fuel to the gold fever fires but not necessarily accurate information on how to actually get them to their destination in one piece.[17] More often it was a case of stampeders relying on their own instincts and good fortune to find competent guides to help them contend with dangers along the way. Physical and mental toughness were prerequisites. "This is the law of the Yukon," a poet exclaimed, "and ever she makes it plain: Send not your foolish and feeble; send me your strong and sane."[18] Pantages fit the bill. "The Klondike stampede was made to order for Pantages."[19]

Some time in 1898, Pantages left San Francisco and landed in Seattle.[20] With his savings, he purchased the necessary equipment and provisions there, which, if he followed the experts, consisted of 800 pounds of flour, 400 pounds of bacon, 300 pounds of beans and 20 pounds of "evaporated potatoes."[21] "If the prospector can afford it," the recommendation continued, "he should add to this outfit one rifle, one shotgun, one gill net and a supply of ammunition."[22] It is not known if Pantages took this advice. He turned his attention to finding a steamer for the coastal journey to Alaska. He would have no problem. Transportation services of varying quality suddenly appeared as a result of the gold rush. Seattle's Mayor

W.D. Wood quit his post to set up his own steamship and riverboat line to the north for just that purpose.[23]

It was a five-day ride through extraordinary scenery. "The magnificence of the inland passage with spruce-clad mountains rising into the clouds, every peak and precipice dripping water in cascading streams and plumed falls."[24] Before arriving in Skagway, the ship chugged past Ketchikan, Wrangell and Petersburg, stopped in Juneau, and then proceeded past Haines. Ships were hurriedly unloaded and passengers disembarked, and then the vessels headed south to pick up more dreamers. There was no indication prior to the trip that Pantages was the gambler type, yet on the steamer he supposedly lost his entire life savings to professionals and landed in Skagway with only 25 cents in his pocket.[25] At this point in his life, it seems characteristically irresponsible for him to lose his life savings. Like all Pantages fables, it must be taken with some skepticism, but it cannot be entirely dismissed.

Another story seems even less probable: Prior to leaving Seattle, Pantages wrapped a pair of mukluks (boots) with an old *Seattle Post-Intelligencer* newspaper. Arriving in Skagway, he was spotted leaving the boat with the newspaper and a miner offered him $5 for it. Another one raised it to $10. Pantages, surprised, "took a look at the old newspaper under his arm. He looked at the miners. 'It's not for sale,' he announced and started toward the village."[26] That night, it was announced that a cheechako (a slang term for a newly arrived person in the mining districts of Alaska or northwestern Canada) from Seattle would read a copy of the *Post-Intelligencer* for $1, gold. The dance hall was filled with 350 miners who thrilled at the news from outside. Since Pantages was illiterate, he had someone else do the reading.[27]

Given that copies of the *Seattle Times* and the *Post-Intelligencer* were available in Skagway for a quarter each, it seems bizarre that anyone would pay a dollar in gold to have a paper read out loud unless there were many other illiterates in town. If anything can be drawn from the episode, it may be that soon after arriving in Alaska, Pantages had an epiphany: It was better to provide a valuable service to the miners than to dig for gold. He said many years later, "I found out there was more money to be made in giving the miners what they wanted, than by competing with them in the gold digging."[28]

White Pass lay ahead for Pantages. Unlike the steeper but shorter (32 miles) Chilkoot Pass served by nearby Dyea, White Pass was a longer (40 miles) but more gradual trail for the less intrepid.[29] In either case, the end goal was the long, snail-shaped Lake Lindeman. Once at the lake, it was

2. Apprenticeship

a short trek to Lake Bennett and the final leg of the journey: a long, 500-mile river ride of equal beauty and danger to Dawson City. If Pantages had immediate plans for the inland journey, he decided to park them for a while and find employment as he took stock of his situation. He landed a job with Harriet "Ma" Pullen, who ran an eponymous boarding house in Skagway.

Pullen, a determined entrepreneur, represents the lesser-known feminine business side of the gold rush. She had arrived the previous year from Puget Sound as a penniless widow "with four children, seven dollars and a knack for making wonderful pies out of dried apples."[30] Her way with horses and knowledge of five native dialects made her a suitable candidate for work in the frontier town, yet her first job was cooking. This was an acceptable role for women, who at the time were limited in their employment opportunities: prostitutes, cooks, nurses and dancers. More entrepreneurial women could "set up restaurants and grub tents," operate laundries, run missions and schools, and keep house.[31] Pullen was different. On the side, she baked pies for which she became well-known, and a thriving business followed. Seeing the flood of prospectors pouring into Skagway, she started a freighting business to help miners haul their equipment through the pass—"one of only a few women ever to attempt to do so."[32] It was likely on this basis that she hired Pantages, with his salary being room and board. The job meant that he learned about the route to Lake Bennett and Dawson. He soon picked up enough information about the Pass "to foist himself on a party of tenderfeet as a guide."[33]

Guides on the White Pass were a common sight, both profitable for them and necessary for the stampeders who desperately needed help for the arduous journey. Each stampeder packed roughly 2000 pounds of food and equipment for the journey that required animals, sleds and the cheechakos themselves to carry the tonnage over the passes. Winter was the preferred time for the cross, since it allowed sourdoughs (another of their many colorful nicknames) to use of sleds to move the loads. It also avoided the mosquito attacks of summer. It took between one to two months to make the journey from Skagway to Lake Bennett. Photos from the era show long snake lines of grim, deathly faced human beings in various poses of suffering and determination on the mountain slopes. The sheer physical dimension of the trek astonishes the modern eye; that so many attempted it reveals its hold on desperate imaginations. If it is indeed the last of the mass runs at fortune by ordinary hordes to be witnessed in the American experience, perhaps it was an act of mercy that corporate interests took over the prospecting for gold after the rush and spared ordinary souls the chance at freezing to death.

The journey to Dawson also revealed Pantages' wiles, will and ingenuity. These traits had almost certainly surfaced prior to his gold rush days, but the records of his feats and adventures now truly reveal themselves. He enters history with some certainty, and his movements now have greater clarity. There is still the fog of mythologizing or speculation, but no longer a faceless speck floating on the vast ocean of humanity. He becomes Alexander Pantages, Klondike legend. His last name had changed by the time he arrived in Alaska. Many immigrants had done the same when entering the U.S. through Ellis Island.

This doesn't mean he escaped his immigrant past. As he discovered in San Francisco, ethnicity had its rewards: He got a job catering to the milling, multifarious strands of humanity in Skagway's bustling docks. The frozen north offered another version of the Bay, even as foreigners still struggled under social and racial discrimination of one kind or another. During his entire time in the Yukon, Pantages never quite shed the "Greek" immigrant or "dark, swarthy" label.[34]

Anyone could become a guide; it just required knowing a little more about the journey than the ordinary cheechako. For Pantages, being a guide also meant that his trek to Dawson City would be paid for. It was pure Pantages, squeezing as much profit as he could from his circumstances. The climb involved a series of camps in which weary stampeders rested themselves, their animals or their guides. The pitched tents and lean-tos of these temporary settlements kept out much but not all of the cold. Coffee and a hot breakfast in the morning made up for sleeping on frozen pillows. Day after exhausting day the prospectors would make the same, slow progress across the ice, then settle at a camp at night, and repeat the next day. As the hikers approached Middle Lake and with it Shallow Lake on the descent to Lake Bennett, the knowledge brought relief that this part of the journey had mercifully come to an end.

From Lake Bennett there was a thrilling boat ride down several hundred miles of winding river, yet with the reassurance that thick snow or ice would not be under the miners' feet. They faced many raging whitewater rapids, including Whitehorse, Five Finger and Rink Rapids. There were large embankments of vertical rock on both sides of the river. At Lake Bennett, stampeders also faced the Canadian Northwest Mounted Police, who only allowed those they felt had the requisite skills, equipment, finances and know-how to continue the journey to Dawson. Unprepared amateurs were deemed too high a risk for the Mounties, who worried about the chaos, financial costs and instability they would bring to Canada—not to mention deaths. There was also a political element to the Mounties' presence, namely a bitter border dispute then raging between Canada and the United States. The Canadian authorities worried after the discovery of Yukon gold that hordes of Americans would overrun the area, giving the U.S. an edge in the dispute. Both territory and sanity had to be preserved, hence the sudden presence of the Canadian police. They would not take kindly to con artists or anyone trying to sneak past them. It was their land and they had to protect it. Having ditched his supplies and with few financial resources at hand, how would Pantages get past their stern eyes?

Even at the age of ten in 1898, it was evident that Joseph P. Kennedy was a doer. He loved to take broken clock parts and assemble them into a working piece. Some wondered if he would turn this tinkering ability into a business. One account claims that in his yearbook at Boston Latin, it was predicted that he "would make his fortune in 'a very roundabout way.'"[35] At eight, he led a group of boys "into a military regiment to march in a Memorial Day parade."[36] He also created a youth baseball team, called the "Assumptions" after his elementary school, without official sanction, and he filled the roles of captain, business manager and star player. With money he made selling newspapers, he secured uniforms and equipment against rival teams like the Playfairs and the Olympics. Joe rented a playing field and charged admission. "The games drew so many people that he hired a ballpark and sold tickets, turning a profit."[37] The man who would later storm Hollywood got an early start in the business of making money.[38] The nuns at his school noticed that Joe loved math and solving equations.

His parents' East Boston home "was not the grandest on the street, but it was large and imposing, at the top of the hill, on a double-wide lot, with a deep, wide backyard that sloped down to the water."[39] It was where his grandparents settled, where his parents were born, and where he and his two sisters lived out a prosperous life. His father P.J. Kennedy, a powerful ward boss in Boston and saloon owner, ran two liquor warehouses and even a coal company. He became a founding member of a small bank, Columbia Trust, eventually to play a significant role in the rise of his son's fortunes. Although Joe may have acquired important business skills from his father, one man who knew both of them remarked, "Joe Kennedy inherited his father's business acumen, but not his soul.'"[40] The old man was known as shy and soft-mannered, averse to flash and publicity, preferring to do business in polite conversation. Joe was the opposite: charming, bold, pugnacious, with a big toothy grin that was both a weapon and a disarmer of skeptics. He was attractive, too, his future wife describing him as "tall, thin, wiry, freckled, and had blue eyes and red hair."[41] Kennedy sold papers to make money, and to ingratiate himself to his friends who did the same and with the community. He also clerked in a candy store, sold peanuts to tourists on an excursion boat, the *Excelsior* (no relation to the one that brought gold to San Francisco), and made department store deliveries.[42]

Despite their personality differences, he worshipped his old man. "He had loved nothing more than accompanying the handsome, black-haired, mustachioed ward boss to torchlight parades, picnics, and outdoor rallies."[43] Interestingly, Joe had nothing to say about his mother. Another source claims that relations with his father were chilly and that his mother adored him.[44] To Mary Kennedy, "Joe was the measure of all things."[45] Despite the adoration, she "spooned out her affection to Joe like a tonic that had to be taken in only the smallest of doses."[46] In a photo of Joe taken when he was seven, he is shown in a dress and a bow around his neck. Later he commented about the picture to his son Ted: "[O]bserve … the piercing eyes, the very set jaw, and the clenched left fist. Maybe all of this meant something!"[47]

Kennedy was acutely aware of his ethnicity. Inner Harbor separated his family's enclave as well as many other Irish Catholics from Boston proper and its Protestant Brahmins who dominated the city's life. The help his father provided to so many desperate Irish Catholics was to Kennedy's thinking both naïve and foolish. "[A]ll I could see was their predatory stare," he later recalled about the hordes that always called on his father for help and advice.[48] He saw his father suffering emotionally and financially from this attention and from his penchant for helping the downtrodden. One Kennedy biographer noted, "Joe decided early on that he would build his life on his own foundations without depending on the loyalty of any place or institution."[49] He would be a lone wolf, he surmised, relying on himself. It was a quality that by design created enemies. In his Hollywood years, this came with consequences.

As Kennedy enjoyed boyhood in 1898 and Alexander Pantages rushed headlong to fortune in the Yukon, William Randolph Hearst led the United States into war. Or so his critics charged. Whether he actually did or not is immaterial; more important is the way he wielded his stick of an expanding newspaper chain to affect public perceptions about the events that led to the Spanish-American War. Part of the reason for his excessive drumbeating to military action was simply because his archrival and despised competition, Joseph Pulitzer's *New York World*, also led its own crusade against Spanish-controlled Cuba. Yet at the same time, the *Cuba libre* campaign reveals Hearst's extraordinary flair for the theatrical, elements of which he used to damn so many in his long career—which would include Alexander Pantages.

With his *San Francisco Examiner* a success by 1890, dramatization of news became central to the Hearstian way and with it the ability to color ordinary Americans' minds. No major American publisher had quite perfected this dramatic skill with such boyish enthusiasm and journalistic vigor as Hearst. By 1895 when he took over the placid *New York Journal* (with funds from his mother, Phoebe Hearst), the now adult Willie excelled in "his adolescent removal from reality and his great theatrical gifts."[50] The "Wizard of Ooze," as he was dubbed by critics, dancing in the mud of newspaper sensationalism, knew how to excite the human senses.[51] One Hearst biographer claimed that the *Journal* "was a demanding, sophisticated paper by contemporary standards," even as it excelled at, or abused, the art of the dramatic.[52] If drama could work for the Bible, Shakespeare and Dickens, surely it could enliven the modern American newspaper—that was the reasoning, according to one Hearst editor (who had moved over from Pulitzer's *World*).[53] "The emphasis on drama—that is, on actions and the people who did those actions—often included an element of sensationalism."[54]

Dramatizing the news came at a cost. Hearst adopted this sensational style with such outlandish intensity that his staff reporters often expressed concern that his newspapers appealed "to the emotions, the lower phases of intelligence, and the baser instincts of readers, and disguising this by playing up occasional intellectual interests of real value." Or, even worse, that he "was deliberately trying 'to color, misinterpret and even falsify current happenings.'"[55] Hearst snarkily wrote, "The modern editor of the popular journal does not care for the facts."[56] More worrisome, for those inside and outside his organization, was that he alone was capable of determining what was best for Americans to read.[57] Hearst proudly stated that "an event becomes news only when journalists and editors decide to record it."[58] Historian Marc Norman again alludes to the level of creative license taken, the stories being given, "a poignancy they might not deserve, characters and a plot, the emotional satisfaction of fiction."[59] A commentator had a different interpretation, suggesting the "'Hearst method has all the reality of masturbation.'"[60]

Cuba weighed uncomfortably on American consciousness, just 90 miles from Florida. An independence movement of one kind or another had long festered on the island in the nineteenth century, decades before the *Journal* and the *World* took up the cause. It is interesting that apparent Spanish cruelty only started soon after Hearst and Pulitzer got interested in the island's liberation, although Spain's misrule of the island was no secret.[61] "Cuba ... had become a land of fire and famine, an example of savage cruelty and wanton barbarity," one historian attested.[62] In 1895, Spain responded to rebellion and deteriorating conditions by imposing martial law, which only made matters worse. With the *Journal* and *World* demanding Spain's withdrawal from the island, it was bound to get messy for the once mighty empire. Under the new leadership of the Spanish General Valeriano Weyler y Nicolau, Cubans were shoved "into camps bereft of food supplies and sanitary facilities; thus disease and death were ever constant."[63] When yellow fever broke out in the camps, the Weyler regime struggled to provide an adequate response. For Hearst, *Cuba libre* turned into a personal, national, political and commercial crusade. He referred to Weyler as "The Butcher" or "The Wolf."[64] "The American newspapers," Weyler declared in response, "poison everything with falsehood."[65] Yet Weyler's own tactics pushed many residents of the island into revolution while also increasingly winning for Cubans the sympathy of the American public, thanks to the efforts of Hearst and Pulitzer.[66]

Pulitzer's *World* rang its own anti–Spanish bells' for example, when it claimed, "Spanish soldiers habitually cut off the ears of the Cuban dead and retain them as trophies."[67] Painting the Spanish as savages "who lacked the moral sensibilities and self-restraint of civilized men" further enhanced the drama of the events.[68] It was a theme that much of the coverage emphasized, creating further evidence of Spaniards as the heavies or antagonists. Hearst's *Journal* and Pulitzer's *World* were now locked in a titanic struggle for New York publishing supremacy unique in the annals of press history. While the competition enlivened journalism at the time, perhaps even giving succor to muckraking reporting that incited much-needed social and industrial reform in the U.S., it also placed facts before a firing squad.[69] "It was the first instance of that effective use of newspaper propaganda on a large scale."[70]

Neither the White House nor Congress was ready for war, as inviting a diversion as it might seem at a time when the nation's economy still reeled from the financial meltdown of 1893. To force the issue, Hearst and Pulitzer employed theatrics on a grand scale. Hearst knew that to sustain his readers' interest and attract new readers, he needed to dramatize the affair: identify heroes or protagonists, antagonists and recognizable plots. "What made Cuba such a compelling story was the fact that events on the island lent themselves to Hearst's favorite plot line."[71] "The hero-villain concept of the war was simple, easy to grasp and satisfying."[72] He also had to find, or manufacture, "some 'outrage' to arouse sympathy."[73] His entire publishing philosophy boiled down to: "Portray the human condition as it is and offer a special accolade to the brave."[74]

The brave tended to be males while their victims were females who needed men's protection. This demarcation was not merely a trait of Hearst, but emblematic of the American culture at a time when "manly" characteristics were requisite for full citizenship.[75] Hearst simply took this macho trait to surreal heights, thanks to the powerful megaphones (newspapers) at his disposal. For American press correspondents in Cuba, the island's women were to be depicted as pure and innocent victims of Spanish lust while Cuban men were nothing less than chivalrous and brave.[76] When not portrayed as ruthless vultures in the coverage, the Spanish came across as "effeminate aristocrats, best embodied by their queen regent or boy king," thus lacking the manly sensibilities needed to effectively govern.[77] And if Americans did not intervene in the conflict, this meant the U.S. lacked the manliness necessary to maintain its political prowess. This was jingoism mixed with racist implications, and it "was trumpeted throughout the land."[78]

With a villain in "Butcher" Weyler, Hearst needed a protagonist whom readers could root for. In a common refrain utilized throughout his publishing career, he preferred women for this role. There was a paternalistic, chauvinistic element to this enterprise; presenting women as natural victims who needed Hearst's intervention glorified him in the process, a sort of latter-day prophet for the weaker sex.

The exercise of Hearstian power rested on "manly character, something defined in different ways but generally in reference to contrasting ideas about womanly attributes."[79] In selecting a female victim, Hearst showed off his strength and courage while capturing the readers' sympathy with tales of physical abuse of an innocent, helpless female. In this case, it involved an attractive teenager named Evangelina Cosio y Cisneros. The operative word is *attractive*. Hearst had a predilection for using comely females in his papers as eye candy. Like leading ladies in movies, they had to be beautiful in order to capture his readers' attention, as part of his winning strategy of "not only informing but entertaining readers, since they wanted both."[80] In turning news into staged dramas, he "became producer, director and stage manager for the greatest of journalistic melodramas."[81] Later, when he ran his own Hollywood film production company and repeated these roles, it was simply a natural progression.

Cisneros was the daughter of a Cuban rebel. She was 18 when the island uprising exploded in the spring of 1895, and her father was captured and sentenced to death. Accounts differ regarding Cisneros' arrest more than a year later; it may have involved her luring a Spanish colonel to her cottage, where rebels captured him only for the Spanish army to rescue him and arrest Cisneros.[82] Another claim involved Cisneros taking part in an insurrection, for which she was arrested.[83] *Journal* readers were fed an entirely different story, one almost certainly made up, involving her "being imprisoned for defending her chastity against a lustful Spanish colonel."[84] According to a *Journal* reporter, "she was confined among degenerates in the filthy Recojidas prison and in all probability was doomed to a 20-year term ... for her purity."[85]

The competing *World* found that Cisneros was treated better than other prisoners and even had her meals brought in from outside the jail.[86] More important than the facts was that Hearst had his heroine. "The life and liberty of a sorely persecuted girl martyr" became Hearst's passion.[87] "Hearst comfortably played the role of Sir Galahad rescuing a helpless maiden."[88] Appeals to various U.S. leaders followed, asking their help in demanding that she be freed. He made special pleas to American women. "We can make a national issue of this case," he barked to a *Journal* staffer. "It will do more to open the eyes of the country to Spanish cruelty and oppression than a thousand editorials or political speeches."[89]

Petitions poured in, including "from women of intelligence and prestige who should have known better than to act on an unconfirmed newspaper report."[90] Hearst had his own reporters attempt to bribe her jailers, which resulted in the Spaniards tossing his lead writer out of Cuba. Employing a method he later used effectively against Pantages, Hearst inflamed the public's anger over Cisneros. The *Journal* noted on August 19, 1897: "The unspeakable fate to which Weyler has doomed an innocent girl whose only crime is that she had defended her honor against a beast in uniform has sent a shudder of horror through the American people."[91] As a Hearst biographer noted, "Evangelina Cisneros had become a symbol of wronged innocence in the United States."[92]

In August 1897, Hearst sent the "gallant soldier-reporter" Karl Decker to make another rescue attempt.[93] Decker rented a flat next to the jail, where on the night of October 7, he and a small group of confederates planted a ladder across to Cisneros' cell, drugged her jailers and fellow prisoners, and whisked her away. More recent evidence indicates that a U.S. Embassy official in Havana, who six months earlier had been suspended on charges of excessive drinking, surreptitiously gave Cisneros a small file to cut her window bars, allowing her to escape the night of the daring rescue.[94] The *Journal* played up her freedom with stunning headlines three days later: "MISS EVANGELINA CISNEROS RESCUED BY THE JOURNAL."[95]

Other newspapers hailed the event, while the trade publication *The Journalist* noted the episode resembled a "medieval romance [more than] nineteenth century journalism."[96] Hearst then brought "this truly beautiful young girl," as he called her, to the U.S., where she met a variety of dignitaries, including President William McKinley in the White House.[97] The ratings, in the form of newspaper sales, went through the roof. "While others talk," Hearst famously claimed, "the *Journal* acts." And he had Cisneros to thank. Years later he boasted that his New Journalism, dubbed "Yellow," "had been instrumental in the evolution of journalism because it was more sensitive to public opinion."[98] His detractors regarded it as manipulation of public opinion. His own son wrote, "He went all out to help start the Spanish-American War in 1898."[99] Many objected to this style of journalism, including his own family; his mother, Phoebe Hearst, refused to allow her son's *Journal* into her house.[100] The trustees of Newark, New Jersey's, Free Public Library banned both the *Journal* and the *World* from its readings rooms.[101] Many mainstream paper editors regarded Hearst and his publications as a plague upon their profession.

The U.S. was now primed for war. In January 1898, after a Senate debate on Cuba, President McKinley sent the warship *Maine* to Havana. It was stationed there for about a month when suddenly on February 15, 1898, a series of explosions destroyed the ship and took with it the lives of 266 Americans. Sabotage was immediately blamed; only much later did investigations reveal that the explosions likely took place on the boat itself and were not caused by an outside force.[102] Readership climbed. On January 9 of that year, *Journal* sales had totaled 416,885; after the *Maine* exploded, it shot up to 1,036,140. By June and July, when hostilities were in full bloom, it reached over 1,250,000. No American newspaper had ever reached such dizzying heights.

It was a formality that Congress finally declared military intervention on April 16. Five days later, Spain cut off relations with the U.S. and on April 24 declared war on the U.S. War was now real, no longer newspaper fiction, thanks in no small part to Hearst and Pulitzer. Government by newspaper, or at least "war by newspaper," had been realized. Journalism would never be the same again. Hearst even visited Cuba as a reporter, filing stories from the front.[103] "I think the standing of the paper will profit by my being here," he wrote his mother. "Other proprietors are safely at home," he added in a dig against Pulitzer.[104] He even managed to take some Spanish prisoners while he was there. The *Journal*'s war ended in August. Interestingly, the U.S. efforts to liberate Cuba from Spain did not extend to the negotiations for peace. Having won the war, the American side had little to do with the Cuban revolutionaries who had first agitated for it. It was an American victory, not a Cuban one. The win also netted the U.S. control over the Philippines and Hawaii.

Hearst and Pulitzer had gone to extremes to outdo each other, verging on the absurd. They suspected each other of stealing news scoops. Hearst reported on the tragic death of Colonel Reflipe W. Thenuz in the fighting. Pulitzer printed a complete story on "the battle of Aguadores detailing the heroics of Thenuz and his subsequent death."[105] The *Journal* promptly revealed that the colonel was a fictitious anagram that spelled, "We pilfer the nuz."[106] Pulitzer came to regret the circulation wars and the role he played in whipping up public frenzy for the invasion. "It has not been to the advantage of any newspaper in doing so," his business manager wrote. "The *World* feels that it is time for the staff to learn definitely and finally that it must be a normal newspaper."[107] On the other hand, Hearst basked in his triumph. "Truly, the victory in Cuba was brought about by a broad-based public demand," he said, facetiously adding: "Let us always remember the power of an informed public mind."[108] It regarded the Cisneros rescue as "the final stage of the modern newspaper" in which it rights the wrongs of society.[109] "It does not wait for things to turn up," the *Journal* boasted. "It turns them up."[110] Missing from the discussion was the participation of American Embassy staff and other sympathizers. Without the support of these individuals, the "journalism that acts" would have amounted to nothing.

Just as satisfying for the young publisher was that he had also bested the powerful Pulitzer, who faded after the episode. Hearst now stood atop the publishing world, a czar and molder of public opinion. He had shown that sensationalism in reporting attracted a sizable audience, and in the process "he had touched the levers of national power."[111] It was an aphrodisiac that he never quite gave up, and one the man who had "re-invented the wheel of journalism" never learned to master.[112] In muckraking journalist Lincoln Steffens' words: "His papers 'appealed to the people'; yes, to their 'best interest,' and to their worst.'"[113]

Somehow Pantages led his group from Skagway to Dawson. "The party made it over the White Pass trail, escaping the dangers of the precipices and the infantile paralysis epidemic then raging."[114] Another version is simpler: "Alex scaled the snowy mountains and slipped by the Mounties."[115] Pantages likely passed the Mounties' inspection because his physique made him look rough and hardy. There were probably fewer rules about guides than there were about prospectors, "despite the fact he had neither a grubstake [supplies] nor passage money to show the mounted police."[116] Once past the Mounties, there was the task of building or acquiring a boat to carry his charges across Lake Bennett and down the treacherous Yukon River—difficult tasks for a seasoned guide, impossible for a novice like Pantages. Yet, in either case, it was necessary, since it was expected of a guide to haul his passengers to Dawson.

Pantages opted to build his own boat. This was not as audacious as it seems; others were doing the same all around him on the lake, so the equipment, the tools and the knowledge were there. But getting this knowledge without having to pay for it proved a challenge. His charges would be watching; if he came across as incompetent, not only would they likely abandon him but they might furiously demand their money back. It was a defining moment. Pantages "wandered about a riverside camp, watching the experts whipsaw lumber from the trees, arguing with the experienced boat builders, telling them what they were doing wrong, soaking up information while they explained why their methods were right."[117]

What this bit of verbal trickery produced was a craft of some seaworthiness, "a boat that looked like a boat," even though it "listed dangerously."[118] To curious onlookers, he said of the uneven boat, "Well, this job's half done."[119] He fashioned another boat, this one only slightly better. But it suited his purpose and he fastened the two boats together. He invited his passengers aboard. Somehow they all made it to Dawson. "Pantages later confided to a friend in Seattle that his method of shooting the rapids was to close his eyes and trust that he was too young to die."[120]

What Pantages stepped into in Dawson City was another world, a parallel society that brought out the best and worst of humanity, often simultaneously. His previous experiences may have helped him acclimate to the roughhouse city more easily than other newcomers, but the circumstances were no less dire than what he had experienced in San Francisco. He drifted from one thankless job to another: "dishwasher, saloon porter, general handyman and janitor."[121] He even tried his hand at selling coal oil to miners. Nothing satisfied him, at least, not for long.

The sign over Charlie Cole's Saloon in Dawson City advertised for an "Expert Mixologist" at the inflated sum of "$45 per day."[122] As Pantages did on the cargo boat and with the Mounted Police, he talked himself into the job, having never mixed drinks in his life. "The money convinced him he was an expert and he soon became one, not only at mixing drinks but in such specialties of the Alaskan barkeep as pressing his thumb on the bar to pick up stray grains of gold and spilling a little dust on the ingrain carpet under the scales when he weighed out payment for drinks. After a good day a shaky man could fluff an ounce from the carpet."[123] Many bartenders coated their fingers with resin and scraped the dust into special pockets under their long white aprons.[124] This practice was called "singling out," and it was dangerous if the offending waiter was caught by customers. Another one involved "doubling out," described as the act of refilling half-empty bottles with water and collecting for the full bottle. Both customers and the house were cheated in this practice, which, like the other scams, involved both a bartender and an accomplice dancer.

Pantages' mind worked in other ways. Mindful of improving the operation, while increasing his wages and trying his hand at theater management, he suggested that Cole turn the saloon "into something of a boxhouse [a saloon with theater], with a real stage and a regular orchestra. Cole did and the place prospered."[125] Another account gives more details to this sudden change of fortune for Pantages. A boxer Cole had booked for a sold-out prizefight failed to show, and Pantages offered to take his place. "I'll save the pot for you, Charlie," he told the owner. "I'll fight the guy myself."[126] He did and he won in a knockout, his one and only return to boxing. A grateful Cole made Pantages a manager and gave him a ten percent interest in his show.[127] The *Dawson Daily News* announced on January 2, 1900, that Pantages was the general manager of the Cole's Opera House.[128]

Pantages invested in a stock theater company, which promptly failed. Salvation came from an unlikely source—a dancer who came to be known, perhaps mistakenly or in an act of theft, as "Klondike Kate" Rockwell. Their relationship, both professional and personal, changed the trajectories of their lives. The area had many colorful characters with names like Evaporated Kid, Circle City Mickey, Siwash George, Dog Salmon Bob, Silent Sam Bonnifield, the Kansas City Kid, the Rag Time Kid, French Curley, Nelly the Pig, Limejuice Lil and Spanish Dolores.[129] But few stood out like the Queen of the Klondike, as Rockwell was also called.

On October 4, 1876, she was born Kathleen Eloise Rockwell in Junction City, Kansas, but died as Kathleen Eloise Rockwell Warner Matson Van Duren, adding married names as if collecting fine furniture. She was born in one marriage but raised in another, her stepfather a divorce attorney and later judge in Spokane, Washington. It was there that Judge Bettis "lived his role as a wealthy nabob to the fullest, swaggering about town in a high silk hat and cutaway coat, and flourishing a gold-headed cane."[130] The family occupied an impressive mansion where "Kate grew into a spoiled child, unrestrained and rambunctious, riding horseback and camping outdoors."[131] On one occasion, she opened the grand family estate to one hundred folks who had lost their homes in a neighborhood fire. The incident infuriated her mother and scandalized the region.[132] She also got her classmates to skip school and provided them with ample supplies of food from her father's charge accounts. "It wasn't that I was bad," she later recounted. "I was just imaginative and full of life and the excitement of living."[133] For a time as a teenager she lived in a convent in Chile.

What she liked to do best was sing and dance. After her mother divorced a second time, they found themselves without money in New York. Despite protests, Kate took to the stage to help pay the bills. Soon she joined vaudeville shows that took her across the country and discovered that part of her dues as a showgirl involved enticing customers to drink. It was a rude awakening for the young Rockwell, but she quickly warmed to the practice. She was in Seattle on July 17, 1897, when the *Portland* steamed into town. Within two years she found herself on the way to the Klondike. The Mounties forbade women to ride down the rapids of the Yukon River, considering it both unladylike and too dangerous for them, so she dressed as a boy and tried to jump from shore onto a boat. She slipped and fell into the freezing water. A Mountie yelled after her, but she was pulled aboard the boat and it sailed down the river.[134]

Rockwell secured a job with the Savoy Theatrical Company which, "with 173 performers and a full orchestra, was the largest theater troupe to perform in the Klondike."[135] The Savoy became the entertainment magnet to Dawson and the region. "The cavernous building came alive with the whir of the roulette wheel, clinking of glasses, shuffling of cards, and band music under the glow of coal oil lamps illuminating the room."[136] As a star, Rockwell lived in a room above the theater. Performing was only a part of the work. As she had discovered earlier, she also operated as a "percentage girl," dancing with the lonely miners and plying them with alcohol. Klondike Kate, as she was now known, performed her tasks well. "My best night I earned $750, mostly just for talking to a lonesome miner," she later boasted.[137] The show began at 8:30 p.m. and the women ended their shifts at ten the following morning.

It seems that Kate and Alex, as she called him, first met at Cole's. They worked as a team—waiter and dancer—"relieving drunks of their gold dust in private boxes after the show."[138] For Rockwell, the "stocky, tough and robust" Greek immigrant was also "slick, handsome and smooth-talking."[139] They made an odd pair: the flamboyant, boisterous, red-haired Rockwell with the "well-proportioned" Pantages with "large dark eyes" and olive complexion.[140] While other Dawsonites dressed roughly, he was clean-shaven, parted his hair in the middle, smoked cigars and wore imported silk shirts thanks, according to Rockwell, to her largesse.[141] Yet he could be "ingratiatingly servile" in one moment and "insolent, indifferent and taciturn" the next.[142] He rarely smiled, was brutally cold, and was not given to idle chatter. "His mind worked in dollar signs," Rockwell biographer Ellis Lucia claimed, perhaps vindictively.[143] But Rockwell was in love. "In the spring," she later claimed, "we'd go picking poppies together on the banks of the Klondike. And we'd made plans for the day when we would later marry."[144] Those marriage plans would come to haunt both.

They were kindred spirits. Both were adventurous, had left home, appreciated the outdoors, wandered in distant lands, loved entertainment, and saw in Dawson a chance to establish their careers.[145] To Lucia, she was an artist, yet "she had difficulty deciding what she was or who she was."[146] She became known as the "Queen of the Yukon," but it is not clear when the moniker "Klondike Kate" was attached to her. Rockwell is accused of stealing it from another "Klondike Kate," a well-known and upright authoritarian Yukon character named Katherine Ryan. Because of the dancer's reputation, the latter was chagrined.[147]

Ladies of the night and entertainers (often one and the same) kept alive the whole creaking apparatus of the city of Klondike. They provided what little human warmth was available to the residents and the miners, and momentary escapes from relentlessly dangerous yet singularly boring lives. As much as Rockwell tried to be something other than eye candy for lonely miners, as her business dealings with Pantages reveal, she ultimately never rose above the limits of her chosen career. "Her sexy, flirtatious glances made many Yukoners feel that Kate turned a trick here and there, and she probably did," her biographer detailed, "for Kitty Rockwell never claimed to be pure as the driven snow and Dawson was Dawson in any woman's language."[148]

Pantages and Rockwell were kindred souls, even if their relationship frequently veered toward breaking up. The social environment of the area contributed to the couple's instability, but their own individual ruthlessness must also be factored into the personal tension. They were enablers of each other's worst traits, accusing each other of infidelity, selfishness and exploitation. They provided social status to one another at the expense of emotional stability. He needed her financial prowess while she craved his physical male companionship. Each recognized the courage in the other, both having left civilization to find fame in a dilapidated outpost with no hint that either would find success. At a time when few women had what we today would call careers, Kate blazed a trail in one of the few areas open to talented women: vaudeville. Their relationship worked, at least professionally, even if it could not last personally.

For much of the late nineteenth and early twentieth centuries, "vaudeville was at the heart of American show business."[149] Opera, concerts and Shakespearean theater had their own cultural demands and pretentions; not so vaudeville. It was accessible and cheap, closer to the everyday lives of ordinary folks. Vaudeville, as one historian put it simply, "was a people's culture."[150] Although forms of vaudeville had been performed centuries prior and in several places across the globe (Cairo, Bombay, London, Shanghai, Mexico City and London), it perhaps it reached its zenith in the U.S. and is thus associated with it. Musical and variety acts adapted much more easily to the political winds in post–Revolutionary America; they were able to change to fit the mood of the times more swiftly than traditional drama and melodramatic theater shows that could raise the ire of moralists.

As immigration increased in the U.S. in the nineteenth century, the new arrivals brought with them their Old World customs. "In the old country, the immigrants' idea of a good time included beer, ale, liquor, music and dancing."[151] Yet operators realized the value of attracting women and children to their shows; thus they sought respectability over notoriety, and in doing so increased vaudeville's popularity. Vaudeville grew in size and reach, attracting a greater range of talent along the way. A network of artists, with bookers and agents, traversed the entire country with the help of expanding railroad lines. Much of the model for the development and expansion of movies was earlier set in place by vaudeville. As vaudeville historian Frank Cullen noted, the profession was one of the few in the country that encouraged talent regardless of ethnicity or gender.[152]

"In a vaudeville show, you could have everything: from the puritanical to the licentious, from the patriotic to the anarchistic; from idolaters of wealth to egalitarians."[153] Despite its roots in medicine and minstrel shows of one kind or another in the Middle Ages, vaudeville was a peculiarly American art form. "The vaudeville form suited a nation where nothing could be taken for granted."[154] It presaged the coming of films with its ability to exploit the technologies of the era, particularly railroad and telegraphs to move acts around the country. It was perhaps the first major

American entertainment institution that encouraged ethnic and female performers. "Diversity, tolerance, democracy, the worth of the individual—all these could be learned within vaudeville's halls, even if the lessons were being absorbed unconsciously."[155] It was also the perfect visual titillation for an industrializing nation that asked that its workers' entertainment come simple, noisy, earthy and hard.

Vaudeville began with a "dumb" act involving a non-verbal skit (so that late arrivals would not feel they had missed anything), followed by the main or star-billing act or two, and concluding with the "chaser," an interesting yet boring number that was meant to clear the halls for the next round of viewers. There could also be transition acts between the three main draws, and the star-billing could be multiple acts, but in general the pattern was maintained.

The vaudevillians' life was never settled; only when they reached such status as belonged to Rockwell could life become reasonably comfortable. It included enduring physical duress, like that of Harley Mankin, the "Frog Man." A contortionist ("snake" in vaudeville parlance) with extraordinary ability, he physically tortured himself for the sake of his career. One of his famous acts took seven years to perfect and involved sitting on a table like a frog in front of an audience, lifting one leg over his head and then pushing it down so that it touched the table.[156] For minority performers, there was also racial exclusion. "No African-American entertainer lived or worked without struggling against hatred, bigotry and the denial of opportunity."[157]

Rockwell's status and reputation demanded she be the main attraction. Her combination of striptease and improvisational dance with music produced a hypnotic effect. For her famous Flame Dance, she unwound 200 yards of red chiffon, spinning to a lone violin playing Ravel's "Bolero." "The stage became a sea of fire from the twisting, spinning, whirling girl weaving in and out of the yards and yards of soaring cloth."[158] The audience sat in a rapturous stare. "Kate's head spins with a frenzy she knows is reaching deep into her audience."[159] It was powerful and mesmerizing, but the act didn't pay the bills. Alcohol did. Rockwell's claim that she once earned several hundred dollars in a day, "mostly just for talking to a lonesome miner," was ostensibly true but the earnings were grossly lubricated with alcohol.[160] The dance halls were designed for the express purpose of alcohol consumption: liquor bar and gambling tables in the front, theater and dancing area in the rear. Above the dancing area were the boxes for customers who could afford them. This is where the dancers as eye-candy became dancers as unofficial therapists for the lonely miners: The ladies dispensed their listening skills with copious amounts of alcohol.[161]

There could be as many as 28 women working the dance floor. Each time a woman danced with a man, he would have to buy a drink ($1) for himself and her. She could accept the drink, in which case she received no further remuneration for the dance. If, however, she refused, as often was the case, she received a token that was redeemable for 50 cents. Since dances were short, this meant an industrious girl could earn $20 to $30 in tokens per night. The big money was in enticing miners to the boxes, where she offered champagne at $80 per quart, for which she received 25 percent commission. It was here that Rockwell excelled.[162] She was, as the *Seattle Times* noted, "a triple threat—a good actress, a graceful dancer, a clever 'box rustler.'"[163]

Pantages and Rockwell were "not above cheating men out of their money."[164] This took the form of serving watered-down champagne. Few inebriated customers complained.[165] Theater mogul Pantages would later cheat actors out of their contracted salaries, carrying on what he had started in the Yukon. As duplicitous partners, Kate and Alex worked well together. Kate was many things to Alex, but the most important was the one for which he had come to the Yukon: She bankrolled his dream to own his own business.

The Orpheum Theater that Rockwell helped Pantages purchase was not designed for a lengthy future.[166] Like most Dawson dwellings, it was built for the moment. It burned down three times.[167] It was cheaper to build it flimsily and risk it being burned to the ground than to spend more on a finer construction at the start. Pantages had few concerns about its design or architectural soundness; his interest was in turnover. The more customers and performances the better; the tills, not the façade, counted. In this regard, the Orpheum was a success. Pantages "talked of his dream of owning a string of theaters across the country."[168] He learned to observe his audiences to see what they wanted and then, after hours, he swept the floors for gold dust.[169] He did well, or at least, well enough, despite the fact that he was tied to his lover. "In his growing good fortune he tired of his association with Kate Rockwell."[170] Pantages rebuilt his theater; but when new gold discoveries were made elsewhere, he recognized that the Yukon's salad days were coming to an end. It was 1902. The gold rush had lasted five years. For the couple, discussions turned to the next chapter in their lives. They had lived together, and she assumed they would settle down and consummate their relationship.

Then a prim and proper 17-year-old violinist from an upstanding California family, Lois Mendenhall, suddenly appeared.

3. Mogulhood

When Alex Pantages realized it was time to leave the Yukon, the isolationist Kate Rockwell refused to go.[1] She had found her niche in life, was financially rewarded for it, and wanted her paradise to last forever. "I began my day's work with an hour in a gymnasium to keep in trim," she later recalled. "'I had my own horse and in the summer I'd drive like wild through the strangely beautiful country.'"[2] The former tomboy could not have been happier. She had also grown exceedingly comfortable in her lavish lifestyle, "partying and drinking on an increasingly lavish scale." She didn't take kindly to his suggestion they leave in the spring of 1902. "Leave?" she replied. "And miss all the excitement? There isn't another place like this in the world and I love it."[3] "And I was named queen of it all."[4] The queen was overseeing an increasingly deserted city with the "magic of the Yukon" already wearing off.[5] The great tidal wave of human entrepreneurship, madness and greed that was the gold rush had now faded and miners were returning home.

There are two versions of what happened next. In one, she packed up and headed south while Pantages remained in Dawson to shut down their remaining business interests. She sailed to Seattle and contemplated her options there, visiting local theaters to get a sense of the leisure landscape in the smelly lumber town. But it was a chance to see films that set her mind ablaze. She was struck and awed by "how many nickels and dimes people paid to view the flickering pictures that often sent them away with sore eyes and headaches."[6] Rockwell had found motion pictures. A quaint little nickelodeon theater was available for $350 in nearby Victoria, British Columbia.[7] She promptly bought the operation, added live vaudeville acts, including her own performances, and the show-house produced a profit. When Pantages arrived in Seattle a few weeks later, he was startled to find that she had moved to Canada. He angrily berated her for taking on the foolish venture of showing films. Yet a few months later, he copied her exhibition formula—offering both vaudeville and films—by opening the Crystal Theater, a storefront operation, in downtown Seattle.[8]

In the second version, Pantages convinced Rockwell to do a grand tour across the U.S., including stops in New York and the booming oil towns of Texas, while he stayed in Alaska planning his next move. In her biography she is strangely silent about her time in Texas; it seems she became romantically involved with a gambler and might have married him, even though he mistreated her.[9] If a lawyer's letter to Pantages is to be believed, Alex managed to repair their relationship. "Sincerely I do trust that no one should ever dim the horizon that now shines in resplendent adoration in the mind's eye of your Katherine."[10] The lawyer approved of Pantages going "to the far east [and] carrying her safely back to the northern wilds that she might replenish the treasury."[11] Together again, they next traveled to Nome, Alaska, where new gold discoveries had been made. They briefly reopened the Orpheum, but he decided that he needed a more stable business environment to fulfill his vision of a chain of theaters. He headed to Seattle while she stayed behind. If her version is to be believed, Pantages avoided discussing marriage with her.[12]

Both versions reveal cracks in their bond. The strains of their unstable careers exacted a price, but there were other factors pulling them apart. She may have borne a child with him, but hid the fact under the pretext that it was the baby of a "young tubercular girl" she had befriended but who died giving birth.[13] Kate had abandoned the baby boy for a time, but returned to raise the child, Lotus, until he was three. She then gave him up for adoption. She also eventually paid for his college education, and the young man became a successful engineer.[14] Pantages never spoke about the baby, although curiously he later adopted a child of his own, perhaps out of guilt for this turbulent period in their relationship. Aside from Kate's infidelities, there was her growing dependency on alcohol. He had a friend write to her in his name: "Katie, I wonder if you will this time sincerely keep your promise and not drink any more."[15]

While he started his Seattle business ventures, she was on the road "where she could hear the applause of the crowd and be a part of exciting things."[16] He wrote begging for funds. "Business is quite good with me, but still always bear in mind that Papa is always in need of ready cash and ever willing to put your savings alongside of his so as to make a good showing."[17] She sent him money, but they did not discuss anything outside the theater business. It was a strange new twist to their bond. "I have begun to realize that you are speeding on your way, separating ourselves from each other by many wiles," he wrote.[18] In another missive, he admitted that he was "getting fat as a pig," because he had "no one to fight and fuss with."[19]

In 1905, Rockwell continued to travel the vaudeville circuit, including stops in Alaska. In Texas, she shared billing with a 17-year-old violinist. The slim and attractive Lois Mendenhall hailed from a prominent Oakland family who "considered Pantages a secure if somewhat tarnished businessman."[20] The violinist was featured at the Crystal. After a year away, Rockwell returned to Seattle, only to find Pantages "strangely cool and aloof."[21] She put this down to his stress at trying to make the Crystal profitable, but when she went to Spokane, where she was regarded as a celebrity, she unexpectedly received a letter from a friend. In it she read that Pantages had married Mendenhall on March 12 of that year. Stunned and enraged, she fell into depression.

Pantages' marriage to Mendenhall promised a more stable, saner world than what Rockwell offered him. Mendenhall was everything that Kate was not: quiet, serene, reserved. In addition, Mendenhall's elitist family could prove useful in establishing his business career. "It wasn't until I met Lois that I knew anything much about good women," he said in a statement, in an obvious dig at Rockwell.[22]

Whether she read this account is not known; she had enough contacts in the theater world to have heard it second-hand. His comments unsettled her further and she drank more heavily.[23] A letter from a friend who knew them both from Dawson encouraged her not to fall apart but to stand up for herself. "Don't throw your life away because of one man," she told Rockwell.[24] She gathered herself and, taking the friend's advice, on May 26, 1905, filed a $25,000 breach of promise lawsuit in King County Superior Court. "USES HER MONEY, THEN JILTS THE GIRL," the headline blared on the front page of the afternoon edition of the *Seattle Times*, the same day the suit was filed.[25] To the *Times* reporter, Pantages at first denied even knowing Rockwell. Finally, after being pressed, he acknowledged Rockwell as a "former acquaintance" but he laughed off the lawsuit. "Why, it's silly to think of me being sued for breach of promise. I am a married man. Married men are never sued for breach of promise."[26]

The suit brought national publicity, causing the "real" Klondike Kate, Kate Ryan, great misery, since friends and acquaintances assumed the case involved her. Rockwell used the courtroom as a theatrical stage, making a grand entrance on her first walk to the witness stand. Under oath she related details of her years spent with Pantages, and no doubt a sympathetic onlooker would regard her as the victim in the case. Newspaper coverage of the trial brought out details of their romantic and working relationship that stained both their reputations. The case dragged on, "titillating the world with allegations and countercharges."[27] Suddenly, when it appeared that she might win the case, she authorized a dismissal to the suit and promptly left the state. Since both sides' lawyers worked the case on contingency, the legal teams were left without compensation. They responded with further legal action, forcing Rockwell and Pantages back into court for additional testimony. Finally, a year after initially filing the lawsuit, the court dismissed Rockwell's allegations, but Pantages agreed to pay her a settlement, reputedly around $5,000.[28] Her desire, as she stated in her biography, to "bring Alex to heel" had failed.[29] It was a blow, affecting her work and zest. Eventually, she escaped the demands of performing and the painful aftermath of the failed relationship by moving to the central desert of Oregon with a dog and becoming a rock collector.[30] She still carried a torch for Pantages, but the bleak yet strangely beautiful desert was a temporary salve. Rockwell and Pantages would not see or speak to each other for 23 years, until his trial for sexual assault in 1929.

The Seattle where Alexander Pantages arrived in 1902 was considerably smaller than San Francisco, and in many ways culturally inept but with pretensions and promise of greater sophistication to come. Yet, in an odd way, it felt like home to him. He could have returned to California after the Yukon days, but perhaps he understood he would be a tadpole in a vast lake there. He had been in Seattle twice before, once after his Panama adventures on his way to San Francisco and then prior to his journey to Alaska, so he was familiar with the rowdy sawmill town on Puget Sound. It shared plenty of edgy entertainment elements with Dawson and San Francisco's Barbary Coast, enough perhaps to make him feel he had not left either of his former residences. Skid Road, as the downtown gambling and saloon area of Seattle was known, had "a reputation for toughness rivaled only by the Barbary Coast."[31]

Seattle had been built over native settlements and was sustained by a seemingly endless supply of timber. With the arrival of the railroad lines in the 1870s and '80s, and worker gangs (Irish and Chinese), the population became more ethnic. The laborers worked hard and played equally hard, and business grew to cater to their earthy tastes. Prostitution and gambling existed with the backhanded approval of local police. "I say, and I challenge contradiction," one local politician offered, "that there never was such a rotten nest anywhere on the face of God's footstool as the police court of the city of Seattle."[32] Payoffs were made and eyes averted to the many illegalities in the city.

For Pantages, police corruption and prostitution were of little concern. Throughout his life, he survived and even thrived in whatever environment he landed in. For Pantages, Seattle offered cheaper rent than San Francisco, expanding business opportunities and a lively theater scene that ignited his competitive spirit.

In 1902, when he opened the Crystal, he was just another entrepreneur determined to make a go of his venture. Movies were a struggling medium in search of their cultural niche when he rented the 18 × 75-foot space on Second Avenue ("little more than a shelf," one theater historian claimed).[33] He added benches and a projector, rented some films, secured a vaudeville act, and opened his doors to the public. "He was his own manager, booking agent, ticket taker, and janitor."[34] It was also the "first 10–20–30 cent vaudeville house in America."[35]

In offering both film and vaudeville—"vaude-film"—Pantages got the best of both worlds. If popular films were not available or simply not to his liking, he could rely more on vaudeville, and vice versa. He knew vaudeville, less about films, so he entered new territory with motion pictures. The cost of renting films was considerably lower than what was required to sustain vaudeville acts—the talent, musicians, electricians, stagehands, etc.—but the return was the same.[36] It took an astute manager to handle the exigencies of both fields and succeed. "The Crystal did well from the start, and Pantages milked every penny from it."[37] On Sundays there was no performance schedule, just what he determined it to be. He could cut a stage act in half; and since projectors at that time offered no mechanism to regulate the speed, he ran through a film so quickly it was difficult to appreciate the scenes. "Turnover was all that mattered."[38]

At the time, movies were usually played in silence, with audiences talking through performances, sometimes rowdily so. Projectors were small and dim, the images on the screen relatively small, and the seating blocked viewers' sightlines. Movies were inferior pieces of entertainment, one reporter claimed. "The flicker was hard on the eyes, men pleaded, and the villain was foiled and virtue triumphed in what appeared to be continual snowstorms."[39]

The movie business itself was chaotic and unregulated. Anyone could set up a movie theater, and many did—on a whim. A newspaper account of one such instance exemplifies this wild spirit: Eugene Levy came from the family that owned Cooper & Levi (despite the difference in spelling), outfitters to the Klondike prospectors during the Gold Rush. When the store was sold in 1900 after the gold madness abated, Eugene entered the real estate business. But he was not happy and looked for other ventures. One day he walked into the exclusive Concordia Club in Seattle and began chatting with a stranger planning to open a motion picture theater in town. Levy had never seen a movie.

"Is there any money in it?" Levy asked the stranger. The stranger said that there was.
Very much? Enough.
Was the stranger sure? The stranger was sure.
Ah, deep, calm faith—that is how Levy got into the theater business.[40]

Levy was part of the expanding group of movie theater owners in the city, adding to its crowded entertainment milieu. At the time, Pantages could not have known that films would become a hugely popular art and significant new industry. He had Rockwell's successful example in Victoria as a model, as well as the few movie theaters already playing in Seattle by the time his Crystal was in operation, but no one was sure where movies were headed. And there was plenty of competition from other venues in a lively and robust theater scene (perhaps second only to New York in the number of performances at any one time) that made movies seem a very risky bet. Seattle offered 180 saloons, many of them box-houses with theaters attached.[41] There were also several legitimate theaters, with many of the leading stage stars of the era stopping there for performances. After the initial burst of excitement surrounding movies (at the time, these were nothing more than short features, under two minutes, that mostly highlighted filmed vaudeville stunts of one kind or another), films were relegated to the box-houses.

Several months before Pantages opened the Crystal, the city's first devoted film theater, La Petite (or La Petit or Le Petite—its spelling varies), had opened. Like Pantages' operation, it was a simple affair: nothing more than a converted storefront with chairs and benches, a bed-sheet for a screen, and a hand-cranked projector. When Edison's Unique Theater opened not long afterwards, showcasing films of "Teddy Roosevelt grinning, William Jennings Bryan shaking his mane, sporting figures like Jim Jeffries, or models displaying the latest in bustles and bathing suits," a hint of the future seemed to be on display. In time, Seattle would become known as Movie Town, U.S.A.[42]

While there may have been earlier films screenings, Thomas Alva Edison's public showing of movies on April 23, 1896, to the New York audience at Koster & Bial's Music Hall was the one that made history as being the first in the nation. New Yorkers were stunned at what they witnessed. Although the movie projector demonstrated that night was invented by others, Edison's name appeared on it and the public presumed it was his creation. This event achieved instant notoriety. Edison wasn't a scientist at all, claimed art historian Kenneth Clark, but a "supreme do-it-yourself man," yet one who had a strong interest and affinity for adding to his bank accounts.[43] "So enthusiastic was the appreciation of the crowd long before the extraordinary exhibition was finished that vociferous cheering was heard," the *New York Times* gushed the next day.[44] It was for many "the real birthday of the motion picture as a form of public entertainment." The problem for Edison and others was how to turn the novelty into a real sustained business.

At first, Edison thought films could be exploited for educational purposes. He later wrote, "I had some glowing dreams about what the camera could be made to do, and ought to do in teaching the world things it needed to know—teaching it in a more vivid, direct way."[45] He would also later claim that movies might become central to home screenings by the wealthy. What the great inventor and his staff hit upon were peep shows—upright, rectangular boxes about the size of a stool—in which viewers could watch 90-second films, as if looking into a microscope.

These shows were magnets, drawing in the curious who wanted to see human beings move in a world that up to that time had been static and frozen. The peep-show demonstrations had a powerful, mesmerizing hold on audiences, and similar peep-show screenings popped up in cities across the country. Edison made hundreds of these boxes, and just when it seemed a business model to showcase movies was settled, it sank into near oblivion. People tired of the novelty (usually vaudeville acts, complete with bowing at the end), and the peep shows that mushroomed across the land closed. Certainly the risqué nature of many of these acts titillated men, but it did little to attract women and families. What cultural inspiration Edison unleashed on that spring day in Herald Square in 1896 had in a few years become chasers at the end of vaudeville acts telling audiences it was time to leave the theater.

There were attempts to revive films after the peep show era, but they were sporadic and of no immediate cultural impact. Saloon owners showcased films as a way to draw customers and sell drinks (early versions of a sports bar), but these efforts proved disastrous. The first movie projectors were not very bright and required complete darkness to show films. The results were accidental trips, spilled drinks and worse.

In 1898, a 29-year-old mechanical tinkerer named Dell Lampman tried to replicate Edison's wildly successful movie screening at Koster &

Bial's, but in a less ornate and therefore more accessible setting. He rented a basement in downtown Seattle and let in "Alaska Gold Rush–bound miners to witness the miracle of moving pictures."[46] Cost of entry was a dime. He featured a "series of films—celluloid strips that averaged between 10 and 25 feet in length and amounted to only a few seconds of screen time each." They ranged from a man walking, to local scenes, such as gulls "against the skyline" and "a steamer puffing to dock."[47] While these attempts did not set the world ablaze, they did reveal what could be done with films. These efforts encouraged others, and in time nickelodeons began.

Pantages' Crystal was part of a larger wave of new nickelodeons across the country. A variety of entrepreneurs entered the film exhibition business, including women, long regarded as second-class citizens and agitating for greater participation in society. One was a competitor of Pantages.[48] Sally Chandler Sloan was her name and, her husband having died in 1896, she was left with some cash that she converted into the country's first movie theater circuit.[49] With the help of a male partner, she followed one of the first movie theaters in the country in 1898 with a chain of theaters in Seattle, Spokane, Portland and Vancouver, B.C.[50] Two other Seattle theaters owned by women have been forgotten by history.[51]

While little is known about Pantages' Crystal as it operated, information about Sloan's operations provide clues as to how these early motion picture theater entrepreneurs ran their show-houses. Sloan's theater in 1898, perhaps only the second theater in the country to be devoted entirely to films (the first being the Vitascope Hall in New York City), featured a 25-foot canvas hung from the ceiling, a gramophone used to play music if a song was featured in a film, as well as the Lumière film projector that a stranger had left her.[52] Films were rented from between $300 to $500 per week. Sloan operated the gramophone. A cashier-projectionist and a young boy to hand out bills rounded out her list of employees.[53] In short, labor costs were very low, and as a result ticket prices were also reduced.

The cheap admission price attracted those who did not patronize higher-priced theaters, including workers and immigrants who enjoyed the frivolity and escapism of motion pictures without any need for cultural pretension or major hits on their wallets. Entire families went to the movies at the same cost as one adult occupying the cheapest seat in a stage theater presentation. The swelling of cities due to the industrialization of the nation provided the customer base that theater operators needed to stay and grow their businesses. In 1900, the population of Seattle stood at 80,671; ten years later, it was 237,194, a near-tripling of its size.[54] This extraordinary growth allowed Pantages to realize his dream of a circuit of theaters, not just one.

Movies in Seattle also benefited from local leaders' desire to clean up the city's reputation for licentious entertainment. The peculiar geography of Seattle (like Rome, built on seven hills) created odd bedfellows between its industrial zones and entertainment district. The "Tenderloin" district, with its abundance of saloons and box-houses showing burlesque, was located in a swamp where ships loaded processed timber for export from nearby lumber yards. This meant a steady supply of workers (and drinkers) to the Tenderloin, or "the line," an "arbitrary limit set by custom rather than ordinance, beyond which the Tenderloin was not supposed to trespass."[55]

This arrangement bothered city Brahmins whose cleanup of the town's licentious and alcohol-infused reputation was a major goal. This meant promoting more family entertainment. Movie theaters popped up above the line; no alcohol allowed, respectable shows preferred and matinees added to distinguish them from the less savory versions below. Already movie theaters competed with the city's growing number of stage theaters: adding film spaces to the mix meant a highly charged competitive environment. Pantages learned to give back as much as he got, chiefly against his main rival, the powerful and well-connected John W. Considine.

The local social elite loved the Chicago-born ex-cop Considine, whose only personal vice, at least before arriving in Seattle, apparently was chewing gum. Considine began his theatrical career in Seattle as a doyen of the Tenderloin, operating illegal gambling houses with the help of bribes to the police chief and beat cops. After a shoot-out with a former police chief (he was acquitted in a notorious murder trial), Considine turned respectable. Seattle's theatrical Mercedes to Pantages' Ford, it was Considine who lured the leading actor of the time, Sarah Bernhardt, by promising her a chance to go bear hunting. He turned a remote, distant outpost in the northwest corner of the United States into a destination for top performers. Pantages didn't have the money or connections to compete with Considine, so legend has it that he cleverly and ruthlessly outfoxed him by using his brains instead. Some of the stories seem more apocryphal than real, but their colorful plots indicate the intense, rancid atmosphere in which they competed. More realistic and likely is that Pantages outdid his rival by simply offering the same acts but at half the cost.[56]

Once, as a story goes, Considine booked a famous violinist and his small orchestra. Realizing this would hurt his business, Pantages found out the arrival time of the orchestra at the train station and sent a driver with instructions to pick up its equipment. When the company arrived, the driver politely explained that Pantages sent him as a courtesy so that in the future he might consider booking his act with him. Suitably impressed and grateful, since Considine hadn't arranged for any such pickup, the violinist watched the driver load all the instruments onto the truck. Later that night at his hotel, the violinist got a call from Pantages, who told him if he did not change his performances to a Pantages theater immediately, all his equipment would be destroyed, including his prized Stradivarius. The violinist was furious, refusing to change his play dates since contracts had been signed, and demanding the instruments back. He threatened to call the police. Whereupon Pantages picked up his Stradivarius and cut a string. More would be cut if he did not change his mind. The violinist and his orchestra performed at a Pantages theater. "Pantages was the soundest psychologist in the theater," one vaudeville historian exclaimed; "that is to say, he was the best showman."[57]

Some challenges had little to do with competition. City planners had long seen Denny Hill (named after an early city settler family) as an impediment to Seattle's expansion. It rose just north of the main downtown area, a physical barrier to any expansion of the city's thriving financial core. It had to be removed. It lay just a few blocks to the north of the Crystal, and major work on removing it took place between 1902 and 1911. A thriving business district was soon transformed into an eerie landscape of giant anthills in the middle of a burgeoning city. Many businesses in the area closed, including theaters, and those that stayed open faced major headaches in the inconveniences the demolition created for their customers, who walked on muddy wooden planks or dusty sidewalks. The city's dry cleaners were happy. According to *Polk's Directory*, in 1904 there were 18 theaters operating in the city; the next year the number had dwindled to ten.[58] Rather than contracting, Pantages expanded in this period.

In 1904, Pantages added his second theater, the Pantages, not far away from the Crystal. He had done sufficiently well from the Crystal "to open an establishment of which he was proud enough to give it his name."[59] In 1907, the Pantages was remodeled and its grand reopening featured his wife playing her violin "in a manner which won for her hearty applause."[60] Several top billings and two short films (*The Policeman's Boots* and *The*

Canadian Lumber Industries) were also featured in the festivities.[61] That same year, Pantages opened the Lois, named after his wife, across from the Crystal. The chain's growth was aided by the city's expanding line of electric trollies that crisscrossed it like a spider's web. Newspaper ads extolled new homes conveniently close to the Electric Car Line and minutes away from downtown.[62] Trolleys were a new urban development that helped cities expand outward. They moved people around cheaply and efficiently, and brought families downtown for shopping and entertainment. Pantages and other theater owners benefited. He set up an operation based on crowd movement and flow, following the "path of least resistance."[63] He might be next door to his competition, or across the street. "I'll take the overflow," he reasoned.[64]

With a few theaters under his control, it was just a short step toward a bigger circuit. In theory, the success of one operation inspired the building of another; the extent to which he borrowed money to finance the construction of new theaters is not known. The growth was rapid. The San Francisco earthquake and fire in 1906 gave him the chance to expand into California. It must have seemed a golden opportunity for him to return to his first American home as a rising theater mogul. The same year as his San Francisco operations, he opened the Empire Theater in Saskatoon, Canada. Three years later, he added sites in Colorado and Missouri. In 1910, he bought the former Plymouth Congregational Church in downtown Seattle and converted it into a Pantages theater by 1915. Alliances with other theater operators in the Midwest greatly expanded the brand, as did more sites in Canada. By 1919, he had added Pantages houses in Salt Lake City, Los Angeles, Kansas City and his easternmost site, Memphis. A "gentlemen's agreement" may have prevented him from going farther east. There were also operations in Fresno, Chicago, Detroit and Cleveland. At its height in 1926, the Pantages circuit owned 36 playhouses and controlled another 42. His was the largest independently owned theater chain in North America. The dishwashing basin in Cairo was a distant memory.

It was the explosive popularity of movies that ultimately made the Pantages circuit possible. The once lowbrow entertainment had transformed into a draw for a growing line of audiences every week. Part of the allure lay in the cheap entry of movie theaters as already noted, but also in films themselves becoming longer and more sophisticated. Gone were the bear acts and stripteases, replaced by films with a greater emphasis on story, characterization and plots. By 1908, there were 8000 movie theaters across the country; three years later it was 11,500 and by 1914 the number of theaters

The Pantages theater in Seattle was the second in the operation soon to expand to dozens. Pantages was not afraid of competition, which he tended to swallow or outlast (*University of Washington Libraries, Special Collections, UW6576*).

skyrocketed to 18,000, "with seven million daily admissions."[65] The appetite for films was insatiable.

Yet even as movies grew in stature and popularity, Pantages did not give up vaudeville. Instead, he made it more efficient and squeezed as much profit out of his touring acts as possible. He opened booking offices in New York and Chicago for new acts, who received contracts stipulating "14 weeks or more" of performances. Popular acts could be kept on for many more weeks but those that turned away audiences could be easily removed. Theater acts began in Canada as test runs, then moved to the Midwest. When the acts got to the West Coast, however, their salaries were abruptly reduced by 25 percent. "Most of the performers faced with this situation took the pay cut to keep from becoming destitute in a strange and unfamiliar area."[66] For women performers, especially those with children, it was especially cruel. "Many a vaudevillian's child slept in a wardrobe or trunk drawer," and had to adapt to the wandering life.[67]

Reducing actors' salaries was common in the industry, but it was not publicly known. Pantages preferred to be known for banqueting his actors after performances, not arbitrarily cutting their wages. Citing a principle that if you make the people working for you feel contented, they will do better work, Pantages provided his performers a banquet table at the basement at the Broadway Pantages in downtown Los Angeles.[68] How extensive this practice was in his other operations, or if it was offered other than on Sundays, was not disclosed.

Many wondered about his meteoric rise. His polemics with the Considine chain and others were established facts, but in a revealing interview during his empire's expansion, he downplayed the battles. The "vital, propulsive personality [with] the face ... of a guileless Cupid" conceded that he had to be his own boss.[69] "I work from eight in the morning to ditto the next day, if need be," he added.[70] It was his ambition that perhaps sets him apart. This "vaudeville Napoleon" had big dreams: "I shall not be happy till I own a chain of houses from the Atlantic to the Pacific—from the Tobaggans to the Everglades."[71]

Unlike other theater owners, Pantages never relied on the word of agents or managers to book vaudeville acts. Before signing contracts, he had to see and feel their impact on audiences for himself. Pantages always placed himself in the position of a customer at his theater, asking his staff to pay close attention to audiences and to understand their needs. This customer-centric focus was not shared by Pantages' rivals. But there was one more element needed to crown the empire, to make Pantages Pantages: a Jewish immigrant architect from Scotland.

By 1910, Pantages had come to recognize that audiences were not only interested in what a theater showed on the screen, but what it looked like from the outside. Each theater tried to outdo the others in style and elegance. Soon "theater buildings became the temples of the 20th Century American city."[72] These movie cathedrals changed the way motion pictures were perceived and helped to develop them as a mainstream cultural art form. One of the key figures behind this movement was Pantages' chief architect, J. Marcus Priteca.

Priteca was born in 1881 in Glasgow, Scotland, to a middle-class family and schooled at Edinburgh University while on a five-year apprenticeship with an architectural firm. "I was feeling pretty smart and I got into an office discussion about a city in the United States called 'Seetle,'" where the Alaska-Yukon Pacific Exposition was to take place, he later told a reporter.[73] His boss at the firm insisted that "Seetle" as he spelled it was on the Yukon River. "I knew this was wrong, but was unable to find Seattle on any international map."[74] Photographs of the city with its wooden sidewalks and overhead wires revealed to Priteca that "this was virgin territory for a young architect."[75] He decided to pay the city a visit, and by early July 1909 he arrived in Seattle only to be arrested for smoking a cigarette (pipes and cigars were allowed).[76] It didn't dissuade him from staying. "I fell in love with the city, especially the excellence of the brick work and architecture," he wistfully recalled.[77]

Priteca was a draftsman at a Seattle architecture firm when he had a chance meeting with Pantages. (There are a few versions of this encounter and it's not clear where it took place, in Seattle, headquarters of the Pantages chain, or elsewhere.) The meeting led to his design work for the new San Francisco Pantages Theater in 1911. It was certainly an inspired choice on the part of Pantages. Considered a "scholar" in his field, Priteca had the wisdom and knowledge to be "thoroughly acquainted with the various styles and distinctive periods of architecture." More importantly, he had the "unusual power of modifying and combining the qualities composing them."[78] The extraordinary two-decades-long partnership that resulted created some of the most beautiful theaters ever constructed in the United States. He designed 30 Pantages theaters. Referring to himself as just a "vaudeville architect," the now cigar-smoking Priteca devoted himself to exterior pomp and interior elegance with "gracefully curving balconies, sloping floors, and good sight lines to the stage from every seat in the house."[79] "Seeing is hearing," he proclaimed.[80] The goal, following Pantages' business philosophy, was to create "fantasy lands where a pauper could feel like a king or queen, if only for a few hours."[81] A theater, Pantages reasoned, had to pull the overworked soul out of humdrum daily reality and into a shimmering world of fantasy and wonder. In 1926, when the San Francisco Pantages was remodeled, the 2500-seat interior was one of the largest built at the time and the theater was instantly considered a masterpiece. Often the theaters that Priteca designed for Pantages included operational offices above them.

Other operators had similar ideas, since competition was heating up. In 1911, Polk's Directory listed 34 Seattle movie theaters. In 1912, James Q. Clemmer opened the Clemmer Theater in downtown Seattle, considered to be "the first building in the country constructed from the ground up specifically for exhibition of motion pictures."[82] Three years earlier he had taken over his father's Seattle hotel and converted unused space on the first floor into the Dream Theater, where "in a stroke of brilliance, he put in a pipe organ and hired a young fellow … to pump out tunes to accompany the silent films. It is believed that this was the first instance ever of using a pipe organ to accompany motion pictures."[83] In New York City and Chicago, ornate movie palaces began to spring up in the same decade. The days of storefront operations had ended.

Pantages preferred classical designs—what later came to be known as "Pantages Greek." Priteca had a fine sense of the classical, but always imbued the style with modern touches. An architectural historian wrote that Priteca had the "ideals of old world architecture and possesses the resourcefulness and initiative which enable him to meet the demands of the new world."[84] He preferred exterior work in terracotta or brick, since these two materials were flexible enough to offer a variety of ornamentation. The outside attracted the eye, but the inside replenished the soul, according to this thinking. In 1915, Priteca designed the Pantages Theater in Seattle in classic Renaissance style with ornate cornices, an interior dome that was "sprayed with real gold leaf" and spectacularly lit, and stained Tiffany-style glass.[85] The theater's white glazed terracotta façades were "architectural expressions of fantasy and delight."[86] "It was aimed almost perfectly at the clientele Pantages wanted to reach," Priteca related about the Seattle Pantages—those "who were hungry for entertainment but who lacked money."[87]

Even as Priteca rendered ornate theater designs, the cost-conscious Pantages kept tight reins on the budget. "Any darn fool can build a million-dollar theater with a million dollars," Priteca fondly remembered one of his boss' favorite expressions. "But it takes a good one to build one that looks like a million dollars and costs half that amount."[88] Costs were also kept low by often using the same contractors on the building sites and by maximizing seating, typically ranging between 1200 and 1600 seats. Priteca had a free hand, but he knew his boss' preferences and rarely strayed from them. In practical terms, the focus was on detail, such as Priteca personally designing the interior seating for optimal sightlines while simultaneously providing the best acoustics possible. It is difficult to separate where Pantages ended and Priteca began, but the design work, from exterior to interior, from stage to side boxes to lobbies and ticket booths, was all the work of the immigrant architect. Every aspect of the theater was carefully planned: state-of-the-art stage lighting, sheet-metal dressing rooms ("Actors are harder on things than any other breed of man") and smaller stages and reduced orchestra pits that required fewer stagehands and musicians.[89] Priteca also designed Jim Crow seating, claiming that Pantages had to bow to the racism of the era.[90] This resulted in lawsuits that were settled, according to Priteca, on "very generous terms—

very uncharacteristic for a businessman with such a tight-fisted reputation."[91]

The Vancouver Pantages in 1914 was another example of Priteca's brilliance. With its 1800 seats and French Renaissance elements, it was "considered at the time to be the most richly embellished and efficient theaters in the Pantages chain."[92] In 1919, the two combined together to build a milestone in the operation: the seven-story Pantages theater in downtown Los Angeles. The "beautiful eclectic Beaux Arts edifice" marked a huge departure for the pair, since it combined an elegant new theater and a new direction for the Pantages theater empire.[93] "Mr. Pantages has decided to make his headquarters in Los Angeles," it was reported.[94] Five year-old Carmen Pantages was on hand to turn the first shovelful of dirt for the new edifice. It was in this building that he would be accused of assaulting Eunice Pringle. As the Los Angeles structure was underway, a new Pantages was planned for Salt Lake City and "six other houses in various midwestern cities."[95]

But nothing can compare to the Hollywood Pantages (note that the very title omits the need for Theater; the name Pantages itself had effectively replaced it). It was the crown jewel of their partnership, one of the finest theaters in the country, and certainly the most architecturally influential of all Priteca and Pantages' buildings. He abandoned his preferred classical expression and instead chose an Art Deco design to "best exemplify America at the moment."[96] The attempt "centered on motifs that were modern—never futuristic," he would later explain, "yet based on time-tested classicism of enduring good taste and beauty."[97] Perhaps the centerpiece to the Hollywood Pantages was its foyer, a "flamboyant version of Art Deco ... one of the first such interiors in the history of motion picture theater architecture."[98]

When the theater opened on June 4, 1930 ("undeniably Hollywood's most fabulous theater"), Pantages was lying in the hospital ward of Los Angeles County Jail.[99] That night, while Pantages languished in bed, "Hollywood witnessed the greatest, most glamorous, and last movie palace opening in its history."[100] It was a magical moment, as the "invited guests—nearly every movie star in Hollywood—stepped from their limousines onto a red velvet carpeted sidewalk and saw for the first time the lavish marble and gold entrance, lit from the elaborate 18-foot ceiling by hundreds of tiny bulbs."[101]

The Hollywood Pantages was not simply the last of the great theaters built by the theater mogul and his brilliant designer; it was the end of an era of movie palaces. With the Great Depression swallowing the nation, people's attentions turned to other matters. Yet throughout the years afterwards, Pantages and Priteca maintained contact. On his first night in jail after being convicted in the first trial, Priteca joined him.

Pantages and other immigrants literally built the movie industry with their labor-beaten hands. It is difficult to separate movies from immigration. No discussion of the growth of films can avoid the huge influx of immigrants that took place in the last two decades of the nineteenth century and the first two of the twentieth. Foreigners populated both the audiences in the expanding nickelodeon circuits as well the ranks of its pioneer film producers, who were rapidly turning movies into a burgeoning industry. This fact was not lost on nativists who by 1919 saw the movie industry as a subversion of traditional culture. The emerging culture wars provide the background and the basis for the Pantages rape trial in 1929.

"Migration," immigration historian Roger Daniels wrote, "is a fundamental human activity."[102] This reminder would do little to quell the anxiety caused by the influx of foreigners at the time. Between 1880 and 1924, more than 22.5 million foreigners arrived in the U.S. In 1910, the foreign-born portion of the nation's population stood at 14.7 percent, a figure never before or since surpassed.[103] In 1920, out of the total U.S. population of 105 million, 14 million were foreign-born and 22 million more had at least one foreign-born parent. The total figure of 36 million represents more than a third of the entire population.[104] In 1880, New York had 500,000 foreigners, and ten years later "40 percent of the city's population was foreign-born."[105]

Social consternation against foreigners was nothing new to the U.S.; waves of English and German newcomers in the 1830s also provoked a nativist reaction.[106] But it was the sudden appearance of the darker-skinned southern and southeastern Europeans that caused increased tension and even violent reaction. In the 1840s and '50s, the Know-Nothings opposed immigration.[107] It has never been easy being an immigrant in the U.S., but in some periods there was more discrimination than in others.

The vast numbers of new arrivals that overwhelmed the nativist comfort zone and apparently threatened the nation's culture if not its survival were not the only cause of disquiet in the land. The initial wave of Dutch, English, French and German in the seventeenth and eighteenth centuries was gradually replaced by the Irish and, by the end of the nineteenth century, southern and eastern Europeans (Jews, Greeks, Slavs, Turks, Italians),

Chinese and Japanese. For many nativists, this skin change was a corruption from the original groups that established the American republic; the Anglo stock replaced increasingly by darker, stranger and less-educated types who seemed less than perfect specimens to carry the republican experiment forward. The new arrivals helped to justify increasing use of exclusionary laws, "special taxes and other statutory burdens" imposed on immigrants.[108] Congress reacted to the nativists' angst by restricting immigration, as it did with the Immigration Act of 1917 that "expanded the principle of exclusion based on national origins."[109] After 1920, the rate of immigration did decline significantly, even though it took the Great Depression of the 1930s to effectively slam the door on newcomers.

Ideas floating in academia and the public sphere at the time about the superior Caucasian race found fertile ground in the minds of nativists. A "frequent contributor to *The Saturday Evening Post* contrasted the 'old immigrants' (from Northern Europe) with the 'new immigrants' (those from southern and eastern Europe)."[110] The old migrants, he stated, "were able to blend into the melting pot," but the newer ones entered "the country simply to earn money."[111] Because they were illiterate, they were "difficult to assimilate." Social science at the time purported to back up these claims: "[N]ew 'scientific studies' argued that immigrants from places like Austria-Hungary, Russia, Italy, Turkey, Lithuania, Rumania and Greece were inferior to earlier immigrants from Northern and Western Europe."[112] It was on these grounds that the 1911 U.S. Immigration Commission report declared the "New Immigrants from southern and eastern Europe" to be "high inassimilable" and "that their presence caused a variety of social problems."[113] In short, they constituted a "degenerate social stock."[114] The report did its best to increase the social stigma against the new arrivals by manipulating estimates of "mental illness, crime, family breakup, transiency, prostitution and labor problems among Italians, Jews, Slavs, Greeks and other recent arrivals."[115]

The "old-new" dichotomy, Daniels noted, is overblown and fails to capture the real differences between earlier waves of immigration from the founding of the Republic to 1820 and afterwards. The earliest immigrants were mostly from rural areas, while after 1820 they tended to be from urban environments (including Pantages, who spent time in Cairo). Likewise, family immigrants of the past were gradually replaced by single male adults, more in line with the needs of spreading factories at the time. According to historian Richard Hofstadter, "The United States was born in the country but moved to the city."[116] Immigration from northwestern Europe continued after 1820 but was gradually supplanted by southeastern

Europeans.[117] In looks, tenor, feel and actions, even smell, the new Mediterranean arrivals stretched the boundaries of established decency.

There were misunderstandings on both sides. Greeks rallied around their social institutions that separated them from mainstream society as forms of self-protection, while Americans saw in the Greek immigrant a distant, bizarre figure seemingly impossible to assimilate into the dominant culture.

A central focus of attention was the *kafenia* (coffeehouses) that sprang up across the U.S. These were usually simple affairs of old chairs and plain décor (sometimes with flags of both Greece and the U.S.), familiar and comfortable spaces for Greeks to interact with other Greeks. In rural Greece, kafenia served as community hubs where celebrations of one kind or another (baptism, wedding, funeral, etc.) took place, as well as a postal mail stop, community meeting place, government information center and even a place where new communication technologies such as the gramophone and telephone were first introduced. In the U.S., the kafenio not only was a balm to soothe the lonely Greek immigrant in an alien culture, but also a social means to find work, housing and even romantic partners. It was "central to the lives of Greek male workers," and they spent a considerable amount of time there when not working.[118] Others regarded the kafenio differently. "The coffee houses are as exact a reproduction of those in Greece ... as one could hope to find," a distinguished sociologist from Yale offered. "There is the same vile atmosphere and the same crowd of big, able-bodied loafers with apparently nothing to do all day but smoke, drink, play cards and talk."[119]

The Greek immigrant who came to the States did so for one reason: to escape poverty and make money. "It cannot be overstated that the overriding motive for Greek migration to the United States was economic gain."[120] But these aliens were also tough and determined to succeed, sometimes at the expense of other immigrants. The results could be tragic. A young Greek immigrant from "the mountains of Roumeli" worked for the Colorado Fuel and Iron Company at $1.75 for a 12-hour work day in 1907. "On his first day of work he had beaten a Bulgarian almost senseless. The Bulgarian had hidden the shovel in a pile of coke when the shift changed, as the custom was, and the young Greek thought he was trying to get him fired."[121]

Press coverage of immigrants was not always "monolithic nor particularly consistent," but it tipped toward the critical.[122] Thus an editorial in the *San Francisco Chronicle* could note that the "undesirable Greeks may become loyal and useful American citizens ... but must always remain a race apart."[123] In communities with large Greek populations, this discrimination was particularly rancid. Thus it was that a historian could claim, "The word 'Greek,' as used by the newspapers of White Pine County, Nevada, often signified all recent arrivals from Southern Europe; it was synonymous with 'alien,' 'troublemaker,' 'inferior' and 'not white.'"[124] Newspapers played a critical role in venting and giving expression to anti-immigrant sentiment. A sampling of the characterizations of Greeks printed in Utah newspapers in the years just before and after World War I include "'scum of Europe,' 'a vicious element unfit for citizenship' and 'ignorant, depraved and brutal foreigners.'"[125] "The anti-immigrant propaganda of the World War I years and the early-twenties' campaigns against the South European immigrants by newspapers, the American Legion and the Ku Klux Klan completely turned the isolate Greeks inward."[126] For the "best and the brightest" of the time, the Anglo-Saxon, Aryan, Teutonic or Nordic groups, simply "had superior innate characteristics."[127] In 1894, the founder of the Immigration Restriction League put the choice more bluntly: whether the nation should be "'peopled by British, German and Scandinavian stock, historically free, energetic, progressive, or by Slav, Latin and Asiatic races [Jews, etc.] historically downtrodden, atavistic and stagnant.'"[128]

World War I did much to toughen nativist resolve against the foreigner, in part as a reaction to the loss of American blood and treasure in troubled Europe. Only shortly before America's involvement in the war, the cultural eruption of D.W. Griffith's *Birth of a Nation* on the nation's movie screens brought a resurgence of the racist Ku Klux Klan that further poisoned racial relations. This movie was screened to President Woodrow Wilson. Wilson told a group of new naturalized citizens in Philadelphia: "You cannot become thorough Americans if you think of yourselves in groups. America does not consist of groups."[129]

Mixed into this sulfuric brew was concern about the spread of communism after the Russian Revolution of 1917. Many Greek immigrants had become radicalized under agitating labor union organizing, and even as this movement helped to assimilate and eventually helped them escape labor employment, it also further distanced newcomers from mainstream America. And "the most radical layer of Greek America society was its working class."[130] Greek-American radicalism was associated with both the notorious Industrial Workers of the World (IWW, or the "Wobblies") and the Communist Party. Many Americans felt that Greeks and others were simply unfit to participate in American republican democracy. Many academics concluded that "democratic political institutions had developed and could thrive only among Anglo-Saxon peoples."[131]

The angst against non–Aryan immigrants also speaks to subtle digs against their more "effeminate" cultures. For Protestant Americans, the sight of Catholic or Greek Orthodox immigrants with their strong emphasis on the Virgin Mary may have struck a less-than-masculine note. At a time when manliness was an important part of the American political ethos, as noted during the discussion on the Spanish-American War, this gave nativists further proof of the inability of foreigners from certain parts of the world to be suitable for democratic engagement. "In the late nineteenth century, men from across the political spectrum generally agreed that democratic government rested on the manly character and fraternal spirit of male citizens and political leaders."[132] Many professions open to immigrants were "effeminate" ones like the service and cleaning industries.[133]

Over time, the earlier hordes of immigrants that had been derided found a way to assimilate into the culture, as difficult and violent as it was. Each new wave of immigration challenged assumed racial categories, which created social hostility. As historian Matthew Frye Jacobson wrote in *Whiteness of a Different Color*, "The contest over whiteness—its definition, its internal hierarchies, its proper boundaries, and its rightful claimants—has been critical to American culture throughout the nation's history, and it has been a fairly untidy affair."[134] Even as this challenge took place, the particular nationality of foreign migrants underwent an ethnicization of their race simply by their contrast to the more "colored" minorities present in America. Without the presence of the so-called "darker races," white ethnicity or the process of "becoming white" might not have existed.[135] This process, as benign as it appears on the surface, did not remove the discriminatory social stigma attached to newcomers; it simply created the societal conditions by which the "ideal ethnic" might become more acceptable and therefore less culturally threatening to the country's dominant Anglicized group.[136]

There is a "complex and often painful interaction between white ethnicity and racial hierarchies on the one hand and historical and cultural memory and social acceptance on the other."[137] Always present are racial and social divisions that are hardest to overcome: the difference between the morally and rationally superior whites versus the "cultured ethnics" (immigrants, refugees, etc.) whose irrational and inferior behavior supported social marginalization.[138] "Classified within the underbelly of whiteness," a Greek-American scholar adds, "the undesirable immigrant is subjected to the disciplinary gaze of the dominant."[139]

As difficult as the conditions were, Greeks spread their wings across the nation. There were Greeks in coal mines in Ludlow, Colorado (where a tragic labor strike occurred), shoe factories in New England, fruit markets in Chicago, saloons in San Francisco, in Greek Orthodox churches in Florida and Louisiana, and even in the halls of Congress (the first Greek-American representative, Luca Miltiades-Miller, was elected from Wisconsin in 1891).[140] Despite these impressive accomplishments, the grand experiment in making a nation out of so many different groups had run into serious problems. While Fourth of July parades and speeches extol the virtues and greatness of our immigrant past, beneath the barbecue rhetoric rests an unsettled question: How can so many disparate races and groups vying to live in America get along? Especially when some of those groups—Greeks, Jews, etc.—held the keys to the nation's dream factories and its movie theaters, and thus a vast portion of the nation's growing cultural production. The battle lines were set for the coming culture wars.

4. Mt. Olympus

By the end of the second decade of the twentieth century, Alexander Pantages was a formidable presence of the stage world. He had survived the 1910s while many other operators had folded. Due to the break-up of Thomas Edison's film trust, the film studios had coalesced in the warm, sunny climate of Southern California and were on their way toward greater control of movies. In time it would lead to monopoly control of the business—from production to distribution to exhibition.[1] As a large, independent operator of movie and vaudeville theaters, Pantages was well-positioned to face the onslaught of consolidation. Not that it would be easy, but by 1920 he certainly had the financial strength and spread of his theaters to blunt competitors.

There were challenges along the way. The great financial panic of 1907, World War I and the influenza pandemic of 1918–19 were a few of the problems he faced. But somehow, through wile or luck, he managed to emerge even stronger. Even his biggest competitor in his early days in Seattle, John Considine, had faltered by 1914. The man who by then was chewing five pieces of gum at a time saw the collapse of his own theatrical empire. One of his partners in the operation was declared insane in 1913 and his mortgaged theaters soon came under tremendous pressure. He sold his theaters to a larger theater holding company, Marcus Loew, but a year later it was returned to Considine. He was fast running out of cash, and with war breaking out in Europe and a nervous public following the events, theater box office receipts fell. The New York Life Insurance Company foreclosed on his most valuable possessions, and the great Considine circuit was relegated to history. When his son John Considine, Jr., later married Carmen Pantages, old animosities were forgotten.

Pantages' career blossomed and so too did his personal life. After the tempestuous days with Kate Rockwell, Pantages found stability with Lois Mendenhall. After their 1905 marriage, three children followed: Rodney

(1905), Lloyd (1907) and Carmen (1910). At some point—it is not clear when—there may have been an adopted fourth, Trixie. In 1907 he had a well-known local architect, Arthur Lamont Loveless, design a house overlooking downtown Seattle at 803 East Denny on Capitol Hill.[2] It was not the largest or most stately in the city, but certainly it was a fine house and set a tone for his rising status. The two-story structure with the large stairway entrance on the corner with Harvard Avenue and Greek columns along the front portico suggests the grandeur that was later featured in his theaters. But evidently he was not satisfied with the house. In two years, he and his family moved to a tonier part of town, Madison Park, into a Tudor revival mansion complete with garage doors with curtains.

Little is known about Pantages' personal life. Likely he preferred it that way. He became a U.S. citizen some time after he opened the Crystal Theater. "Pantages had become an excellent swimmer, an avid hockey and lacrosse enthusiast, and a dancer."[3] But there the record stops. There is no indication, for example, whether he obtained a driver's license, or joined any local business associations, or had friends outside of the profession.

His relationship to the local Greek-American community remains equally mysterious. The initial Greek immigrants to Seattle originated from the eastern Aegean island of Leros and tended toward occupations in food-related professions, such as restaurants and grocery stores.[4] By 1915 there may have been 2000 Greeks residing in the city.[5] Like other diaspora groups in the U.S., they formed local community and political organizations, but the main focus tended toward the creation of bodies related to the building and maintenance of Greek Orthodox churches. Seattle's Greek-American community formed a Greek Club in 1909, followed in 1913 by a Greek American Political Club.[6] But it was the Greek Community of Seattle, incorporated on October 30, 1916, that took on ascendancy as it set about constructing the Saint Demetrios Greek Orthodox Church.[7] There is no record of Pantages' involvement with financing the construction of Saint Demetrios. And while he helped bring family members from Greece to Seattle (where he promptly put them to work into his theaters), there was very little other contact with the former homeland.

All his attention, energy and focus were apparently devoted to growing his company. If it's true that he worked "an average of 16 hours per day," then there was little time for anything else.[8] But as with the disputes regarding his birth year, it is not always clear who was the real Alexander Pantages. He could be a "true friend" to his employees, but did not hesitate to cheat his actors out of their pay.[9] Instances of lawsuits resulting from the reduction in pay made it into the newspapers, but the attention they received was small compared to the lengthier columns that extolled his integrity. According to an unpublished biography, Pantages beat out two competing concerns for a new theater in California. The developer behind the project chose Pantages over the others because he found him honest and sincere. "'I shall tell you why I made the agreement with you instead of the other men,' he told Pantages. 'They undoubtedly represented more money than you, but I felt that you have been telling the truth.'"[10]

This same Pantages, possessed of extraordinary business prowess, had a darker side. His willful disregard for convention revealed itself early, when he ran away from home without warning and had no strong guilt about doing so. Later, in his dealings with Kate Rockwell, he may have taken advantage of the relationship despite her own failings. When he was out of work in the Yukon, she reputedly "supplied him with money so he could smoke 75-cent cigars, wear $15 silk shirts, and generally live the life of ease."[11] On the subject of marriage to Rockwell, he was always circumspect. "She desired marriage, and Pantages would have no part of that."[12] Later she accused him of taking her money to open up his first theater. He lowered the fees he paid his actors, and he was not above refusing preferred seating to African Americans.

Vaudeville had been his life until 1920 but now films beckoned, as did being close to Hollywood. He let it be known that he would be producing his own films, which would be showcased at the new million-dollar theater that was completed in downtown Los Angeles that year. It was a heady time for the Pantages chain. He would soon announce plans for a chain of movie theaters and even a film production company.[13] In a display of his growing wealth, sons Lloyd and Rodney in 1919 were pictured in Los Angeles in their new Templar Speedster automobile, the equivalent of a Lamborghini today.[14]

It was a wise career move on Pantages' part: Being closer to Hollywood and movies made sense at a time when vaudeville was rapidly losing its allure. After this move, Pantages finally accepted the primacy of movies over live stage. He would be closer to the movie industry and could therefore ingratiate himself to the studios. And it may have helped, too, that the landscape of Southern California and its continuously warm weather reminded him of the old country he had left. But in 1922 he suffered a nervous breakdown.[15] Little is known about it, yet it represents a sea change in his behavior. From then on, he took the kind of chances that he may never have taken before. There may be a direct connection between the nervous breakdown and the events of August 9, 1929.

Some time during the 1920s, Pantages acquired the reputation of a man with a wandering eye. His own lawyer, Jerry Giesler, accused him of such. There were trips to Mexico with young starlets, some of them under-

When Pantages moved his headquarters to downtown Los Angeles around 1920, his stature as both a vaudevillian and movie exhibitor was well established and he had become a national figure (*Marc Wanamaker, Bison Archives*).

The Pantages family's move to Los Angeles brought its members into contact with glamorous Hollywood stars. In this photograph, Marlene Dietrich stands next to Lloyd Pantages (*Marc Wanamaker, Bison Archives*).

age; even a rumor that his wife Lois suspected him of cheating on her. She supposedly hired an attorney and a private investigator in 1927 to prepare for a divorce, according to an *Los Angeles Examiner* story during her own trial for manslaughter two years later.[16] No divorce proceedings resulted. "Pantages considered himself somewhat of a ladies' man and liked to hire acts with girls in brief costumes."[17] It is reputed that the San Francisco Pantages had a penthouse where he entertained the talent, including some of his showgirls. Stories emerged of angry husbands accusing Pantages of having designs on their wives. Pantages always denied such claims and he had the legal muscle to back him.

Assignations of one kind or another were not new to show business. The intensity of the work, the abundance of attractive talent, the long spells between performances, the travel, the sheer boredom of the profession, and the insecurity of the field lubricated social relations. Some took the practice to great heights and in doing so brought opprobrium on Hollywood.

Heightened immigration was only one issue; American culture itself was being upended. The numbers speak for themselves. In the case of Greek immigrants, in 1880 there were only 500 in the U.S. By 1910 there were 167,000 and 500,000 by 1940.[18] Such an immense and rapid influx was bound to cause social unease. The industrialization of America drew immigrants into the country and sucked workers (many of them farmers) from rural areas into cities. This internal migration may look innocent on the surface but underneath it churned deep social stress. Not only did the farmers who migrated to work in the factories adjust to hourly wages (many of them happily so, given the unpredictability of their existence), but so too did the families who had to deal with the absent male in the home. "For the first time," one historian wrote, "the central activity of fatherhood was sited outside one's immediate household."[19] This increased the power of the mother, which did not sit well in some conservative quarters of the American public. "At the turn of the [twentieth] century, cultural critics attacked rising maternal influence, along with urbanization and immigration, as having a feminizing effect on American political, cultural and religious institutions."[20]

For many, the move to urban centers meant greater cultural choices. During this shift, many leisure pursuits—from baseball and football to vaudeville and traveling circuses, to name a few—rose in popularity and social stature. These leisure events took place in rural areas, too, but they came to be associated with urban centers, since the larger concentration of populations was able to support them. The greater diversity of populations in the city meant that entertainment focused on the lowest common denominator to reach the largest possible number of people. It was a form of secularization born from a simple business desire to make more money.

Many traditionalists regarded this expanding form of entertainment as favoring hedonism. It was an old concern. During the American Revolution era, leaders worried that the new republic would, if its morals went unchecked, go the way of the Roman Empire. Where once "only a tiny fraction of the people had ever seen a show or been professionally entertained," now diversion became the norm for millions.[21] How could a nation weaned on entertainment be able to run the industrial age?, some asked. "'The men of our country,' the head of the Philadelphia Gear Works proclaimed in 1926, 'are becoming a race of softies and mollycoddlers; it is time we stopped it and turned out some regular he-men.'"[22] Entertainment was getting in the way of the nation's work ethic.

Movies did not cause these changes, but they were blamed nonetheless. Where once folks gathered for the Sabbath, this "gave way to the Sunday drive or baseball game or movie or other pleasurable outing."[23] Some cities banned baseball games on Sunday through blue laws, but it was a losing battle. City leaders failed to understand that it was not simply a matter of eliminating Sunday competition for the church services; the reality was that religious devotion was falling in the U.S.[24] Groups like the Holy Rollers attempted to revive old-time religion with some modicum of success. Even business people urged a return to "old-time values." One of them declared that "the essentially sound and more dependable elements of American citizenship" require a "return to the God, the Bible and the fundamental principles of our forefathers."[25]

Vaudeville and films suffered from the same blue laws eliminating shows on Sunday. It was not merely intended to hurt theaters where they were most vulnerable—the box office—but also to send a message to movie producers about the power that traditionalists held. At the Pantages Theater in Seattle, there were 2000 patrons per weekday; that number tripled to 6000 on weekends. Eliminating Sunday showings meant a revenue loss of 30 percent for his operation. One theater owner noted, "When this law was made Washington was a territory" and not a state; it was only enforced beginning in 1908.[26] Pantages was drawn into the controversy. In his "somewhat broken English," the theater owner noted the consequences: "I tell you it would be very bad; it would ruin the town.... If people, especially the young people, don't have the theater to go on Sunday, what they going to do?"[27] Authorities' ears were deaf. Many theater owners protested in Seattle, and a few arrests were made, with some actually going to trial (all found not guilty) before the laws were quietly rescinded and theater owners went about their Sunday business again.

It was a taste of what was to come.[28] Ruralists "worried about the erosion of standards of public morality."[29] "Cultural tensions between big-city and small-town values were voiced frequently ... [and some] members of the small-town middle class felt that their cultural influence was threatened by the growing dominance of urban businesses, entertainments and codes of behavior."[30] "Urban" was a code word for foreigners, particularly Jews. It is instructive that from the beginning of the American colonies, "Puritans had fought constant, jealous battles against the theater, fearing its competition as 'the Devil's Church.'"[31]

By the early 1900s, the Devil's Church was represented by Hollywood. It was a convenient target; after all, how could the Jews and other prominent immigrants fight back? And it was on these grounds that one pastor, Dr. Wilbur Crafts, proclaimed a "jihad" against the "devil and 500 un–Christian Jews" who ran Hollywood.[32] It did not help the movie industry's image that many Americans believed "everyone connected with the industry was a libertine with the morals of a mink."[33] Despite revenues obtained from movie theater advertising and the popularity of film stars in their pages, mainstream newspapers reflected the general unease about the "loose" morals of Hollywood and its sinful ways as expressed by self-styled guardians of public morality such as various women's vigilance committees and vocal Protestant ministers. They claimed that Hollywood "was directly responsible for many of the dramatic changes in American society since the motion picture was invented," and these included a "rising divorce rate, a rise in juvenile delinquency, and what they saw as a general flaunting of traditional values by American youth."[34]

The entire nation's moral collapse was laid at the door of Hollywood. Not only were many of its managers Jews born in Eastern Europe (movie moguls such as Adolph Zukor of Paramount and William Fox of Fox were Jews born in Hungary), but they also represented the sordid movie industry that challenged traditional mores. Much of this challenge was taking place in mainstream society, and movies simply reflected those changes. But because they made the changes visible and brought them directly before audiences, movies needed to be controlled. It was out of this concern that the first production censorship codes emerged in the 1920s. Interestingly, at about the same time there also emerged regulations regarding public health. The "standard regulation of these two fields [films and health] "points to an important parallel: both institutions were reshaping the public sphere with the aim of preventing the spread of bacterial, moral and ethnic contagion (via film spectatorship or urban squalor) and both were dedicated to the 'Americanization' of immigrants."[35]

For some time, women had agitated for an increasing role in society, such as the right to vote. They also led efforts that later resulted in the prohibition of the sale and consumption of alcohol. The First World War brought the issue of women's greater social participation to a head. Popular culture today assumes that Rosie the Riveter is associated with the Second World War when in fact she starred in the first. "The First World War had created jobs for women, and they had tasted independence, even if the jobs were now going back to the men; as a result, though, there was a large-scale revolution in domestic life." Hollywood, like other cultural industries, reflected this change. "The old order fought a bitter rearguard action, but girls all over American were emulating their screen idols: they smoked, drank, petted, used makeup, rolled their stockings, cut their hair, abandoned their corsets and petticoats and with them a large amount of Victorian hypocrisy."[36] This new distaff freedom seemed well connected to movies, either as inspiration or as expression, or both. Thus, to the general public, Hollywood represented the new egalitarian, free-swinging future.

Suppressing sex in American culture kept a grip on national morality. Removing the lid on sexuality meant automatic moral decline without considering the potential liberating qualities and more honest gender relations this could spawn. It was easier to banish sex to the underground than to discuss it in the open as adults. "[B]efore the movies," film historian Robert Sklar wrote, "the art of love played almost no part in the culture's public curriculum. In movies, however, it became the major course of study."[37] Women's need for greater social participation changed perceptions about the nature of sexual relations in society. No longer would women be satisfied with mostly domestic roles. They wanted to do the same things as men, to be truly equal. Films, as made-up worlds, were in a position to show them the way. As recounted in Alexander Walker's *Sex in the Movies*, Hollywood, by its very nature as appealing to the masses, could bring this gender liberation to the local bijou.

Into this context came the "vamp" (short for vampire) film. Many cultures make room for women who do not abide by traditional domestic capacities, but none of them had the power and reach of movies to spread its message around the world. In vamp films, a seductress dominated men and poisoned their morals, celebrated her sexuality and got away with her crimes. At its height in the 1910s, the vamp film presented women with images that disregarded traditional norms and created further fissures in society. There were several practitioners of this film role (Valeska Suratt, Virginia Pearson *et al.*), but no one captured the imagination quite like the daughter of a tailor from Cincinnati. Born Theodosia Goodman and under the skillful marketing hand of Fox studios, the once "circumspect and demure" woman had become Theda Bara, a man-eating femme fatale and product of exotic Middle East background.[38] This was simply another form of white ethnicity (making Middle Easterners "palatable" to American audiences) and abject stereotyping, consigning sexual mystery to that region's inhabitants. This stereotyping was later used to spectacular effect by Rudolph Valentino's "Arab sheik." By sulking provocatively and lasciviously across the nation's screens, Bara became a powerful, yet unintentional, erotic symbol of feminine liberation. Because movies for many women had become "a peculiar kind of 'real world' with which they identified in intensely personal ways," this type of symbol could be transformative.[39]

Film studios cared not one iota about such liberation; their goal was box office draws, and they succeeded. The vamp proved so lucrative for Fox that waiting in the wings in case Bara's ego swelled was the statuesque figure with the ethereal name, Valeska Suratt. Vamp films were decidedly less popular with traditionalists. "The self-appointed custodians of the country's morals particularly lamented the evil influence of the movies; by pointing to Hollywood, 'sin city,' they justified their contention that not only the films were evil, but that the filmmakers were in league with the devil."[40] Waiting to pounce on any transgressions was that paragon of virtue himself, William Randolph Hearst. If anyone took journalistic and commercial advantage of the culture wars, it was Hearst.

On the balmy morning of Saturday, September 3, 1921, famed film comedian Roscoe "Fatty" Arbuckle set out from his home in Hollywood with two friends and headed west toward the Pacific. He had several cars at his mansion: a silver Rolls-Royce, a Renault roadster, a Cadillac town car, a Hudson limousine, and a Locomobile Sportif. But the one he chose for the trip to San Francisco (the Las Vegas of the era) was perhaps his favorite: the Pierce-Arrow Model 66 4-A, a $34,000 automobile at a time when the average flivver sold for $370.[41] He had driven it enough times that it had come to be known as "Fatty's car," or for others, the "$25,000 gasoline palace."[42] Only about 1250 Pierce-Arrows were built between 1910 and 1918, and of those only 14 remain today, including Arbuckle's.

He was joined on the trip by two fun friends, actor Lowell Sherman and director-writer Fred Fishback, an immigrant from Bucharest, Romania.

His Paramount bosses expected him to participate in its annual "Paramount Week" beginning the next day when its stars paraded through the city and joined in film premieres—in Arbuckle's case, *Gasoline Gus*, playing at the Million Dollar Theater in downtown Los Angeles. Paramount was then the most powerful movie studio in Hollywood. It was the first nationwide feature film distributor when it was established in 1914; three years later, led by a former furrier and Jewish furniture upholsterer, Adolph Zukor, it was on its way to becoming a powerful producer, distributor and exhibitor of motion pictures. Arbuckle's best friend, Buster Keaton, recently married, wanted him to join them on a yachting cruise to Catalina Island. Arbuckle brushed off both studio and friend to head to central California and to descend into hell paved with the journalistic assistance of William Randolph Hearst.

The man who left Los Angeles that fine morning was at the apex of his career. As Greg Merritt recounts in discussing the tragic events that followed, Arbuckle was then the most successful film actor in the industry. He was making a million dollars a year, the first to do so, an astronomical figure but also a testament to the growing power of film as the dominant cultural form in the U.S. and increasingly around the globe. By 1921, the former product of a broken home had acted in 150 films and directed more than 70. He was born in Kansas but grew up on Santa Ana, California. He was 12 when his mother passed away and he was shuffled to his sister's family, then to his abusive, alcoholic father in Watsonville, California, only to discover that his old man had abandoned him. He worked at odd jobs in a local hotel in exchange for room and board. He had already acquired the sobriquet "Fatty" (at 12 he weighed 180 pounds), but he also had a fine singing voice that led him into vaudeville.

The future California Highway 101 that Arbuckle and company took that Saturday was mostly paved. The path once blazed by Spanish missionaries and traders, "El Camino Real" ("Royal Road"), had its own share of dangers—steep, winding curves and careless drivers—but the scenery more than made up for them. It was a far cry from his intense film work over the previous few months. He had recently completely three feature films simultaneously; in 1921, he had made six features in only seven months. He had worked hard and he now needed to relax hard.

All three men were married. In Arbuckle's case, his 13-year marriage to Minta Durfee hung by a thread (they had been separated the last four and a half years). The weekend was not meant to strengthen their matrimonial lives. Alcohol flowed in abundance, a sure sign that their time in the St. Francis Hotel in San Francisco was not to study the finer details of the second law of thermodynamics. "I am convinced," Arbuckle proudly proclaimed, "that the fat man as a lover is going to be the best seller on the market for the next few years. He is coming into his kingdom at last."[43]

Prohibition against the production, sale and consumption of alcohol in the U.S. was only 20 months old, yet its enforcement was already being flouted in San Francisco, where bars continued the trade. Arbuckle's Hollywood mansion was well stocked with liquor, and on the Pierce-Arrow that day there were 20 bottles of it.

The choice of the St. Francis itself was not coincidental. The "Grande Dame of Union Square" was well used to hosting the rich and famous, with liquor flowing freely. The largest hotel on the West Coast at the time, it pumped fresh air into its rooms every eight minutes, had its own orchestra and school for youngsters, even its own Turkish baths with heated saltwater. It was a world unto itself, highlighted by a ten-foot Magenta grandfather clock from Vienna in the lobby. The Pierce-Arrow pulled up to the hotel late that Saturday afternoon. Arbuckle and his friends were weary, but not too exhausted to take delivery of four bottles of gin and Scotch from nearby Gobey's Grill. The hotel had its own illegal bar in the basement—a speakeasy—for those who preferred drinking away from their rooms. Arbuckle's secretary had rented three rooms for the three friends on the twelfth floor of the St. Francis, 1219, 1220 and 1221. Arbuckle and Fishback shared 1219 while Sherman had 1221 to himself. The room in between, 1220, was to welcome guests.

The next day, the threesome did some sightseeing and visited a few of Arbuckle's friends in the area. They then ate and danced at Tait-Zinkland Café, which also featured a cabaret. They stayed late there, with with Sherman inviting one of the showgirls, Alice Blake, to their room the next day. On that same day, three guests checked into the nearby and equally elegant Palace Hotel: publicist Alfred Semnacher, his friend Maude Delmont and a struggling 27-year-old film actress, Virginia Rappe.[44]

One more figure had to enter the drama for the story to be complete: a women's clothing salesman named Ira Fortlouis, also staying at the Palace. He knew Fishback, and when he spotted Rappe in the hotel lobby he immediately inquired about her. On Monday, when he visited Fishback in 1220, he rhapsodized about the stunning Rappe, and soon she was invited to 1220. At noon that day, Rappe showed up to the suite. After introductions and small talk, she called Delmont and invited her to join the boozy scene on the twelfth floor. Blake also appeared, joined by a fellow cabaret girl, Zey Prevost, daughter of Portuguese immigrants. Arbuckle called the hotel staff and ordered a Victrola to play 78 RPM records. The party, whether accidental or purposeful, was now in full swing. Both Arbuckle and Sherman were in their silk pajamas, with Fatty in a thick brocade robe that reached to his ankles.

Another guest, a friend of Arbuckle, Mae Taube, arrived for what was to be a drive in his Pierce-Arrow, but seeing the free-flowing liquor, she abruptly left. Semnacher also stopped by to pick up Delmont and Rappe, but the two women were having too much fun to leave. Semnacher left instead with Blake, who returned to the party after her dance rehearsal was cancelled. At the time of the tragic events, there were six figures in 1220: Arbuckle, Sherman, Rappe, Alice Blake, Zey Prevost and Maude Delmont. Twelve more bottles of booze from Gobey's were ordered. And the day was still young.

Arbuckle startlingly asked whether anyone would join him in jumping out of one of the suite's windows. "If I would jump out of the twelfth-story window, they would talk about me today, and tomorrow they would go to see the ballgame. So what's in a life after all?" he asked facetiously, if not a little vacuously. It wouldn't take long to find out the answer. At one point, Arbuckle found himself seated next to Rappe. There were many similarities in their backgrounds: loss of a mother early in life, absent fathers, ties to San Francisco, and mutual friends. At some point, she excused herself to go to the bathroom in 1221. There she found it locked, with Delmont and Sherman inside in a moment of passion, so Rappe went instead to the bathroom in Arbuckle and Fishback's shared room. At some point before three p.m., Arbuckle marched into his room and locked the door behind him.

The events that followed would be disputed, but the few points that were in agreement were that Arbuckle found Rappe lying in his bathroom floor, picked her up and took her to bed. He then showered and shaved for a later appointment, and saw that Rappe was miserably ill in bed. He came out of 1219 to let the others know that Rappe was ill and called the front desk. At this point, Delmont and Sherman emerged from 1221 and went into 1219 to see what was going on. The hotel doctor examined Virginia and concluded she was suffering from too much alcohol in her system. Her condition worsened, but not until the following Thursday was she taken to a hospital—one that specialized in maternity cases.

The next day, she was pronounced dead. An autopsy was performed and all her pelvic organs removed before she was taken to the city coroner.

By this point, Arbuckle had returned to Hollywood. Within days, he would be charged with murder.

Hearst waited breathlessly for such moments. Arbuckle would become the Spanish in Cuba, and before the journalistic dust settled, one of the greatest film comedians in the world had his career ruined before his eyes.

On September 11, 1921, readers of the Sunday edition of the *San Francisco Examiner* were startled to see a photo of a forlorn Arbuckle, one foot casually crossed over the other, being booked at the Hall of Justice with the screaming headline "ARBUCKLE IS CHARGED WITH MURDER OF GIRL; ACTRESS' DYING WORDS CAUSE STAR'S ARREST."[45] He had driven from Los Angeles the day before with his lawyer and $5000 in cash for bail, but no bail was set for the "murder of beautiful Virginia Rappe, motion picture actress."[46] Shortly after his arrest at 11:45 p.m., he was escorted to city jail where, "tight-lipped and grave," he "passed through the ordeal of questioning, arrest and incarceration in a cell without a single word. Not a trace of the famous million-dollar smile was in evidence."[47]

From the first day's news coverage of Rappe's tragic death, the narrative was visible: Arbuckle was painted as a party animal given to wild excess, while the overwhelming evidence as reported in the newspaper greatly tilted toward his guilt. This narrative simplified the case for readers, providing easily identifiable heroes and villains, but at the cost of fairness. Arbuckle represented the worst side of Hollywood, the one that many nativists had been railing against for years. Yet, according to an Arbuckle biographer, he "didn't have a sexually active life outside his marriage, at least, because self-consciousness about his weight made him shy around women.... Arbuckle may have been the most chaste man in Hollywood."[48]

Here, according to the press, was a vivid example of Hollywood corruption and immorality at its most blatant, resulting in the death of an innocent and beautiful woman. A less attractive female might not have seemed like the tragic loss that Rappe was.

Reminders of Arbuckle's loose, partying ways were spread throughout the *Examiner* coverage, with such terms as "wild party," "uproarious affair," "fatal party," "lurid occurrences," "hilarious drinking party," "rough party," "booze party" (in headlines) and "drinking party." The full extent of his partying lifestyle was revealed in a side story under the headline "Arbuckle Always Keen for Parties, Say Friends." "The party's the thing" was, according to witnesses, "the keynote of the life of Roscoe Arbuckle."[49] During a time when the consumption and manufacturing of alcohol were forbidden, the repeated emphasis on liquor and wine at the party suggested the extent of Arbuckle's flouting of rules. Hollywood, the reader no doubt would be led to believe, abided by its own rules and behavior, different from the rest of society. The driver of "freak cars," the article began, was as famous for "the scores of parties" as he was for film comedy. These celebrations took place "at clubs, hotels, inns along the roads and most of all at his palatial home" and included "[b]anquets, teas, breakfasts, dinners, entertainments, motor parties, weekend parties, house parties, lawn parties and other parties galore."[50] Interestingly, "at a big dinner at his house, to vary the entertainment," he "staged a 'dog wedding' and even more fantastic ideas were carried out from time to time."[51] For moral crusaders like the Reverend Robert "Fighting Bob" Shuler, Arbuckle represented the height of depravity and immorality.

While he may have entertained and made millions laugh, clearly Arbuckle had a celebratory side that exceeded normal societal bounds—at least, according to the *Examiner*. Arbuckle's exuberant, eccentric social behavior may have been normal in an industry given to creativity and youthful excess, but for the rest of society, his after-work antics raised concerns about the morals and lifestyle of Hollywood's elite. It was cleverly captured in a revealing photo from the previous Sunday in which Arbuckle is shown leaning out the window accompanied by a beaming "unidentified" woman, its headline demanding, "Who's Girl With Arbuckle?"

Rappe was a devotee of parties herself, but in the *Examiner* pages she was transformed from a party junkie to an attractive, vibrant young woman whose future was snuffed out by the predatory Arbuckle. In one photo spread in the Sunday coverage, she was shown in several past film roles, suggesting not just an ordinary beauty, but also a busy, hard-working, multiple talent, including a fashion designer. Her own eccentricities were also revealed, but in muted form. She derided traditional women's roles while simultaneously causing a sensation with her attire. On one travel vessel, she and a friend danced the "nightie tango" in "nightgowns worn over evening dresses."[52] Despite insistence from the medical doctor who performed the post-mortem examination that there was no evidence of sexual assault, surrounding stories in the initial coverage painted a different picture.

The *Examiner* featured an article next to the headline piece announcing Arbuckle's arrest that was no less damaging. "Girl Rational When She Named Actor, Says Nurse" the headline beamed, describing Rappe's apparent deathbed statement. "I am used to seeing people die," the somber piece quoted the nurse in the dramatic opening paragraph. "That is my business. I see them die all the time."[53] Thus establishing her seriousness, she proceeded to reveal how the "beautiful girl" passed away "with the final words on her lips—'Get Roscoe—follow this to the finish.'"[54] She later admitted that "Get" meant only that Arbuckle should pay her medical bills.

Rappe "didn't want me out of her sight," the nurse said. "From the time I took the case to the instant of her death, she was continually calling me to listen to what she had to say."[55] The article not only portrayed the nurse as serious, but also as "scrupulously desirous of being fair." Dying patients can be delirious, she suggested, but she knew the difference between hallucination and rationality. What Rappe said about Arbuckle was spoken when she "was apparently in full control of her mind."[56] The nurse went on to claim that Rappe did not want any publicity around the affair, lest her fiancé, movie director Henry Lehrman, find out about it. "If he knows of it, he will throw me down," the nurse quoted Rappe. She also admitted that the girl was too intoxicated to remember the details surrounding what caused her death, suggesting Arbuckle had taken advantage of her inebriated condition.

Arbuckle's lawyers advised that he make no statements to the police or the press (it was left to his accusers to talk to reporters). While legally sound, from a marketing standpoint the advice was poisonous. The same fate later befell Pantages. One of Arbuckle's lawyers even "refused to admit that he was prepared to defend Arbuckle or that the actor stood accused of a crime."[57] Meanwhile, his accusers vocally voiced their thoughts about his guilt. Even the autopsy, according to the Hearst paper, revealed evidence of violence, although it was not certain if the injuries occurred before or after Rappe's death.[58]

Less than a day after his arrest, the bad publicity already affected distribution of an Arbuckle film. While the managers of two San Francisco theaters that pulled his films "did not want to be understood as passing judgment upon Arbuckle before he has been given a hearing," the accusations left them no choice.[59] Even the Palace Hotel, where Arbuckle planned to stay on his return to San Francisco to face the charges, refused him entry. "The Palace Hotel does not care for his patronage," a hotel spokesperson bluntly announced.[60]

The next day, Monday, September 12, 1921, readers saw a sketch of a dark and gloomy Arbuckle in jail on the *Examiner* front page under the bold headline, "WITNESSES GUARDED; INTIMIDATION FEARED."[61] Surrounding his forlorn sketch were three pieces, only one of which had a byline, indicating the extent of Arbuckle's transgressions. The main story quoted a police detective who flatly declared, "We are going to convict Arbuckle of murder."[62] He added, "Witnesses whom we have examined today will leave no doubt as to his direct responsibility for Virginia Rappe's death."[63] Reminding readers of Arbuckle's wealth and evil ability to affect the outcome of the case, the detective noted, "Arbuckle has a load of money, and we are taking no chances on his reaching any of our witnesses. That is why we are keeping these persons under cover."[64] The phrases "wild drinking party" (repeated) and "fatal party" reiterated the excesses of the previous Monday's events.

To further damn Arbuckle, Rappe's fiancé was given front page coverage. Henry Lehrman had directed and befriended Arbuckle in the past. "Arbuckle is a beast," Lehrman declared, recalling former days. "That's what comes of taking vulgarians from the gutter and giving them enormous salaries and making idols of them."[65] In a hint of the culture wars raging, he added, "Such people don't know how to get a kick out of life except in a beastly way. They are the ones who ... participate in orgies that surpass the orgies of degenerate Rome."[66]

To further separate Arbuckle from ordinary society, the San Francisco daily provided a long column detailing his first night in jail. This "disconsolate figure" did not expect to end up in Cell No. 12 after his drive from Los Angeles.[67] In the morning, having lost sleep, he pleaded with his fellow prisoners to borrow soap, a towel and a comb. Then, as if already deeply affected by the proceedings, he swore to the other prisoners that he was "through with booze."[68] The article did not record the reaction, but it did note one comment that got a response from his jailers. Arbuckle insisted that bed-clothing be brought in from the outside. He was told bluntly that he would have to accept the accommodations as they were, just like any "ordinary prisoner."[69]

While a few individuals came to his defense, including his wife Minta Durfee, long separated, such support was cited only in side stories with little if any literary flourish, often formal statements copied verbatim from police reports. The *Examiner*'s journalistic attention was given more to Rappe than Arbuckle. Thus in the case of Monday's coverage, a mysterious woman appeared with Fatty in the picture of the pair in the hotel window, identified as Mrs. Mae Taube, and her statement revealed her displeasure at the goings-on at the party. "I do not believe there was any attack upon Miss Rappe ... as far as Arbuckle is concerned," it concluded. "I have seen him frequently and he has always been a gentleman and never told risqué stories in the presence of women."[70]

As the *Examiner* news coverage continued, with the plot template established from the outset, it became essential to keep the stories relevant and the headlines screaming. A bulldog had grabbed Arbuckle by the throat and would not let him go. The next step in the process involved testimony before a grand jury to determine if a trial was warranted. In his many years as a newspaper publisher, Hearst had perfected the cheesecake display of women in his pages—whether in gowns, swimsuits or the latest fashion—and even in a murder case such as this, that stereotypical display never stopped. Rappe became the cheesecake; her smiling photos, seen from the very first day's coverage, were repeated. It was not hard to see the irony: The film comedian known for bringing laughter to millions had snuffed out not just a life but one as happy and joyous as Rappe's.

With a constant reminder that the events that led to Rappe's death involved a "booze party," the *Examiner* showed itself not just a major daily American newspaper but an instrument of morality upholding the nation's laws. Film exhibitors and executives cloaked themselves in the blanket of moral indignation over Arbuckle's fate for the obvious reason that it was good business. Even the Woman's Vigilant Committee, a talking shop more than an effective organization upholding the rights and defense of women, decided to take up the case, effusively declaring that the "disgraceful matter ... has aroused our women" and would not rest until the person behind Rappe's death was punished.[71]

As later revealed in the Pantages case, Hearst idolized women. For all his apparent progressiveness as a former politician, he was staunchly old-fashioned in regard to the roles women should play in society. A steady diet of his newspaper coverage reveals the superior virtue of the traditional domestic female over the sex-chasing viper. The photo montages of the smiling Rappe were only one example of this thinking put into practice; Hearst wrapped women in the garb of no-wrong, in the process turning ordinary, fallible human beings into saints. It played out, too, in the appearance of Arbuckle's wife arriving in San Francisco with her mother to give support to her accused husband, despite being associated with the murdering lothario. It was one more example of the halo that Hearst placed upon women.

The most damaging photo montage in the *Examiner* revealed Arbuckle in the middle of a large spider's nest, two large wine bottles beside him, surrounded by seven women involved in the Rappe case and under the title, "THEY WALKED INTO HIS PARLOR."[72] This image graphically captured the essence of the *Examiner*'s damning condemnation of Arbuckle as no other single piece of coverage ever could.

The coroner's jury held him responsible for Rappe's death, and further recommended that public officials do all in their power "so that San Francisco shall not be made the rendezvous of the debauchee and gangster."[73] More than 300 women of the Vigilante Committee gathered to insure that this "most outrageous case" be fully prosecuted.[74] There were also reports of attempts at bribing or influencing a key witness to the events being investigated by the district attorney, no doubt the nefarious work of Arbuckle's camp. The "booze party" from earlier *Examiner* coverage evolved into the "famous booze festival at the bidding of pajama-clad Roscoe ('Fatty') Arbuckle."[75] As a result of such accounts, the president of the Screen Writers Guild pronounced that Arbuckle's movie career was over.[76] And yet another photo of a smiling Rappe pictured her at her Los Angeles home with her pet dog under the banner, "Before the Fatal Trip."[77]

The *Examiner* followed the "booze line" between Hollywood and San Francisco, complete with a photo of Arbuckle's $25,000 car totting 20 bottles of alcohol. It took a past photo and, adding booze to his cargo, turned it into a weapon of attack. Meanwhile, in Thermopolis, Wyoming, a group of "150 men and boys, many of them cowboys," shot up a movie theater showing an Arbuckle film and seized the print, burning part of it.[78]

For days the *Examiner* had followed the trail of Rappe's body as it made its way from San Francisco to be buried in Los Angeles. It claimed that 8000 people came to view the deceased "gray-haired matrons with their daughters; men in overalls, who stood hat in hand and school girls, with braided hair down their backs—all inspired by love"—an act reserved only for the nation's greatest citizens who had passed away. The large crowd owed its size no doubt to the *Examiner* and other newspapers' coverage; they had turned Rappe into a great star such as she was not, and perhaps could never have been. Stardom had blithely eluded her, until her death at the hands of Arbuckle. Now she was very famous, this tragic figure of innocence and beauty, and viewing her body took on overtones of national patriotism.

Those readers who paid close attention to the coverage may have been startled by the results of the preliminary hearing in which Police Judge Sylvain Lazarus declared a charge of manslaughter against Arbuckle rather than the murder the prosecution had implored. The judge upbraided the district attorney for substantial lack of evidence: "The only witness in the entire case," he thundered, "who have any direct testimony bearing upon the guilt or innocence of the defendant, was the nervous hotel chambermaid," and that evidence involved sounds emanating from the hotel room with Arbuckle and Rappe.[79] Yet readers were subjected to a litany of innuendo, false statements, unsubstantiated evidence and hearsay throughout the case. The prosecution's leading witness, Mrs. Delmont, apparently intoxicated at the time when Arbuckle and Rappe were in his room, was considered too unreliable to testify. She had declared, for instance, that she had seen Rappe go with Arbuckle into his room, when other witnesses said that Delmont was in another room at the time and could not have seen Rappe and Arbuckle. Delmont would later be arrested on a charge of bigamy.[80] The first doctor to inspect Rappe's body noted only one bruise on her arm, and not the many that were later noted by other physicians and the coroner.

When the trial began on November 14, 1921, it seemed almost anticlimactic. "In the thousands of communities where mirth and laughter in the past have greeted the Arbuckle films," wrote the *Examiner*'s Oscar H. Fernbach, "sits the vast audience which from today on will watch the unreeling of a moving picture in which he again is the center."[81] When the court lacked drama, it was replaced by that constructed on the pages of the *Examiner*. "The world is a great audience," declared one *Examiner* reporter, "comparing notes on Fatty."[82] Whether in Salina, Kansas, or Paris or London, the same query is asked: "I wonder if he did it?" The same reporter, regarding the machinations of selecting a jury, later declared, "Men play chess with men, for the life of a man."[83] When witness Zey Prevost came to testify, the reporter described her this way: "Clad in blue broadcloth trimmed with black braid, a fur hat with gold brocade and wearing furs to match, she entered the courtroom with a supercilious smile and climbed into the witness chair."[84] As the trial rolled on, the reporter added: "Outside the Hall of Justice the rain falls steadily, making the streets ebony mirrors, reflecting yellow lights. Inside the jammed courtroom where Roscoe Arbuckle is being tried, the air is stale and murky."[85] Roscoe's youngest brother was married during the trial, but Roscoe was unable to attend the ceremony.

Fireworks did emerge, including testimony that Rappe had a habit of feeling sharp pain after drinking and also of ripping off her clothes, which she did in Arbuckle's room. A doctor who examined her prior to her death reported that Rappe confessed she had been drunk and "did not remember much what had occurred."[86] The doctor also testified that he saw no bruises on her body, contradicting statements made by others. Another witness testified that a detective had visited her and discouraged her from being a witness for the defense.[87] When Arbuckle finally testified in court, he calmly related the events of the day and "was not a whit shaken in his asserting" during cross-examination.[88] Fernbach wrote, "It was claimed ... by many of the spectators, this is the first case in the history of greater trials in the United States in which a defendant was so confidently and so completely surrendered to the guns of the prosecution."[89]

Arbuckle stated that he had gone to his room to prepare to leave for an outing, locking the door. He went to the bathroom only to find Rappe "prone on the floor and violently ill."[90] He brought her to one of his beds. He went to the bathroom, and when he returned, he found she had fallen on the floor between the beds. He lifted her onto the larger bed. He then went to the adjacent room to seek help.

For the first time in the *Examiner* coverage, shortly before the verdict was reached, Arbuckle is shown smiling in a photo of a spectator shaking his hand under the banner "COMEDIAN GETS HANDSHAKE."[91] That smile soon was erased when the jury of five women (women having won the right to join juries only four years previously) and seven men (including a cement contractor, candy dealer, accountant and explosives expert) failed to reach a verdict after more than 44 hours of deliberation, with ten voting for acquittal and two for conviction. It would drag on for several more months, each time laying a new knife into Arbuckle's career.

The second trial began on January 11, 1922, and there would be many more moments for Arbuckle to carry out his favorite "courtroom occupation of tearing up sheets of paper and piling the bits in neat little mounds on the table before him."[92] During the start of the new trial, and over 2400 miles away in the nation's capital, Postmaster General Will Hays announced his resignation from President Warren G. Harding's administration to take up a $150,000 post representing movie studios in Hollywood. Hays would later pound the final coffin into the nail of Arbuckle's movie career.

The *Examiner* coverage of the second trial was muted compared to the first. Fewer headlines and less space were devoted to it. Gone were the photos of a grinning Rappe and a sullen Arbuckle. Witnesses for the prosecution who were convincing in the first trial suffered from "impaired memories" in the second.[93] When jury deliberations began on Wednesday, February 1, 1922, District Attorney Matthew Brady declared there would be no third trial if the final decision was anything but unanimous. Jury discussions continued on Thursday. On Friday, another tragic event roiled Hollywood and once again brought its morals into question: the murder of film director William Desmond Taylor.

After 45 hours, the second jury (one woman and 11 men) voted 10 to 2 to convict. Brady changed his mind; there would be a third trial after all. Most jury members simply did not believe Arbuckle's story. Arbuckle's

Eight years before Pantages' trial, famed film comedian Roscoe "Fatty" Arbuckle suffered under the relentless negative newspaper coverage of William Randolph Hearst's *San Francisco Examiner*. This photograph shows him at his first trial for manslaughter, surrounded by his lawyers and (to his left) the prosecuting attorneys (*Marc Wanamaker, Bison Archives*).

lawyers' decision not to put him on the witness stand likely backfired, a mistake not repeated.

The third trial began in mid–March. Brady sensed victory as Arbuckle wearily traveled back to San Francisco from Los Angeles as his lawyers' bills mounted, eventually reaching $150,000.[94] A deposition was introduced in the trial in which a doctor told Rappe in 1914 to stay away from alcohol due to her chronic abdominal pains, remain in bed for several weeks, and undergo a strenuous diet. She ignored all his advice. Arbuckle turned 35 during the third trial but there was little to celebrate. The trial dragged on for more than five weeks, with Arbuckle's testimony serving as the climax to the grueling case. What had taken many hours of often tense and fractious deliberations among the jurors in the first two trials this time came soon and unequivocally. It took only three minutes on Wednesday, April 12, 1922, for the four women and eight men to acquit him. An ovation burst from the courtroom spectators. The jury then issued an unusual statement declaring that a "great injustice has been done him."[95] In the last photo of the coverage, Arbuckle smiled as his wife kissed him.[96] Arbuckle was a free man, but he would never again star in a major motion picture.

Years later, Arbuckle attempted a Hollywood comeback and was given a directing job by none other than Hearst himself, who by this time had his own film production company. Arbuckle confronted Hearst over his newspaper coverage of his trials:

"Why are you giving me a job when you did everything you could to hurt me?"
Hearst's reply was to pat Arbuckle on the shoulder and say, "I don't care what you did, son. All I ever wanted to do was to sell papers."[97]

The great sensational trial was over, with Hearst reaping the profits from it, yet the decade would not end before one more bonanza came to the press baron: Pantages' turn awaited.

5. 1929

The 1920s began brightly enough for Pantages. The son of the grocer from Andros had by the start of the decade built himself a formidable theatrical empire in America. He had reached Olympian heights. His theater chain covered most of the U.S. and extended into Canada. His booking office in New York City insured access to great acting talent there. On August 16, 1920, he completed one of his signature theaters, the lavishly elegant new terracotta Pantages Theater in downtown Los Angeles, which also served as his headquarters.

August 1920 could be considered a peak time for Pantages. He had the theater-cum-headquarters in downtown L.A. to be proud of, but he also could gush to the press about achieving his dream: calling the opening of the theater "the climax of an ambition cherished by Mr. Pantages ever since he left his home in Greece and went in search of world adventure as a cabin boy. It is an ambition that he declares he was born with, and he gives to the statement an almost fatalistic emphasis."[1]

Whether or not this ambition was indeed inherited from Pantages' father, it makes for compelling press copy. There is something romantically quaint about this press account—the kind of joyous mythmaking that served to buttress America as the bastion of free enterprise and success. More significantly, it reveals something of the Pantages ethos: That he could trace his career back to his father, to a man he left behind in Cairo, never to see again, perhaps absolves him of the guilt behind this impulsive act and sweeps it under the rug of destiny rather than forcing him to face it squarely.

This brash but fateful act could even be considered to lie behind his great success as a businessman. "So, there you have the impulse," the article further adds, "which made the career of this Alexander the Great of the variety and vaudeville show."[2] The photo of Pantages that accompanies this *Los Angeles Times* account is perhaps the most famous one of his career, showing a middle-aged businessman in suit and tie, holding a pen in his right hand and delicately supporting his chin with the other. That this should become the standard photo of Pantages—portraying someone who could not read or write English as an intellectual rather than a businessman—is telling in terms of the mythology he liked to spin. During his career, Pantages picked up many monikers. "Christopher Columbus of New Talent," gushed the *Times*, later adding "generalissimo of vaudeville." And, perhaps the one closest to his heart: "Pantages can now sit back and issue his orders in the large fashion of a military Alexander."[3]

Despite the dizzying heights his empire had reached, he fostered an image of a man with his nose to the grindstone. No prima donna, at least in the press accounts, was he. "I am the general manager, and sometimes the bookkeeper, and once in a while I fit dresses on the ushers," he proudly told a reporter, adding, "[S]ometimes I write a monologue."[4] By "writing," he meant dictating to someone else who put pen to paper.

Pantages felt compelled to create the image of a hard-working man. It suited his temperament and perhaps was meant to wash away his immigrant past. It also played into the tenor of the times. The 1920s was a grand era for business. The decade's second president, Calvin Coolidge, ironically one of the least hard-working chief executives in history, had famously said that the "business of America is business." He also said that the "man who builds a factory builds a temple."[5] Or, in this case, a movie theater.

This new "religion of business" had an intoxicating effect on American society, spawning new evangelists like Aimee Semple McPherson, who befriended Mrs. Lois Pantages and helped the mogul wife's through her own manslaughter charges in 1929. Sister Aimee understood that in the 1920s, money was the new messiah and she gravitated toward people who possessed great amounts of it.[6] She instinctively knew that the impact of "business as religion" required a change in the nature of worship; religion in America had to act more and more like a business. It was the tenor of the time that brilliant narcissists like McPherson achieved great popularity and, significantly, notoriety (the two went hand in hand). Luckless in her personal life (her first husband died from malaria while doing missionary work in China, and she separated from her second husband), McPherson found her passion in her own unique brand of religion.[7] Her Angelus Temple had the appearance of a stadium-like movie theater, complete with marquee at the entrance. Reverend Robert Shuler, another vocal, raging prophet, upbraided McPherson for "commercializing religion."[8] He also accused her of "collecting money for church purposes and not so using it."[9] The two had an intense dislike of each other, fueled not only by religious and professional differences, but no doubt by their gender differences. Shuler was an arch-traditionalist while McPherson represented the new wave of socially mobile and vocal women.

McPherson also owned and operated her own radio station, KSFG, to spread her message. In 1926, she drove to Venice Beach in Los Angeles, put on her green bathing suit, went for a swim and never returned. The nation was spellbound. Three deaths (one from suicide) and more than a month later "a bedraggled Aimee appeared at the door of a cottage in Agua Priesta, Mexico, with a fantastic tale of having been kidnapped and held prisoner."[10] The story included an 18-mile hike through a desert yet "without so much as a sunburn" on her face.[11] When it turned out that the sudden disappearance was spent "in a 'love cottage' in Carmel with a married church radio engineer," she was indicted for filing a false police report.[12] The exhibitionist McPherson, who loved to come to court dressed in flashy, theatrical costumes, saw the charges against her suddenly dropped a few weeks later.[13]

Money was important to Pantages, too, but by the time he moved to Los Angeles he had enough of it that he was motivated more by managing his growing business than simply adding to his considerable fortune. "He has never lost the human touch," the *Times* proclaimed. "A procession of people pass through his office all day. Some of them are there on matters of importance—some are there for nothing at all. But Pantages sees them all."[14] His great gift was that he knew how to entertain audiences at time when "Americans wanted to play and to be entertained."[15]

Pantages' "human touch" extended to the way he sometimes treated his actors. Beginning in 1911 at his Broadway vaudeville house in downtown Los Angeles, he instituted the "novel idea" of feeding his cast on Sundays between performances. This was copied in his other theaters. "A notable thing about the Sunday banquet at Pantages," the *Times* crooned, "is that it demonstrates the democratic spirit of the vaudeville performers."[16] It is uncertain, the article went on, if the offer for food extended to inviting the animals of the acts performed at the theater.

By 1910, films were in the ascendancy for paying audiences, yet Pantages held on to vaudeville in his theaters. It was, instead, a non-stop conveyor belt of comedians, singers, animal acts, jugglers, contortionists and dancers. Many of these acts he personally saw. "When I go to the theater," he confessed to the *Times*, "I never watch the audience. I watch the show. I say to myself, if I like it, the public will like it. If I don't, the public won't."[17] It seems he did not believe in test shows, but proudly relied on his own gut instincts. It was either an act of stubbornness or simply the result of experience as he claimed in the article.

Pantages' insistence on personally supervising the acts selected for his vaudeville houses extended to tryouts as well. According to the *Times*, he never tired of discovering new talent or helping those with a smidgen of talent develop further. "While he is rather impatient with the members of the bunk bazaar, he goes to any amount of trouble to help anybody with a grain of talent."[18]

In 1918, the *Los Angeles Times* reported that there were 31 theaters in his circuit, and he was in the midst of planning the new theater that would be completed in 1920 in downtown Los Angles that also housed his offices. He had just completed a theater in Spokane, Washington, and was planning another one in Salt Lake City. As with all his theaters, the signature operation in downtown Los Angeles was designed by B. Marcus Pritcca, his longtime architect and by this time something of his alter ego. The theaters they built in the 1920s could truly be called "palaces," a far cry a far cry from Pantages' first ramshackle storefront in Seattle.

By now, the Pantages family seems to have settled in Los Angeles quite comfortably. The warmer climate may have suited them better than the frigid, soggy, stormy one of the Puget Sound in Washington; perhaps more significantly, they brought their social status with them intact. By the end of 1919, Lois Pantages was noted in the *Los Angeles Times* for giving a violin performance, the "first time in a theater since she retired from public life," to help a boy's orphanage.[19] The change of environment, even the planning of it, seems to have energized Pantages. He was in a flurry of construction, so much so that in September 1918, the War Industry Board asked him to halt the building of his theater in Salt Lake City because of the need for metal to help support the war effort in Europe.[20]

The acceptance of the Pantages family in Southern California society seems especially telling, since there is little to suggest that Pantages was socially active in Seattle. In L.A., the family grew close to Hearst and his mistress, Marion Davies. Marion would be a bridesmaid at Carmen Pantages' wedding, when she married John Considine Jr. Pantages family members were frequent guests at Hearst's San Simeon castle. It is perhaps a striking feature of Pantages' life that he seems to have completely cut off his ties with Greece and his Greek culture, since no records of his participation exist in the Greek-American communities of Seattle or Los Angeles would happen, for example, if he donated to the local Greek Orthodox Church. It is not known if he made contact with relatives back home, or if he did, in what shape or form. For someone as prominent and wealthy as he was, Pantages' name does not appear in any philanthropic cause or activity. During his rape trial, no one from the Greek-American community publicly came out to support him. One of the few was Aimee Semple McPherson, who had become a sort of therapist to the wealthy and mighty.²¹

Meanwhile, Pantages' building boom continued. The circuit that began in Seattle found natural expansion along the West Coast. From an organizational standpoint, particularly for vaudeville, the proximity made sense: It was much easier to move actors and equipment around with shorter distances between playhouses. But the chain grew and distances grew with it; steadily, it seems, so as not to stretch the lines of communication between cities. There was only one way to go, however, and that was eastward. Along the way, Pantages made sure that the theaters belonged to him and were not leased. "All the Pantages houses in the West ... were personally owned by Alexander Pantages."²² Many cities were covered: Minneapolis, Winnipeg, Calgary; Vancouver, Victoria, Seattle, Spokane, Tacoma, Portland, San Francisco, Oakland, Los Angeles and Salt Lake.²³

A 1929 article in *Variety*, which disclosed the sale of his theater circuit to RKO Pictures, also noted, "All the houses except three operated by Pantages are owned." It also cited the following leaseholds: Memphis, 90 years; Kansas City, 90 years; Salt Lake City, 93 years; Vancouver, B.C., 85 years; Spokane, 50 years; Tacoma, 90 years; San Francisco, 42 years; Los Angeles 42 years; San Diego, 94 years; and Minneapolis, 50 years.²⁴

Even with theaters in places like Memphis and Kansas City, "the Pantages circuit is regarded in the East as a western affair." This may have grated on Pantages, whose relentless ego demanded that he expand his

William Randolph Hearst, the destroyer of souls and swallower of reputations. No single man had such an overwhelming impact on twentieth-century newspaper publishing (*Marc Wanamaker, Bison Archives*).

chain to its limits. He may have laid the groundwork for eastern expansion early in his rise as a theater mogul, but certainly by 1920 it was well underway: theaters in Memphis, Tennessee, Fort Worth, Texas, New Orleans, St. Louis, Kansas City, Missouri, and Toronto, Canada, signaled Pantages' movement eastward. It almost has the air of a military campaign, modeled, perhaps, after his namesake Alexander the Great and his sweep across the Middle East.

Then came the announcement of a new theater in Washington, D.C., "the capital city of the greatest nation in the world."[25] Unlike his western operations, the planned theater in the capital was not owned but rather leased. Leasing theaters was common in the Pantages canon of management, but the attempt to do so in Washington, D.C. smacks of a certain desperation to have an operation in the nation's capital. It never materialized. He had to settle for being as far east as Birmingham, Alabama.[26]

On the West Coast, there would be another theater in Los Angeles, this one on Hollywood Boulevard between Wilcox and Cahuenga and costing the staggering amount (if the published accounts are true) of $2 million. Like the theater in Washington, D.C., the property would be leased to Pantages, not owned by him. "It is the plan of Mr. Pantages to erect one of the finest legitimate show-houses in the United States," it was announced.[27]

By the 1920s, the Pantages chain had the reputation of being "the most important independent vaudeville circuit in the country, in amount of weeks offered and territory covered."[28] By weeks offered, this meant the length of bills or acts performed in the circuit; certainly in terms of vaudeville, there was no chain larger than Pantages'. And bookings took place out of New York, Chicago and Los Angeles, in essence covering the entire nation, and lasting up to 32 weeks of performances.

The Pantages circuit "was the first to successfully employ the rotating bill policy, playing bills intact from the Atlantic to the Pacific."[29] And not just American bills; Pantages ventured for acts in Europe "that couldn't otherwise have obtained bookings over here."[30] Whether European or American, the Pantages contract was always the same: It guaranteed "a definite number of weeks, but not stating how long a period [the acts] shall be played."[31] The contract might read "14 weeks or more," but performers came to realize that payment for services rendered were not always consistent for the "14 weeks or more."[32] The performers "knew that six of the weeks would be played at a 25 percent cut. The cuts were usually enforced when the acts reached the Coast."[33] It is on these grounds—not stating the length of the playable acts—that Pantages found justification for not paying actors the agreed amounts. "[M]ost of the [actors] were sore at Pantages," but few it seems did anything about it.³⁴

One who did was the manager of heavyweight champion Jack Dempsey, part of a musical comedy. On February 16, 1924, he sued Pantages for not receiving a substantial portion of the money owed him. Quoted in the *Los Angeles Times*, the manager noted that he received $4000 of the agreed upon $6356.76, but Pantages refused to give the balance.³⁵ On April 16, 1924, he claimed that the money owed to Dempsey was "taken by burglars," and therefore Dempsey was "not entitled to the extra part of the receipts for the week in question."³⁶ The case would eventually be settled out of court.³⁷ Theater circuits were hardly strangers to lawsuits, but it may be the case that Pantages had more than his fair share of them.

Yet by the 1920s Pantages, or "Pan" as the trade journal *Variety* nicknamed him, had also gained a reputation as a controversial figure, "one of the most colorful executives in modern theatre annals."³⁸ His dealing with actors is perhaps only a small element in his checkered reputation, but it did establish him as someone with whom one dealt cautiously. "Pantages was a firm believer in his own convictions," *Variety* noted in 1929, "his own methods, good or bad, and his own righteousness, and also that dough is the great fixer."³⁹ His dealings with others could be rough and domineering: He "laid down the law as he wanted to, with no alibis, no apologies, and no explanations. In his 22 years in show business he never changed his style."⁴⁰

This domineering authoritarianism led to the most complaints against Pantages of any theater operator of his importance. Throughout the trajectory of his theatrical tenure, "there was a consistent line of charges of business abuse by actors against [the] Pantages circuit alleging broken contracts, salary double crosses, illegal cancellations" and various other complaints.⁴¹

The Pantages method involved a preference for dealing with acts directly, rather than through managers. This may explain how he was able to sign contracts with actors, then turn around and reduce payment by 25 percent. In other instances, he was not above taking big acts and breaking them up into the parts that he wanted, and chucking those parts that did not suit his fancy. "For instance, if he liked a dance team in a flash act, but didn't care for the rest of the turn, he would route the whole act out to the Coast and then lift the team and book it alone when it got there."⁴²

Pantages and his staff may have honed these unethical practices to an art form. *Variety* noted that his employees echoed their boss' ethos.

"Few of Pantages' employees and associates were unwilling to follow his example or use his methods," and this extended to booking acts that were owned by members of his booking office staff, or the so-called "office act."[43] This was one "vaudeville booking innovation credited to Pantages, or at least to his booking office."[44] *Variety* described it this way: "This was an act, usually a dancing flash [tap dancing group] or full stage comedy turn drawing a good salary, which the Pantages office itself owned, or in which one of the Pan brokers had an interest."[45] According to *Variety*, he knew about this and in fact used this practice to keep "the booking office crews in line. Pantages played one office against the other, with Chicago keeping a check on New York and Los Angeles, etc."[46] Another account has Pantages himself involved in the corruption: "When open talk of his men grafting from acts was heard, it was also alleged Pan must have split coin with others."[47]

Pantages' public stinginess extended to his professional associations. According to *Variety*, he was a member of the Vaudeville Managers' Protective Association (later the Variety Managers Association) but "he never paid dues. He did not reply to complaints filed with the arbitrary organization and flatly refused to accept any of its arbitrary decisions against him."[48]

It is hardly surprising that for many in the entertainment industry, Pantages was a "lone wolf," as *Variety* called him.[49] He seemed at heart to be a grocery store operator writ large. His mentality and thinking were tinged with entrepreneurial gusto, but he seemed keen to build his business, not an institution. Despite having sons Rodney and Lloyd involved in the business (the two brothers managed the new Hollywood Pantages Theater that opened on June 4, 1930), the company seemed to revolve around his ego.[50] It seemed impossible to imagine the Pantages theater chain without Alexander Pantages.

Pantages built a spate of theaters across the U.S., but the chain carried his personal stamp, and nothing in his life indicated that this would change—even if life had changed around him. He remained iconoclastic, increasingly a dinosaur in an entertainment industry that clearly now favored films over vaudeville. In 1902, when Pantages opened his first Seattle theater in films were a fledgling art form and industry; by the 1920s, with millions going to the local bijou every week, vaudeville seemed increasingly irrelevant. Yet he clung on it like a barnacle. "He favored the combination show, and although he always regarded the [motion] picture as a necessary element, he considered the vaudeville most important and never was anything but a distinctly vaudeville showman."[51] His refusal to change from the combination—film and vaudeville—meant that as vaudeville further dropped in the national pastime rituals, he put the future of his theater operations at risk.

There is no evidence that this was an issue for Pantages; what does emerge by the 1920s is a high regard for his lifestyle and for actions that put his reputation at risk. Even as he preferred "cheap girl flash acts" of the acrobatic variety, his shows were designed for family consumption.[52] Yet his extracurricular activities increasingly found their way into the limelight and brought attention to an unsavory part of his character. If there were hints of this darker aspect of his character before, it certainly emerged by the 1920s.

Pantages was not one to be cowed by bad press; the battles he fought in public could be regarded as minor skirmishes in the larger game of status and wealth. But it does point to another facet of Pantages. He was careful to build up his myth of the poor Greek who achieved the grand American dream, but he seemed careless when it came to his personal life. There was, for instance, the lawsuit that resulted from the soured relations between the Pantages family and Dr. O.M. Justice only because Lois Pantages objected to the doctor divorcing his first wife and marrying another. Dr. Justice sued Alexander Pantages for services rendered and won.

More colorful yet more worrying were reports of his extracurricular activities. There was the case of an estranged husband accusing Pantages of "paying attention to his wife."[53] If the newspaper account of the affair is to be believed, the wife and her sister were at the Pantages Theater after the wife's act (she performed at the theater) ended. The wife claimed that she remained at the theater with her sister discussing business with an associate of Pantages until one p.m., at which time Pantages came and drove all three to a nearby parking lot. Here the estranged husband punched the theater mogul.

The husband's version of the event, published in the same account, was considerably different. In his telling, he had detectives following his wife on the night in question. A detective had seen the man's wife and her sister "run out from the stage door and get into a car." The detective notified the estranged husband, who came to wait at the parking lot where his wife had her car. Shortly after one a.m., the car with his wife and sister and Pantages returned. The man confronted Pantages, telling him "he was a fine one to be going around with my wife."[54]

At this point, Pantages reached for his back pocket, presumably to get a gun; the husband punched Pantages. The associate of Pantages later came over and he too got hit in the face. The willingness of Pantages to spend time with one of his hired actors alludes to another aspect of his character not visible in the press releases. Earlier in the same year, another incident took place that raises questions about his nocturnal activities. In this event, he is returning from an apparent weekend stint in Tijuana, Mexico, with a bejeweled woman and being driven by his chauffeur. Irate drivers testified that they were "crowded" off the highway near Santa Ana, but the chauffeur insisted he was only trying to get away from "highwaymen."[55]

One of the irate drivers stopped Pantages' car. He looked in the rear of the car and saw the bejeweled woman (another irate driver claimed there were actually two women in the back of the car with Pantages). It was at this point that the irate driver saw Pantages pull out and brandish a gun at him. When asked about this incident in court, the chauffeur maintained that Pantages was merely protecting the women and her jewels.

By the 1920s, Pantages had gained a reputation, as Jerry Giesler later claimed, of being an "old goat." According to Arthur Dean Tarrach, his biographer, "Pantages considered himself somewhat of a ladies' man and liked to hire acts with girls in brief costumes."[56] The impact of these revelations on his family is not known, although in the midst of Lois Pantages' trial for second-degree murder following her 1929 car accident, it was revealed that she had hired an attorney and detectives "in preparation for an action for divorce" against her husband.[57]

As 1930 approached, Pantages made overtures to sell his theaters. By this point, the New York Stock Market was reaching dizzying heights, and Pantages may have felt this was a good time to step down from the empire and perhaps relax for the first time in his life. It would be a decision that would have fateful consequences; he would never again reach the glory of the years prior to 1929. As with so many of his other business dealings, there was a public face to the negotiations and a more unsavory one behind the scenes. Business negotiations could be protracted and cumbersome, but Pantages drove a hard bargain. Negotiations seemed to drag on for weeks and months; was this done as a negotiating tactic or simply because he changed his mind about leaving the theater business, or at least substantially reducing his interests in it?

What might be considered a precursor to the sale of his theater operations (some but not all of these operations) was the July 28, 1927, announcement of films taking precedence over vaudeville in many of his West Coast houses.[58] On the one hand, there seems nothing particularly earth-shaking about the announcement; by the mid–1920s, it was clear that films had reached cultural supremacy in the country. Yet, at the same time, it seems an extraordinary announcement. A man who built his fame, wealth and reputation on the back of vaudeville was, in effect, seeing the writing on the wall: Vaudeville was losing its entertainment value. Despite hedging his bets, the direction his theater operations were now taking was obvious: "Under the new policy, Pantages will feature the [motion] picture above vaudeville, except when outstanding vaudeville attractions warrant feature billing."[59]

If Pantages desired to sell his operations, then the switch to film in his theaters made complete sense: The future lay in films, not in vaudeville. And so it was that by early 1929, there were already indications of interest in his operations. One of the most serious came from Joseph P. Kennedy, already a legendary figure in business and movie industry circles. Kennedy came to occupy not just a prominent role in the buyout attempts of the Pantages chain, but in a legend that grew around the rape charges against Pantages.

Like Pantages, it was Kennedy's destiny to reach the top of his profession, whatever profession it might be. Unlike Pantages, there was not one but many: banker, private investor, real estate mogul, movie mogul, civil servant and political operative. But he felt the sting of social exclusion, being Irish-Catholic in an era when American Protestants suspected a "papist conspiracy" to dominate the U.S. and did all they could to exclude Irish-Catholics from the citadels of power.

Even though he grew up as the "pampered son of a powerful and respected East Boston ward leader and businessman," Kennedy carried a chip on his shoulder from the family's impoverished, immigrant past.[60]

Much of this angst was due to the family's history, which he heard enough about growing up in East Boston. His namesake, Joseph P. Kennedy, left Dunganstown, County Wexford, Ireland, some time in 1848 or 1849 to escape the devastating potato famine ravaging the country. British colonialism exacerbated the famine, the effects of which were "near genocidal."[61]

Between 1845 and the 1850s, about a million (out of a population of eight million) Irish died and two more million emigrated to North America. To get to America required guts and stamina. The six-week journey between Liverpool and East Boston on the "coffin" ship was hellish: Human beings "locked together in darkened, unventilated ships" with "hatches battened" and "no room to stretch, no decent air to breathe, and no escape from the accumulating human waste, the scourge of seasickness, hunger and thirst, the stench of decay, disease and dying, and the endless boredom" that were "broken only by fits of panic when storms rocked or fire threatened."[62]

The immigrant Kennedy managed to land in East Boston (then known as Noddle's Island) and immediately began work making wine barrels. He married another immigrant, and soon there was a family, three girls and one boy, P.J. While better paid than most other manual laborers, coopers also worked long and exhausting hours. By 35, Kennedy passed away, ostensibly from cholera but more likely from overwork that damaged his immune system.[63] Suddenly, young P.J. was fatherless and forced to go to work. He was a stevedore for a time (loading and unloading ships), eventually earning enough to buy into saloons. Yet his real love was politics; and as an Irish-Catholic in a town with a majority of his kind, P.J. used his skills as a conciliator to rise in local ward politics.

This was the world into which Joseph Patrick Kennedy was born on September 6, 1888. At the time, the Kennedys lived in a very comfortable home in a fashionable street in East Boston along with other successful families. As the son of "one of East Boston's most prosperous, respected and powerful politicians," young Kennedy had few wants or needs that were not met.

The growing presence of Irish-Catholics caused consternation among the reigning Protestants. In the late 1880s, a Protestant movement grew to reduce the power of Irish-Catholics in the city.[64] The Anti-Catholic Association and the Immigrants Restriction League were only a manifestation of a larger nativist movement against immigration. Around the dinner table, Joe and his sisters, Margaret and Loretta, heard stories of the political discrimination, which left a strong impression on the children. "Those who survived were lean and mean. They were quick of wit and masters of dissembling. They understood political leverage and knew when to attack, when to retreat, and when to hide."[65]

As a youngster, Kennedy dressed well and was an able organizer. He hated his music lessons, preferring to get his "gang" from the neighborhood into baseball games, stage plays (free to spectators) and local pageants, such as his own kids' version of July Fourth and Decoration Day, in which he led a group of his friends to the local cemetery for the yearly celebration. He was an energetic young man with short, reddish-brown hair and a winning smile. The power and influence of a good set of teeth on a career should not be underestimated. American mythology dictates that luck, pluck, hard work and talent lead to success. It says nothing of charm and gregariousness. Kennedy was not particularly interested in his studies, but he replaced his intellectual curiosity with back-slapping, glad-handing, bravura charm. It got him elected class president and a place on the high school baseball team. His desires boiled down to success in all he touched. "Go for it" became his religious mantra, whether it involved stock trades or assignations; it was all the same to him.[66]

Above all, Kennedy was a student of life and social power; to how to get it, maintain it, build upon it. His goal was the mastery of the art of manipulation and financial wizardry. Life—the kind lived on the street and in back rooms and smoky parlors and in other women's beds—was his academy, and few understood it as well as he. He was cunning and devious, but such types make this world move. A poster child for capitalism from an early age, Kennedy discovered that the system he was born into was driven by money and with it its corollary, power. He saw it in his father's dealings and felt it himself in the surrounding culture. As a teenager attending parochial schools, Kennedy found a ready supply of outlets for his excessive entrepreneurial energy, including selling newspapers, peanuts and candy to passengers on cruise ships; acting as an errand boy for the Columbia Trust Company (that he would later head as its president) and even managed a stint in a haberdashery shop. At one point, Joe lighted coal stoves for Orthodox Jews forbidden by their religion to work on the Sabbath.[67]

Utilitarian cultures like America place a premium on ambitious, hard-working souls like Kennedy. So when he became fabulously rich as an adult, hagiography would declare that "he had risen early in the morning and worked hard, shrewdly, and late; he had been alert to opportunities," and so on.[68] As with sausages and laws, what was missing from the picture was the unsavory reality of the necessary behind-the-scenes maneuvering. While others might seek more idealist pursuits, Kennedy knew that any path to success was strewn with broken bones. Others', not his.

As a Bostonian, Kennedy knew the value of a Harvard education, for practical as well as social reasons. But his mediocre grades in parochial schools meant that he "should not have been admitted to any college, let alone Harvard."[69] But Harvard he did attend; and in the murky waters of Bostonian politics, it is likely that political favors greased the way, thanks mostly to his father's connections. At Harvard, he seemed more interested in the social benefits the college offered than in its academics. He graduated with 497 others at the college, 26 of them Catholics and 30 of them Jews, and with a deeply ingrained sense of what outsiders had to do to survive in a Protestant-dominated society: meet the right people, charm them, get the right favors.

A year after graduating from Harvard in 1912, he smelled an opportunity. With the connections gained from his family's political ties, he became a bank examiner in Massachusetts, the first, or so he said, Irish Catholic to do so. He learned the inner workings of the banking industry on the job, which he used to reach the next rung on the social and financial ladder.

The Columbia Trust Bank in Boston was failing. Kennedy's father had a share in the operation, but the son saw more than just saving his family's position in stepping in to rescue it. Instead, he sensed a chance to make a splash in the business world. Working tirelessly, a trait that he displayed more or less for the rest of his life, he raised the necessary funds and in the process got himself appointed president of the bank. Without his father's connections, he might not have become the youngest major bank president in the nation, yet few could fail to be impressed with his determination and risk-taking. These became hallmarks of his growing fortune. "A thousand times," he advised his son, "things don't happen, they are made to happen."[70]

It is not clear when Kennedy first became interested in the movie industry, but by 1919 he had joined a few other young entrepreneurs in buying controlling interest in a chain of 31 movie theaters in the northeast corner of the country, the Maine–New Hampshire company.[71] This came along with the "New England franchise for Universal Pictures" as well as "dabbl[ing] in motion picture production himself on a very limited scale, and though he enjoyed it his efforts were unsuccessful."[72] He may have also been drawn to the film industry for the reasons that attracted so many others, such as its unique ability to attract so many stunningly comely women and the power producers had over them. "Joe's philandering was constant and well-known."[73] For his deeply religious Catholic wife Rose, "sex was for procreation only, while Joe saw it as a way of asserting control and establishing his own self-worth."[74]

The growing stock market in the 1920s gave Joe Kennedy not only a means to increase his fortune, but by joining a Wall Street stock brokerage firm, Hayden, Stone & Co., also an opportunity to learn the tricks of the trade, which he parlayed into sizable profits. The "compelling force behind speculation is the desire to win," he once quipped.[75] While it was a time when even ordinary fools made money in the stock market, and there were millions of them, Kennedy's use of inside trading, stock manipulation and disinformation put him in an entirely different category. "Joe Kennedy learned the ins and outs of the stock market and the ways to manipulate it" that are illegal today.[76] In 1934 when he became head of the new Securities and Exchange Commission under President Franklin

D. Roosevelt, the fox was forced to clean up Wall Street for the chickens he once swindled.

The movie industry gave Kennedy opportunities that few other industries could—a relatively young business with all the inefficiencies and struggle with growth that this entailed, yet also the "fourth largest industry in the country."[77] Along with other movie moguls in the 1920s, Kennedy promoted standardization and vertical integration to squeeze more profits out of filmmaking. He was a natural fit for Hollywood. "With his quick grin, open manner and direct speech laced with profanity exuding a sort of contagious sexual energy,"[78] Kennedy was not the usual banker turned movie producer. "He looked and behaved like a picture man."[79] Kennedy shrewdly realized that Hollywood had a public relations problem. "Hollywood in the eyes of Middle America, appeared a veritable modern Babylon, with Sodom for a suburb."[80] He used this bad image to his advantage.

Some time during his Hollywood stay, Kennedy seems to have struck up a friendship with William Randolph Hearst. Outwardly improbable friends—Hearst the patrician, self-confident and imposing nativist, Kennedy the clawing, ethnic-minded urchin—they both were supreme egotists and workaholics, shared interests in politics, and had mistresses. They were also outsiders to the Hollywood scene, although they easily imbibed its lifestyle. Kennedy would, by the 1930s, if not earlier, become a financial adviser to Hearst, although as with other friends, he set about to take economic advantage of him.

Reputedly at the behest of Will Hays, former Republican National Chairman and Postmaster General under President Warren G. Harding and, starting in the early 1920s, president of the powerful Motion Pictures Producers and Distributors of America, Kennedy was invited to come to Hollywood and "bring to the industry much that it has lacked in the past."[81] Namely, a solid reputation. The movie industry that had been built up by immigrants and rocked by scandals like the Arbuckle case and the William Desmond Taylor murder needed a "white knight," and Kennedy was happy to oblige. "Before Joseph P. Kennedy," historian Cari Beauchamp noted, "no one had come from Wall Street and simply bought himself the presidency of a studio. 'A banker?' quipped movie mogul Marcus Loew, summing up the surprise of many. 'I thought this business was for furriers.'"[82]

He ingratiated himself in the movie industry by arranging a set of lectures by studio heads at his alma mater, Harvard. For the immigrant studio heads, this was quite an honor. "I cannot begin to tell you how it impresses me," one told Kennedy, "coming to a great college such as this to deliver a lecture, when I have never even seen the inside of one before."[83] As an added touch to further his status, he compiled a book of the lectures, under the grandiose title of *The Story of the Films* and, as its editor, promptly sent copies to influential publishers, editors and other figures for publicity. Kennedy could be a rascal, but he was a master of publicity.

Kennedy sold part of his share in the Maine–New Hampshire movie theaters and in early 1926 bought an interest in a mismanaged operation called Film Booking Office (FBO), a production and distribution company. As with his other dealings in the industry, there seems to be a complex story behind it that only added to Kennedy's reputation as the "coming Napoleon of the movies."[84] The British company behind FBO had invested over $7 million for it but Kennedy offered only $1 million to buy it outright. He was turned down cold.[85] A month later, FBO asked Kennedy if his offer was still available.

In 1928, Kennedy sought to buy the 700 movie theaters under the Keith-Albee-Orpheum Theaters Corporation across the U.S. and Canada. Controlling a vast network of theaters insured that Kennedy's films would get showings and with two million patrons daily filing through the KAO chain, this was a plum prize indeed. At first Edward Albee, founder of the company and pioneer in the entertainment business, refused to sell to Kennedy, but by May 10, 1928, a contract was signed. According to Kennedy biographer David E. Koskoff, a few months later Albee came to see Kennedy to make a suggestion, and Kennedy summarily and crudely dismissed him: "Didn't you know, Ed? You're washed up, you're through."[86]

Like a shark, he looked for weaknesses in his prey. His biggest prizes lay ahead of him. He pillaged files of friends and associates for "inside information such as the size of holdings of other stockholders and their financial condition."[87] This information was then used to manipulate stock to his benefit. For Kennedy, the business executive's goal "was to enrich himself, not to make the company prosper."[88] To that end, he merged FBO and KAO into Radio-Keith-Orpheum and sought to acquire one of the earliest moviemaking and distributing companies in the business, Pathé Exchange.

In doing so, he set up a complex stock trading scheme whereby his own personal holdings in Pathé stock would be more than doubled, but common stockholders would be left holding the bag: He received $80 per share while the "little folks—the suckers" as he called them got $1.50 per share.[89] Lawsuits followed, but they were dismissed. One anguished stockholder, Anne Lawler of Jamaica Plain in Boston, wrote to Kennedy: "This seems hardly Christian like, fair or just for a man of your character.... I wish you would think of the poor working women who had so much faith in you as to give their money to your Pathé."⁹⁰

Even his mistress Gloria Swanson paid heavily in her financial dealings with Kennedy. He "contracted with United Artists to produce several Swanson movies," and while the two had success with a few releases, *Queen Kelly* proved a disastrous box office failure. Rather than swallowing the losses himself, as would a normal producer, he instead placed the losses personally on Swanson to the tune of $800,000. Kennedy was always "repaid in full" for his contribution to a movie, while she suffered the losses.⁹¹ For Swanson, it proved to be an expensive romantic liaison.

But according to another Kennedy biographer, Ronald Kessler, what he did to RKO and others was "nothing compared to what he did to Alexander Pantages."⁹² It is this version of the events surrounding the rape charges against Pantages that history best remembers. Kessler claims that in February 1929, "Joe made an offer to buy the Pantages chain for $8 million, the second largest in California," but Pantages refused.⁹³ By this time, "Joe's innate arrogance was now rampant, and when Pantages again rebuffed his offers in April and May in Los Angeles, Joe threatened him with by boasting of his influence in the banking and movie businesses."⁹⁴ It is hard to imagine that Pantages took these threats seriously, as he was himself a stark exponent of the ruthless school of business. But Kessler claims that Pantages soon felt the meaning of Kennedy's threats. "[T]he Pantages Hill Street house, on the northwest corner of 7th and Hill Streets in downtown Los Angeles, found it was being denied first-run blockbuster features from major studios."⁹⁵ By at least one account, Kennedy "set about to destroy the reputation of Alex Pantages, in order to swoop in and take over the chain of Pantages movie palaces when the old man was down for the count."⁹⁶

The Film Daily reported on February 18, 1929, in two separate announcements, that Kennedy arrived in Los Angeles to finalize negotiations with Pantages. Yet in the same issue, in a brazen act of coy gamesmanship, Pantages denied moves to sell his operations. "I've never set a price on my circuit for anybody," he told the trade publication, which noted that he had "70 houses" under his command.⁹⁷ About a month later, the same denial was repeated, begging the question whether Pantages was simply using his intransigence as a negotiating tactic. In a strange plot twist worthy of a detective novel, there is the announcement that Radio-Keith-Orpheum "is negotiating for the Pantages circuit," at the same time Pantages "emphatically denied" that his chain was for sale.⁹⁸ In this latest report, Kennedy is mentioned in connection with the negotiations for the last time; thereafter, only his associate in the negotiations, J.J. Murdock, is recorded in the press.

It is likely that by spring 1929, Kennedy was cutting his ties to Hollywood. This is verified in a brief report in the April 3, 1929, *Variety* cryptically noting that "at the request of bankers, Joseph P. Kennedy will remain on the board of directors" of Pathe, not identifying the bankers nor why they asked him to stay.[99] Thereafter, Kennedy's name no longer appears in business discussions about Pantages' theaters.

The cat-and-mouse game over Pantages' theatrical holdings suddenly ended, as evidenced by a March 31, 1929, *Film Daily* announcement titled "R-K-O-Pantages Merger Reported Progressing." It revealed that the Pantages operation would be folded into RKO with Pantages retaining "an interest in the merged circuits."[100] It specified that the amount involved in the merger was between $15,000,000 and $20,000,000 and would not include the new Pantages Theater in Hollywood.[101] Once again, Pantages emphatically refused to acknowledge the report, saying "I know nothing of any deal being closed."[102]

Then came the bombshell: On April 3, 1929, *Variety* reported the sale of the Pantages circuit to RKO for $8 million. It was a stunning announcement, given Pantages' previous vehement denials about a sale. The deal that was about to be closed stipulated that RKO would take over all "Pan theatres with the exception of the house now under construction in Hollywood."[103] Pantages, the report indicated, would receive "$2,500,000 or $3,000,000 in cash and the balance in stock." The stock would "be put into escrow April 15 and an agreement be made between that period and July 1 with RKO taking over the houses on supervision plan."[104] The piece added this detail: "Pantages insists that provision be made for his son Rodney so as to continue the Pantages name in show business. Just what Rodney will do is unknown but understand will be connected with the operation end of RKO in some way appertaining to his father's houses."[105]

This inclusion belies the notion that Pantages did not want to continue his operation, not in theory but perhaps in practice by maintaining the his name with the theater marquees. Or was he merely trying to find employment for his son? (Curiously for a man who left his own father and broke ties with his family.) Whatever the motivation, a few days later came a hitch. In *Variety* it was stated that RKO was "disinclined to accept Pan's son, Rodney, as an executive in that outfit."[106] As a result, while Pantages claimed that the option given to RKO would remain, he also made overtures to "dispose of his houses to Fox, which organization is reported not particularly interested."[107] If this was brinkmanship on the part of Pantages, he could be accused of taking it to an extreme.

The April 18, 1929, *New York Times* reported that Pantages admitted to the sale of his theaters to RKO. In the switch, Pantages confirmed the deal, which amounted to "approximately $14,000,000 and probably would be completed in two or three weeks."[108] It added that the sale would involve 15 theaters and all of his theatrical real estate, including an 11-story building in Los Angeles.[109] The piece also noted that RKO had taken a "verbal 30-day option on the theatrical properties" two weeks prior to this announcement. It seems that Pantages' previous denials were not genuine.

But negotiations were now taking a different course. *Variety* announced on May 8, 1929, that RKO might end up taking all the Pantages theaters and introduced another player into the purchasing picture, Publix Theaters (later to be associated with Paramount Studios). The article stressed that the deal was imminent. "Just when it may be closed," it assured the reader, "doesn't seem certain, but it is expected shortly."

As the struggle over Pantages' theaters continued, RKO made other theater purchases, including a chain in New York, and showed interest in purchasing others in Ohio and Texas.[110] It seems the chain would not wait at Pantages' door as other independent chains threw in the towel to bigger conglomerates. *Variety* again announced the imminent closure of the "Keith and Pan" deal on May 15, 1929, although in this new pronouncement, RKO would not get all Pantages' theaters: "Other theatrical interests will get the remainder."[111] As before, it was a false alarm.

The role that Kennedy played in the negotiations is uncertain. *Variety* announced on April 3, 1929, that Kennedy would "remain on the Pathé board of directors" but only "in an advisory capacity," perhaps hinting at his exit from the movie industry. If this is the case, then a primary reason behind the purchase of Pantages' chain was missing. In the April and May press announcements, Kennedy's name is noticeably missing from the negotiations, in contrast to the beginning of the process back in February when he figured prominently in them.

Pantages, too, might have wondered what would become of his life if he did not have his theaters to run. The curtain was already closing down on other theater pioneers like himself; not just F.F. Proctor in New York (he sold to RKO) but also the venerable Sid Grauman, whose Chinese Theater in Hollywood had by the late 1920s become a theatrical landmark (the place where stars leave their footprints and hand prints).[112] Was Pantages willing to exit as gracefully as they? On May 29, 1929, *Variety* announced that Pantages sold his new Hollywood theater to Publix which also would take over his flagship theater on 7th and Hill, indicating that perhaps the train to sell had already left the station and perhaps it was too late to back down.

Meanwhile, the RKO deal ground on; the *New York Times* reported on June 7, 1929, that a merger was near: "Negotiations have reached a point where only four or five problems are yet to be worked out, Mr. Pantages announced here today."[113] This was a marked change from his denials only a few weeks before. By July 26, 1929, a deal was finally announced involving RKO purchasing six Pantages theaters (in San Francisco, Salt

Joseph P. Kennedy (left) was considered the architect behind Pantages' ruin. A man of extraordinary will and ego, he came (to Hollywood), he saw and he conquered, including other movie moguls like Jesse Lasky of Paramount (right) (*Marc Wanamaker, Bison Archives*).

Lake City, Portland, San Diego, Spokane and Tacoma) for an amount "said to be between $4,500,000 and $5,000,000."[114]

As the machinations over the Pantages theaters continued throughout the first part of the year, another set of circumstances were put into motion. They reached a crescendo in October, the same month as his trial. The crash of Wall Street seemed an impossibility in early 1929, despite obvious signs that the market had reached a fever pitch. The great fat years of the decade's roaring stock markets were about to come tumbling down, but millions were too blinded by greed to realize the danger. Out of a population of 122 million, 15 million owned stocks. Twenty years before, it was only half a million.[115] Even women, who had traditionally left investing to men, got into the act in huge numbers, perhaps as high as 35 percent of all speculators.[116] It was "blue skies" indeed, as Irving Berlin's popular 1926 song promised. There was talk of "permanent prosperity," although this came from speculators themselves rather than serious economists who were in a better position to know.

Prudent, conservative investments had also given way to margin loans, stunning gains and the near hysteria that the market could absorb drops and still climb. It was a "New Era," many claimed; companies were managed better, the Federal Reserve had stabilized booms and busts, and expanding technological progress meant an unlimited supply of new products that could only make human lives, at least American ones, healthier, better, easier, longer and more vibrant.

Beneath the glitter that was the great bull market of the 1920s was a beast that needed constant feeding: namely, the call loan market that allowed stock speculators to buy stocks but put up only a fraction of their worth with a promise to pay later. Many took this as a free ride on the roulette wheel whereby stocks were purchased with very little money and sold later at a profit as the market continued to rise, which it did most of the decade. This encouraged speculators to invest, and so long as market prices continued to rise, many profited handsomely. Only when the speculation reached disproportionate size compared to the actual economy that the stock exchanges represented, did the system collapse.

Bankers were happy to feed this casino capitalism; they could borrow funds from the Federal Reserve at a discount rate and lend them out at twice the rate. In time, bank loans to the call loan market exceeded those to regular businesses. The "quick, safe, lucrative return" of the call loan market was preferred over those in "legitimate business or agricultural loans of longer duration, lower return and higher risk."[117] Even corporations got into the act; rather than parking their surplus cash in bank deposits, they placed them in the call loan market, getting greater returns but also further feeding the Wall Street frenzy. And the Federal Reserve could do nothing to control this vast stream of ready cash.

It did not help that the excessive speculation had also fed into a mania for mergers and acquisitions and, even more tellingly, an emphasis on holding companies that were little more than "an office housing the corporate and financial records of their subsidiaries," usually in business-friendly Delaware where 10,000 corporations were housed in a single office building floor.[118] As historian Maury Klein noted, only 86 of the 573 active companies listed on the New York Stock Exchange at the time were actual operating companies producing real products. The rest were some combination of holding and operating companies or purely holding companies.[119] Such financial pyrotechnics were designed for internal power and control, not for expanding the nation's economy. There was also insider trading and sweetheart deals between executives and boards of directors whose profits, often untaxed, were beyond scrutiny.

Part of the problem was the Federal Reserve's inability to decide whether it was within its purview to quash excessive speculation on Wall Street. Founded in 1913, it still had not resolved the length and breadth of its mandate to oversee the nation's economy, and as a result it let the speculation continue for fear of treading into the unknown. Its chairman was the health-challenged Benjamin Strong, who suffered from one malady or another, putting him out of commission for months at a time. Strong had famously wondered about the consequences of taking an interventionist role in the equity markets and what this would do to the rest of the nation's economy. But prior to his untimely death in October 1928 he had warned in a letter that the issue of speculation was not merely one of call loan margins, excessive speculation, holding companies or greater public participation in the stock market, but something more fundamental: psychology: "The problem now is how to shape our policy as to avoid a calamitous break in the stock market, a panicky feeling about money, a setback to business because of the change in psychology."[120]

So long as the market continued its astronomic rise, these concerns remained in the shadows. Only when gravity finally exerted itself did the entire edifice tumble down. Farmers in the 1920s generally fared less well than other sectors of the economy, but it was a slowdown in other sectors that by 1928 signaled that the economy was not faring well. Employment fell, as did building construction, railroad freight loadings and the all-important commodity prices.[121] The Fed responded to this by lowering the discount rate, which only further swelled the call loan market. Voices of concern were drowned out by bull enthusiasts, so the markets continued their upward trajectory. The famous astrologer Evangeline Adams, who counseled movie and business elites like Charlie Chaplin, Mary Pickford and J.P. Morgan, blithely predicted in February 1929 that the market would continue to climb that year.[122] Even the normally sedate Andrew Mellon, banker and Treasury Secretary, announced on March 15 that the bond market offered bargains. Rather than advising restraint, the clarion voices were for more buying and speculation, not less.

On March 18, 1929, the Dow Jones Industrial Average went on a downward run for eight straight sessions, and by March 26 it shattered trading volumes as stocks were dumped. That same afternoon, call loan rates reached 20 percent, an astonishing figure and one that alone might bring down the entire speculative house of cards. "The March declines were probably triggered by the high cost of call money," one historian wrote.[123] But cooler heads prevailed, as one large bank pumped $25 million in extra funds into the call loan system, and the danger was averted with call money rates falling to a more reasonable eight percent. The Federal Reserve was not happy about this intervention, since it encouraged the speculation to continue. To outsiders, it seemed nothing could kill off the speculation, which only fed into its apparent invincibility. Steel production rose that spring, even as construction activity and car sales slowed. It was nothing to panic about, yet it revealed an underlying economy perhaps unable to support such dizzying stock market values. A more worrisome matter—one that escaped many investors' attention—was the continued increase in volatility on the market, something that had grown markedly since 1921: from 4.80 points in 1921 to 38.90 eight years later.[124]

Another sharp drop on May 13, 1929, left blood on the Exchange floor. There were more anxious moments that month, but the market soon recovered. From June until its September 3 high, with the Dow shooting to a record 381.17, a tenfold increase from its low in 1920, the market was on a tear. Closer inspection, however, revealed that the advancing stocks were a small group; the majority of shares on the Exchange were below their January 1, 1929, levels. So it seemed to be a false rally. More troubling for the Fed, the intensifying speculation that resulted after the March mini-crash and intervention meant that with the new high in September, the market "had further to fall and the consequences would be more severe."[125] Statistics guru Roger Babson warned on September 21, a bumpy day on the market, of an impending crash, a jeremiad he had been repeating since 1926. The next day, the market responded to Babson's dire prediction by rising—at least, for the dozen or so select stocks that had led the year's rally. Many expected the surge to continue.

In October, they got a rude surprise.

In normal circumstances, the theater sales agreement with RKO would have been a cause for celebration, but there was by July already a cloud hanging over the Pantages family.[126] And this cloud would only darken as the summer wore on. One writer called 1929 "a bad year for the American people [and] a complete disaster for the Pantages family."[127] On June 16, 1929, Lois and her son Lloyd hosted a beach party at her seaside home. Witnesses later testified "they saw no liquor" during the festivities.[128] At some point, after driving away from the party as she headed east on Sunset Boulevard, Lois may have tried to pass another car, only to end up hitting three cars and then smashing into another car driven by a Japanese-American and his family. The driver of the car, Juro Rokumoto, and his wife were severely injured. Mr. Rokumoto later died from his injuries.[129] Five others were also injured. Mrs. Pantages sustained "cuts to her nose and lips."[130]

Lois Pantages' case presaged that of her husband and the start of a few years of soul-wrenching tribulation. The trial that resulted from her car accident provided fewer sensational elements than her husband's, but no less melodrama. It was another case involving a wealthy Hollywoodite, a fancy car (Stutz), alcohol and death.[131] District Attorney Buron Fitts, who would later prosecute Alexander Pantages, took charge of Lois' case. "Fitts declared he was convinced the facts justified the prosecution of Mrs. Pantages," the paper reported, "in view of the testimony of witnesses that the woman appeared very drunk and had struck two other [cars] prior to the Rokumoto crash."[132]

Lois was wheeled in "an invalid's chair" into court on July 17, 1929, to be formally charged with murder and driving while intoxicated. "Still very weak following a month's confinement in a hospital," Lois cut a very forlorn figure.[133] At her grand jury hearing, a police officer who was at the accident scene testified that he "observed a distinct alcoholic odor on her breath" and thought she "appeared under the influence."[134] During the trial, the attending nurse and doctor in Lois' hospitalization testified that they did not smell any alcohol on her breath.

The trial before seven men and five women that began on Tuesday, September 3, 1929, was a family affair. Not only were Pantages and the three children at Lois' side (with Carmen "soon to be a bride"), but the same group of expensive lawyers who would defend Pantages against the Pringle charges were also used to defend her case—something the *Los Angeles Examiner* later noted.[135] According to the defense, Mrs. Pantages was not intoxicated but suffered from "a nervous disorder."[136] The strong public interest in Lois' case—"[m]ore than a thousand persons jostled each other outside the courtroom" to follow the proceedings—foreshadowed what was to come for her husband.[137]

The *Examiner* described the widow, Karuko Rokumoto, as "a quiet, dignified, self-possessed young woman dressed all in black" and said that her three children "look like students, all with their heavy, horn-rimmed glasses." On the other hand, Lois and Alexander Pantages were revealed to be psychological wrecks in the courtroom. If he had been initially cool and aloof to the charges, by the time of her trial he was a different human if the coverage is to be believed. Lois was "thin, nervous, alert" with "unquiet fingers that drum incessantly on the arm of her chair" or "play with the huge stone in her ring."[138] Alexander was a shadow of his former self: "He's gone soft. Flabby. Disorganized. Sometimes he tries to pull himself together and get back to his old confidence. He can't do it. Most of the time he doesn't even try."[139] "And whenever he moves," the *Examiner* added for emphasis, "the enormous diamond on his left hand flashes out a cold, ironical glitter."[140] Condemnation by ring.

Hearst reporter Harry Lang was brought in to add more theatrics ("Mrs. Lois Pantages ... is being watched for signs of insanity...!") in a case with no shortage of drama.[141] Forces outside the courtroom included Reverend Robert Pierce Shuler, who assured his followers that Lois would never be convicted because the jury was rigged. He boldly told his radio listeners that it would be a hung jury "and I can name the man who will hang it.'"[142] The statement promptly landed him in court on a contempt charge. He was convicted and forced to pay a $75 fine.

"Fighting Bob" Shuler was part of a crop of vitriolic, loudmouthed, exhibitionist preachers (Aimee Semple McPherson, Father Charles Coughlin and Billy Sunday being perhaps the most famous) who had a hold on the American imagination at the time.[143] He contributed to the rise of the "megachurch" in American spiritual life, yet even as he pandered to changing social mores, he sought to "preserve traditional Christianity" as a "champion of overage, old-stock Americans in their battle against the wealthy and the corrupt."[144] His brand of fundamentalism was a product of Southern Methodism as it developed in the last decades of the nineteenth century; he wanted a bigger platform and California served that purpose.[145] He connected well to the angst suffered by Midwestern Protestant refugees in Los Angeles since the 1880s.[146] He "managed a perfect appeal to these retired farmers and their families.... They were delighted to have their imaginations stimulated with ideas of sexual and other vices at the same time they were empathically assured of their own superior righteousness and even allowed, as it were, to bringing the wicked to judgment.'"[147] The wicked included Lois and Alexander Pantages.

It was not an act on his part to fight the rich and powerful: Shuler genuinely believed in his crusade, even as he ceaselessly overstepped his bounds as a moral arbiter and needlessly created enemies. Burning bridges meant that he was doing God's work. There was no fence-sitting when it came to fighting evil, and he fought it from the depths of his soul. Shuler became pastor of Trinity Methodist Church in downtown Los Angeles, which he converted into his base of power. When he initially arrived at the church, "he found a discouraged congregation numbering 600 active members and burdened by a $70,000 debt." He wiped away the debt and his congregation swelled into the thousands. Revealing his nativist sentiments, Shuler regarded Los Angeles as "'not dominated by foreigners ... the one city in the nation in which the white, Christian idealism still predominates.'"[148] Shuler arrived in L.A., his grandson wrote, "to convert person *and* city alike."[149]

Sermons became jeremiads against sin and corruption. After a generous gift by a wealthy oilman's wife, he took to the airwaves on a new radio station, KGEF ("Keep God Ever First"). A man with an overdeveloped emotive reflex, Shuler used the powerful megaphone of the airwaves, along with sermons and pamphlets, to shrill effect, swaying elections, railing against the immoral (the movie industry was a favored target) and generally terrorizing the city's political and social elite in a manner never done before. As the *Los Angeles Times*, itself a frequent Shuler target, noted, "If you haven't been denounced by Reverend 'Bob' Shuler, you just don't amount to much."[150] The targets included: the Automobile Club of Southern California for colluding with car insurance companies; the University of Southern California for "licking the feet of millionaires who give them large sums of money"; Jews ("undermining American idealism"); Catholics ("plotting to seize American institutions"); the Los Angeles Public Library (offering books "not fit to read even by 'heathen China or anarchistic Russia'"); the YWCA for promoting "wild dances"; the Presbyterian Church for political collusion; and scores of public officials from the L.A.

Police Department, the country's courts and entire administration, and even the County Health Department.[151] To cite a popular bumper sticker from the 1980s, Shuler wasn't prejudiced—he hated everybody.

Immigrants and the motion picture industry came in for special opprobrium. Like many other nativists, he thought the movies were corrupting the nation's youth. He railed against Charlie Chaplin for his propensity for affairs and for marrying young women ("Is Charlie Chaplin a Born Fool or Did He Cultivate It?" one of his colorful sermons asked).[152] Fatty Arbuckle was another favorite victim, Shuler accusing him of soiling the lives of others with his "colossal parties."[153] Shuler wrote two pamphlets attacking Alexander Pantages, *Millionaires and Hired Girls* (1929–30) and *Eunice Pringle* (1931).[154] According to Shuler's grandson, his pamphlets averaged 60 pages in length and reached thousands.[155]

On the other hand, Shuler recommended in a remarkable show of his nativist sentiments that the Ku Klux Klan clean up public government. The cultural wars were on overdrive. Some of his targets fought back by seeking to shut down his radio station on the grounds of his misuse of the airwaves. Shuler defended freedom of speech or, as he preferred, freedom to "prophesy." Within a short time, the Federal Radio Commission revoked the station's broadcast license.[156] He blamed a conspiracy of the rich and powerful for aiding in the revocation, including Alexander Pantages.

Lois Pantages' three-week trial ended with a guilty verdict of manslaughter on Wednesday, September 25, 1929, at 8:37 p.m. Tears and a collapse by Lois Pantages followed. She faced one to ten years in San Quentin. Taken home, she refused food and water. Aimee Semple McPherson came to the Pantages home to comfort her.[157] When Lois was forced to come to court for sentencing, she arrived in a wheelchair attended by nurses and doctors. Eventually she would escape sentencing and be placed on probation, or as Harry Lang put it: "Mrs. Alexander Pantages will not go to San Quentin."[158] She paid a settlement (the $78,500 check was presented in court during the judge's probation decision; she endorsed it with a hand that shook so terribly that her name was barely legible, Lang wrote) to the Rokumoto family as damages.[159] A photo of the check and Mrs. Rokumoto holding it appeared with the Lang piece.[160] Lois was also ordered to "surrender her automobile driver's license, forbidden the privilege of driving any of her expensive cars for ten years and forbidden to drink intoxicating liquors during the same period."[161]

With the conclusion of Lois' trial in late September, attention turned to her husband's case. It opened at ten a.m., Tuesday, October 1, 1929. "The bailiff's pronouncement barely had ceased echoing," a paper added, "when Judge Fricke created a sensation by ordering the jury panel under guard and to be locked up in all absences from the courtroom."[162] It was a tough but necessary reaction to the intense public interest in the trial.

For William Randolph Hearst, people preferred stories over news. "As a keen observer of the American psyche," historian Ben Procter wrote of Hearst, "he understood that readers needed to identity with a specific event, to sympathize with a tragic martyr, to rejoice with the triumphs of a heroic figure ... [and] to provide the public continually with some stimulant, some 'outrage' to arouse sympathy."[163] He found that person in the form of the 17-year-old dancer known by her stage name Solita Deyo.

6. Mogul's Trial

Eunice Alice Pringle's life was far removed from Alexander T. Pantages'. She was born on March 5, 1912, in Marysville in Central California, the daughter of a doctor and a high school teacher who was hard of hearing.[1] The few facts that emerged about her life came from the rape trial; it was an uneventful life compared to Pantages', one that most jurors would find easier to understand than his. In 1921, her family moved to Garden Grove, roughly around the same time that the parents separated. She attended the high school where her mother taught, performing in plays and also editing the yearbook. Eunice was an only child and, from all indications, she was doted upon by the family. She was also very athletic, playing basketball and soccer and also swimming.

She attended the University of Southern California for one semester and the first six weeks of the second.[2] During her time at USC, she lived in a women's dorm. She likely dropped out of college, where she had studied "dramatics and language," to pursue her theatrical career.[3] By her account, she also attended "the Methodist Church and was a member of the Camp Fire Girls."[4] Since the age of 11, Pringle had been "studying and practicing the art of dancing [and] preparing herself for the stage."[5] "I have had practically no professional stage experience," she told reporters after Pantages' arrest. "Most of my dancing has been more of a semi-professional nature. I danced before the Uplifters Club one time and that was about my most important engagement."[6] She took lessons at a Hollywood dance studio.

It was either at the dance studio or at another Hollywood studio that a friend introduced her to the "short, dark-haired, dark-faced man of 40," Nicholas A. Dunaev.[7] The Russian Dunaev, billed as being from New York, was peddling *The Prince from Hollywood,* a one-act play involving an East Indian prince; in its written form, it seemed a simplistic and crude *ménage-à-trois* scenario of trifling consequence and little dramatic value.[8] It did, however, give Pringle the opportunity to dance and play the piano.

Some time before or after the introduction to Dunaev, Pringle took on the stage name Solita Deyo as an homage to her mother (Deyo was her mother's maiden name). Mrs. Pringle purchased the play from Dunaev for $350, offering her daughter a role as a Spanish dancer. The relationship that developed between Eunice and Dunaev remained mysterious. It was declared inadmissible in the first trial and Eunice refused to discuss it.

According to Pringle's testimony, it was Dunaev who first introduced her to Pantages. It was around May 1, 1929, that Pringle first called on Pantages to book Dunaev's act. From that initial meeting followed many attempts by Pringle to push the play, with Pantages promising to book her act at his theater in Fresno. At one point he reviewed the play at his theater, promising afterwards to book it into his circuit. But later he asked her to join another revue then touring, which she refused to do. More attempts to persuade him followed, each time Pantages telling her to come back another time, a standard line normally interpreted as the polite brush-off. But Pringle refused to back off. "My greatest interest," she would tell the grand jury, "was simply to appear on stage in an act which I know was well-suited for me."[9]

Friday, August 9, 1929, started innocently enough for Pringle.[10] Dunaev drove her to downtown Los Angeles in Mrs. Pringle's car at 10:30 on that balmy 85-degree morning.[11] Pringle wore a red crepe dress, red velvet jacket, sheer stockings and high-heeled red slippers.[12] Pantages' lawyers claimed this outfit was designed to get the theater mogul's attention.[13] Eunice was to see an eye specialist, visit her former residence hall at USC, have lunch and finally pay a call on Pantages.

She entered the seven-story Pantages building and took the elevator to the second floor where the Pantages theater offices were located. The elevator operator remembered her as being alone.[14] In her trial testimony published in the *Los Angeles Examiner*, Pringle claimed she saw Pantages some time after arriving in the main office area. "He went through the office and smiled at me and then later he went through again and spoke to me."[15] He told her he would see her but first had to go to the barber's. He promised to return and speak to her. He then led her into the balcony of the theatre where crooner Eddie Leonard was singing in the musical, *Melody Lane* ("talking, singing, dancing ... offering glorious vaudeville!" the Pantages ad in the *Examiner* on August 10, 1929, proclaimed) and promptly left for his appointment. A short while later, Pantages returned and whisked Pringle into a small mezzanine office between the first and second floors of the building. The tiny space measured four and a half feet wide, 13 feet long and over six feet high ("I could stretch out both hands and almost touch both walls," one witness testified).[16] According to Pringle, there were three chairs and "sort of a cabinet" in the room.[17]

She removed her red velvet jacket, and he asked if he could do the same. He promised to book her act, then took her by the hand, telling her she had lovely hands. He added that she was a wonderful dancer and,

The tiny room where the sexual assault on 17-year-old Eunice Alice Pringle allegedly occurred. The room was described as either a broom closet or a side office. Jury members paid it a visit (*Marc Wanamaker, Bison Archives*).

drawing closer to her, asked if she would be his sweetheart. Rebuffing his advances only excited Pantages, who suddenly went "crazy" and held her tightly to him.[18] Then he jumped up, pulling her with him, and smothered her with kisses and bites. When she screamed, he put his hand over her mouth. He continued kissing her, and using his body, he forced her down onto the floor, still holding his hand over her mouth. She struggled but felt pinned down by his weight. Then began the assault, from which she fainted. When she came to, he was lying beside her. She got up to leave, but he grabbed her and would not let her go. Pringle finally managed to escape, thrust open the door, and rushed out shrieking. This was her side of the story.

"The telephone switchboard operators noted that as Pringle ran past she was ripping her clothes off, not putting them on."[19] She ran out of the building onto the sidewalk, yelling as she went. A police officer about a block away heard the screams and rushed over. He called for backup and led her back inside the building. When two LAPD detectives came to the scene, they found Pantages and his clothes "in completely disarray, with coat off, and parts of his clothing torn."[20] "There's the beast, don't let him get away!" she screamed.[21] Pringle's dress was "ripped down the side … and she was in a state of shock and fear" when the detectives arrived.[22] Pantages was arrested and, along with witnesses and Pringle, was taken to downtown police headquarters where he was charged with two counts of statutory and violent assault of a minor.

Pantages' version of the events that afternoon, as expected, was markedly different. He claimed that she started visiting him earlier in the year, pushing to get her act booked. After some time, Pantages agreed to see it (his office manager had misgivings about the play), but it was "so vulgar and obscene" that he could not stage it and instead offered Pringle "work in another act."[23] Pringle refused to give up on her play and continued to press him on it. On August 9, 1929, Pantages was heading to the mezzanine office when Pringle suddenly entered and shut the door. "You speak to me now!" Pantages recalled her saying, then he claimed she rushed forward and yanked his jacket off him. Then she grabbed his suspenders and pulled him to the floor, causing him to losing his balance. He fell down and she suddenly screamed. Then she ran out and accused him of having assaulted her. "I've never had anything like that against me before," Pantages told police, "and I consider it a clear case of frame-up!"[24] When told that he would be locked up in jail that night, he replied, "I'm not surprised!"[25]

The narrative as constructed by the *Los Angeles Examiner* from the start of the coverage (the very next day, Saturday, August 10) was to idolize Pringle and to demonize Pantages, a strategy effectively and powerfully

6. Mogul's Trial

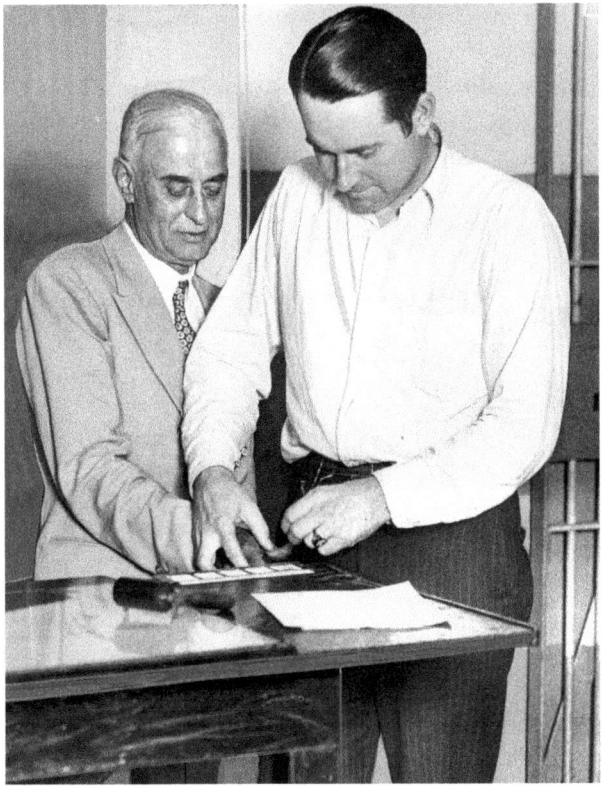

Pantages is fingerprinted after his August 9, 1929, arrest for sexually assaulting Eunice Alice Pringle (*Marc Wanamaker, Bison Archives*).

used in the Arbuckle case. It was the very heart of any suitable dramatic construction: creating an easily discernible protagonist and identifiable antagonist. This simple binary code took the thinking out of the minds of the *Examiner*'s readers and placed into the hands of its editors. All readers had to do was to follow along, in serial form as movies had effectively done, and radio and television were to do later. This was the great secret that Hearst and other press barons peddled: the daily drama of life told in simple, clearly delineated, breathless fashion. Not fiction, since it was based on real events, but "fictionalized reality" that hooked audiences and insured that those printed newspaper copies would sell day in and day out. At first, the stunning story of the Pantages rape allegation received second billing in the *Examiner*'s front page to the main headline and a typically Hearstian publicity ploy—in this case, the Hearst-sponsored lighter-than-air airship, the *Graf Zeppelin*, in its maiden voyage around the world. But soon the Pantages case came to dominate the front page.

Under the headline banner of "Pantages Held on Girl's Charges," on August 10, 1929, the *Examiner* recounted the events of the previous day as well as Pantages' arrest. From the start, greater weight was given to

While Pringle was photographed with her parents, Pantages was captured with his lawyer, defense attorney W. Joseph Ford, who instructed him not to speak to the press. This allowed Pringle, under no such restriction, to share her side of the story and capture the public's imagination (*Marc Wanamaker, Bison Archives*).

Pringle's side of the story.[26] Pantages appears as a solitary figure, but Pringle is assisted by her doting mother, apparently there to give comfort during this tragic and trying time of need. The implication seems clear: no one to help the victimizer but the family rallying around the victim. (The father appeared in later news stories of the case, suggesting the separation with the mother had ended.)

Interestingly, by way of contrast, the *Seattle Times* indicated in its headlines that Pringle was 16.[27] This was not the only inconsistency reported; in one instance, her father was "Dr. Earl Pringle," in another, it was "Dr. Lewis A. Pringle," who received threats against his daughter if she did not drop her charges.[28] The *Times* added that the alleged assault took place at 3:30 p.m. of the previous day. As he would repeat during the entire case, Pantages claimed he was being blackmailed and gave his age as 54.[29] Forgoing the narrative theatrics of the *Examiner*, the *Times* noted that "Miss Pringle" graduated from Garden Grove High School only the previous year and that she was still a USC coed, whereas most other accounts said she was no longer in school.

"She was intensely ambitious, Eunice was, but she was a good girl and was home every night," the mother declared to the press, furthering the image of Pringle as the victim and, thus, the protagonist.[30] As if to further cement Eunice's moral standing, the article added that residents of Garden Grove "last night declared that the Pringle family bears an excellent reputation."[31] Later accounts have the daughter living with the 40-year-old Russian prince turned Hollywood producer Nicholas Dunaev.[32] Pringle later admitted that Dunaev dropped her off at the Pantages Theater on that fateful afternoon. The mother also reminded readers that her daughter "had been promised a booking for her dancing act for over a year," thus offering proof that Eunice had been mistreated by Pantages from the start.[33]

"Examination of the girl last night disclosed a mark on her right shoulder, a badly bruised left arm and a badly scratched and bruised back," readers were told, thus furthering the assumption that Pringle was the innocent, injured party.[34] The examination was part of the procedure that also included grand jury testimony to determine if a trial would result from the case or not.

A sidebar article next to the main story provides additional material to undergird the basic narrative. The sidebar reveals Pringle's version of events and the devastating pain and anguish she suffered. The photos above the sidebar further promote this view: Pringle, hair askew and dress ripped, and with an expression of inner torment and violated indignity, while Pantages stands in his white suit, one foot crossed over the other, cigarette in hand held between his thumb and forefinger, striking a pose that seems detached, almost amused and oblivious to the severity of the charges against him. The contrast between the two principles could not be more striking.

The next day's *Examiner* featured the story "Pantages Freed on $25,000 Bail." In this account, Pringle signs the formal complaint against Pantages. Adding to the impression of his guilt was this announcement: "She has been subjected to a medical examination earlier in the day by Dr. Hannah Beatty, county juvenile physician. Dr. Beatty's report substantiates the girl's charges that she had been attacked."[35] As for Pantages, the article revealed, "Still maintaining an air of entire unconcern, Pantages appeared for arraignment."[36] He claimed that the events were a setup, while the article described Pringle's response: "In near tears, she branded Pantages' charges of frameup an absurdity."[37] The contrast was not simply due to emotional differences; Pringle had direct access to the press while Pantages' lawyers forbade him to speak to reporters. When the press confronted him early in the case, Pantages defended himself. "Say, fellows, you know I wasn't in that room with that girl for a minute."[38] "Don't say anything, Pan," one of his attorneys interrupted. "I don't want him giving out any statement at all," the attorney barked to the press. "I don't want him saying anything."[39]

As on the previous day, another sidebar article gave sympathetic voice to Eunice and her mother. "'All I ask is justice,' sobbed Mrs. Irene Pringle [who was] in a state of nervous collapse following her daughter's charges [and] was under the care of friends yesterday in her apartment.... 'Only a mother who has raised a daughter can understand what this must mean to me,' she continued between spells of weeping, while her daughter attempted to comfort her."[40] But it is Eunice's voice that carries the most emotional appeal to readers, revealed with devastating honesty. "I never had the slightest suspicion of Mr. Pantages," she told the grand jury. He "was old enough to be my grandfather."[41] She went on to explain how he took her hand and in the process changed his demeanor, regarding her lustily. "If it is the last thing I do on earth, I want to pay him back for this terrible thing he has done to me."[42] She claimed that she had been a "good girl" and while she had "boy friends," "never was the friendship any more than passing. I was just in love with two things—my mother and my career."[43] She ended by wishing she were dead. "This most horrible thing has happened to me."[44]

Reports in the August 12, 1929, *Examiner* show that an appeal was made by Eunice's father for "24-hour guard for Eunice because Dr. Earl

Pringle's claim that an attempt was made to enter the ground-floor apartment" where the Pringle family was staying at the time. The family's phone did not stop ringing, and there were also "mysterious phone calls made telling Eunice to get out of town."[45]

There were sworn statements to the grand jury by those who knew Eunice, including an "operatic tenor and well-known radio singer" named Amado Fernandez; he told D.A. Buron Fitts that the girl's reputation "was above reproach."[46] The newspaper reported no such individuals stepping forward to vouch for Pantages—at least, not as reported in the *Examiner*.[47]

Witnesses for Pantages, such as members of his Hill Street theater staff, were not quoted in the *Examiner* as supporting their boss. In fact, the newspaper reports confusion on Pantages' side—as when the paper indicates on Wednesday, August 14, 1929, that his press agent, who was there on the fateful afternoon, suddenly disappeared, along with vague rumblings of "mystery girls" attempting to hush up the entire affair seemingly on behalf of Pantages. Despite the media attention and the emotional toll of the case, Pringle remained resolute in her claims. Thus the *Examiner* reports in this same edition of her physical condition. ("The girl, pale, with dark rings under eyes, had to be supported by her companion as she walked through the corridors of the Hall of Justice into Fitts' private office. She appeared on the verge of collapse.") Readers were reminded: "'Her story doesn't vary one iota,' Fitts stated following his talk with the girl. 'It is exactly the same as she told the night Pantages was jailed.'"

Implicit in this coverage are the descriptions—"pale, with dark rings under her eyes" and "supported by her companion"—that suggest scenes out of a melodramatic movie designed not only to capture reader interest, but also to turn the entire court proceedings into sensational theater.

The blurring between journalism and soap opera was furthered with the arrival of the first byline in the *Examiner* coverage by staff reporter Harry Lang beginning on August 15. Readers might be forgiven for thinking they were reading a screenplay rather than the pages of a mainstream American newspaper. Under the banner headline GIRL FAINTS ON STAND AT HEARING, Lang introduces the setting and characters in dramatic, tense fashion. The reader is almost grabbed by the neck with the words: "Eunice Pringle, the 17-year-old dancer, on the witness stand."[48] No verb, just straight introduction of the protagonist. And then the next paragraph: "At the defendant's table before her, Alexander Pantages, 54, gray-haired millionaire theater man—facing possible imprisonment for the rest of his natural life for what the girl swears he did to her."[49]

Eunice then "faints dead away on the stand." She recovers and continues. Pantages sat solemnly while she testified, the account indicates, also reminding readers that "Pantages had smirked and smiled the night they arrested him; he didn't smile today."[50] A crowd estimated at 500 packed the courtroom. "Courthouse attachés said it was the biggest crowd that's tried to get into a court hearing in a long time ... hundreds milled about the corridors—and a lane had to be opened for Pantages when he left the courtroom. His face was worth nothing, then."[51]

The dramatic elements overwhelm the journalism. First, there was the stifling heat in the courtroom, which Lang reports to be "well over 100 degrees hot."[52] "Women who had struggled to get in, struggled again to get out, before they fainted. Spectators [and] court attachés sat about in their shirtsleeves."[53] Then there is Pringle: "[O]ver on the couch in the corner, by the breath of air that came in from the open window, lay Eunice Pringle, the plaintiff. Eyes closed, face waxen—she might have been dead for all the movement that was in her."[54]

Her father and mother sit by her, fanning her. And for some color to

The accuser in the Pantages trial, Eunice Alice Pringle, seated between her parents, who were separated at the time. Hearst converted her from an unknown into a national celebrity (*Marc Wanamaker, Bison Archives*).

the scene, Lang adds this: "'Seems as though she just doesn't care any more whether she's alive or dead,' somebody whispers, 'since this happened. Strange to see her like this—if you'd ever seen her dancing and bright and merry, like she used to be.'"[55] Then, "Wham! Wham!—a gavel pounds, and Judge Leonard Wilson, the only cool-looking man in the perspiration-drenched courtroom, steps up to the bench. Pantages looks up at him worriedly. 'Case of the People vs. Alexander Pantages,' bawls a clerk."[56]

"Hot." "Fainted." "Waxen." "Dead." "Worriedly." The story threw visual punches with dexterity and ease. Even if she wilted under the immense courtroom pressure, Pringle's testimony clearly damaged Pantages' defense, as it would again during the actual trial in early October. The sidebar article offered a lengthy rendition of the two principals' testimony, the detailed account by Pringle and the somewhat nebulous denial by Pantages. Above this sidebar piece is a picture of Pantages seated imposingly with his bevy of nattily dressed, brooding lawyers around him. Beneath the photo of Pringle, as if Pantages' picture above crushed hers below, is the contrasting photo of Eunice slumped in the witness stand, hand to forehead and looking utterly wrecked and depressed. The unmistakable impression of the lone girl up against the phalanx of expensive and presumably ruthless lawyers could not be missed. The photos only added more sustenance to the idolize-demonize narrative.

And as much as Pantages' lawyers tried to attack her credibility, Pringle resisted. By this point, *Examiner* readers might themselves feel under attack. Perhaps this was the intention—to put the reader in Pringle's shoes. Thus on Friday, August 16, 1929, there is the grilling that Pringle received from Pantages' lawyers. "Question after question they had fired at her—questions of the tiniest detail, evidently in hope that somehow she might become confused, contradict herself, give them an opening whereby to impeach her story. But Eunice failed them.... It was no easy experience for a 17-year-old girl."[57]

If the idolize-demonize narrative needs any further justification, it came in the *Examiner*'s editorial pages on August 14. Under the headline "District Attorney Properly Takes Personal Charge in Grave Prosecution," the op-ed launches into a carefully worded attack against Pantages and the wealthy, presumably Hollywood lifestyle he represents. It is left to the reader to assume that this lifestyle referred to the (Jewish) immigrants who ran the Hollywood movie industry.

Citing the Pantages case as "one of the most important prosecutions of recent years," the editorial bluntly states that the "whole machinery of justice leans heavily upon the courage and intelligence of the prosecuting

Pantages did not take the assault charges against him seriously, claiming he was framed. Here he stands during his arrest with two theater employees, without a care in the world (*Marc Wanamaker, Bison Archives*).

authorities."[58] As if to remind its readers of the stakes and of Pantages' privileged position, it offers a clear warning: "No matter how wealthy an accused person may be, his wealth should not make a particle of difference to the rigor with which his case is prosecuted."[59]

The *Examiner* further radiated its populist tones in the editorial by adding Pantages' wealth "should not of itself carry the implication of guilt, but neither should it give the slightest advantage over the poorest person in the community accused of a similar offense."[60] Standing as the pillar in all this is the heroic district attorney, Buron Fitts, who "is to be heartily commended" and who is "determined to make every employer's office in Los Angeles safe for every young and defenseless girl." And most tellingly, there is the warning that "[o]ur womanhood must be as secure in its virtue as every citizen should be secure of life itself."[61] The admonition to protect "womanhood" is expected of newspapers as guardians of a community's morality. Pantages knew the tide of public opinion was against him because he exhibited signs of fatalism. "No—I haven't any hopes at all of escaping trial on this thing," he admitted in court. "But I haven't lost courage—yet. I won't lose courage—not until the very end."[62]

The opinion piece was designed to justify the melodramatic elements of the case. It may also have been a crude but clear message sent to Fitts by the *Examiner* to prosecute the case to its fullest limits. As a guardian of morality, the *Examiner* had always been close to the D.A.'s office, even when the D.A. in charge had his own moral challenges. Bribery charges would follow Fitts later in his career, but in 1929 his reputation showed no lack of probity. The "soldier prosecutor" had a righteous streak that tended to turn the courtroom into his bully pulpit, and he used it effectively. He had his own predilection for drama, which he aptly demonstrated in the Pantages trial. The Texas-born Fitts' crusader ways may have come early in his life, although they were certainly cemented during his experience as an American soldier in World War I. "At the battle of Argonne in 1918, Fitts' right knee was blown away, and he suffered mustard-gas burns."[63] He walked with a limp for the rest of his life, which added to his crusading spirit. A staunch supporter of war veterans, he used his membership in the American Legion to advance his political and professional career. In 1926, he received the highest number of votes to become lieutenant governor of California, only to resign the office in 1928 when his former D.A. boss, Asa Keyes, was indicted for bribery and Fitts decided to prosecute him.

No battle was too small or too big for Fitts. He understood, as many ambitious types do, the relationship between good publicity and political office. Although he resigned his elected office, he did not abandon politics. He threw his hat into the ring for governor of California after the Pantages trial; thus his crusading ways were not without strategic benefit. But at heart he remained the "soldier as prosecutor" who battled evil, who used the power of his office effectively if not zealously to clean Los Angeles County of its filth. He first prosecuted Lois Pantages as a warm-up to his entanglement with Alexander. His later years were less successful. He too fought bribery charges, was shot at, and at the age of 78 he committed suicide.

Trials of the Pantages type invariably attracted both excessive publicity and notoriety, including the bizarre; the *Examiner* normally published such trifles, but so did even more respectable newspapers. On August 18, 1929, *The New York Times* printed an Associated Press article stating that Roy Keane, an executive of the Pantages theater system, "had been taken into custody as a material witness in an alleged attempt to bribe witnesses to alter testimony in the case."[64] Another witness stepped forward and accused Pantages of trying to attack her in the same "private office."[65] It was revealed the next day by Chief Deputy D.A. Robert P. Stewart that this former usher had been threatened by a man in a phone call, despite the fact that her name was never released to the public: "'You are known and if you don't keep your mouth shut you will be taken for a ride,' the deputy said the man had telephoned."[66] Such claims in the coverage, impossible to verify, seem intended only to add to the drama, and to make Pantages look guilty. In the end, that may be the only purpose of the story. While not quite as sensationalistic as the *Examiner*, the tone of the *New York Times* does not veer from the main script established by Hearst. This could also be said of other newspapers, such as *The Los Angeles Times* and *The Chicago Tribune*.

The *Examiner* coverage of the legal proceedings was only a dress rehearsal for the actual trial that began on October 3, 1929. The same melodramatic overtones, the same screenwriting style by Lang, the same focus on tension and suspense were to follow, as if the court case had now completely morphed into a theatrical production. Pantages was caught in the vise of justice, and he did what any wealthy accused would do: He sought the best legal protection. He retained Max Steuer, "famous New York criminal attorney," to help his own defense as well as that of his wife Lois.[67] It was an attempt to lay the groundwork for what *The Los Angeles Times* called "perhaps the greatest court battles ever witnessed in Los Angeles."[68]

It was showtime.

Ominous signs about the trial's outcome could be deduced from the news coverage early on, similar to the darkening clouds that were gathering on Wall Street earlier in the year. The same day as Pantages' arrest for sexual assault, the stock market suffered its third shock, losing a billion dollars in value. The raising of the discount rate from five to six percent was blamed, along with $300 million credit made available to the Bank of England in its own financial struggles.[69] Wall Street's machinations were the farthest thing from Pantages' mind that day, but it was rotten luck on his part that his fate in the trial strangely paralleled that of the country's economic undoing. The preliminary coverage of his arrest in the *Los Angeles Examiner* and other mainstream newspapers reflected the shock of the event, but it also set the tone that carried into his trial—one that echoed Fatty Arbuckle's fate eight years earlier. In the Pantages case, the nation got another morality lesson from Hearst's papers, which acted as self-appointed protectors of standards in the cities his press empire represented.

The use of photos in the *Examiner*'s coverage was particularly damaging, since it vividly and starkly revealed the dimensions of the case, even as it greatly simplified them. Readers were not required to ponder or reflect beyond the simple narrative of the case: a young innocent girl deflowered by a foreign-born movie theater mogul and sexual predator. All facts, instances, revelations, actions and testimony in the case were made (sometimes forced) to fit this simple storyline. The credo of newspapers that they do not tell readers "what to think but what to think about" holds true, and in this way they give assurance of their all-knowing and discerning ability to publish the truth. But at the *Examiner*, this ability to dispense with "what to think about" included the skillful use of dramatization to heighten interest and to titillate the reader.

The hagiographic display of Virginia Rappe after her death was repeated in the Pantages case by its judicious use of photos, in particular the sultry photo of Pringle's Solita Deyo, under a sombrero, giving no hint that she was a teenager.[70] It was all part of protagonizing and idolizing Pringle. No historical photos of Pantages were ever offered, none could be, since he was the antagonist in this melodrama; to do so would be to humanize him and thus draw empathy from readers. That was reserved only for Pringle. Similarly, readers were treated to a Pringle photo montage: six head shots joined together under the banner "ALLEGED VICTIM, AS CAMERA RECORDS HER MOODS."[71]

This was hagiography of a different sort from what was used for Rappe, since the victim here was alive, but the intent was the same: to turn Pringle into the brutalized victim. It was skillful and effective use of photography, turning an ordinary human being, hitherto unknown in entertainment, into a larger-than-life character. Underneath the photo montage was another picture of Pringle, looking squarely at the camera, her hand pointing to the tiny room where she alleged the assault took place. In these photos, the *Examiner* pressed its own case against Pantages, but unlike in a court of law, the theater magnate was not able to defend himself. In the note accompanying the pointing photo, the *Examiner* mentioned Pantages' "palatial" offices, a not-so subtle reminder of his wealth and power and the forces allied against Pringle. Pringle's forlorn face directly confronting the reader was meant to further the assault's impact on her. Such portrayals could only have been lethal for Pantages' theaters, where business suffered. In contrast to Arbuckle, however, there were no published reports of organized attempts at boycotting Pantages' theaters, so it is difficult to assess the box office damage his operations faced.

The "wealth and power" theme was clearly delineated in the opinion piece about the trial noted above. As guardian of community morality, Hearst made sure that on the scale of justice, morality, and decency not money and influence, had to win. Particular fealty was laid at the feet of Buron Fitts, who is "assuming personal charge of one of the most important prosecutions of recent years."[72] It later emerged that Fitts had aspirations for political office, specifically, the governorship of the state of California. The op-ed noted that the D.A. "must be above the very suspicion of influence," although that likely did not include political ambitions.[73] Ultimately the case was pared to "the person of a young girl alleged to have suffered outrageous violence at the hands of a wealthy man."[74] It did not mention Hollywood by name, but it didn't have to.

There was a fairy tale element to the coverage that cast a further glow upon Pringle. Prior to the case, Dr. Lewis A. Pringle and Lou Irene Pringle had been separated for seven or eight years.[75] "We have been brought closer together than ever before by what has happened," Dr. Pringle said "while his wife nestled her hand in his and smiled through her tears."[76] The photos of the family promoted family unity during a difficult period.[77] In contrast, the lone wolf Pantages appeared to be without a family, therefore outside of its protective womb.

Equally compelling photographically was the presence of "Policewoman Fairchild," not only providing protection and comfort for the teenage Pringle but also giving an official police stamp of approval to the victim's side. The physically imposing Fairchild may have been standard police procedure for court cases involving assaults on a minor, but it certainly gave Pringle a strong presence that could have aided her case. Such visible signs on images appearing in the *Examiner* sent a strong message to readers: A young girl's honor had to be vindicated. A revealing photo in the series starkly expressed this view, involving the principals in the preliminary hearing in mid–August in which a depressed, simply dressed Eunice sat between her mother and Fairchild, while only a few feet away were two Pantages lawyers and the elegantly adorned theater mogul himself, his back to Pringle, casually lighting a cigarette. The *Examiner*'s observation that the lead attorney in Pantages' defense could receive a fee as high as "$500 per minute" exaggerated the vast economic differences between the two principals involved in the case.[78]

Dramatic overtures to protect Pringle's life and any attempts made to get her out of the way heightened the growing suspense of the case.[79] That Pringle was "on the verge of a nervous collapse from the strain which has followed the alleged attack upon her by Pantages" insured that the coming trial would not be short of drama.[80] Pantages contributed his share to the growing interest in the trial when his lawyers asked that the court venue be changed. His attorneys "filed affidavits by more than 30 persons stating their belief that the public opinion in Los Angeles is so prejudiced against Pantages that his trial" would not be a fair one.[81] The motion was denied.

His trial went ahead, in the same courtroom as the one that earlier decided his wife's fate over the accidental death of a Japanese-American gardener. His wife had suffered terribly during her own court case, while Pantages himself had "lost 30 pounds" from the time his ordeal began; he was now "nervous and troubled."[82] If he expected to get any sympathy from the court, he received none, except that one of two charges against him (forcible assault) was dropped and only the statutory assault remained. Suggestively, the *Examiner* noted that during Lois Pantages' trial, all her children were present, while at the start of her husband's case only son Lloyd joined him in court.

The trial began on Thursday, October 3, 1929, in Superior Court, Judge Charles Fricke presiding. The trial combined legal proceedings, courtroom theater, serial drama, entertainment and social revelation. It was a snapshot of a country at war with itself about what constituted an "American" and how it regarded its foreign-born and female members. It was also the last of the great sensational trials of the decade and the end of Hollywood itself being hauled into court. While crimes involving Hollywood elite of one kind or another continued, the Pantages case was the terminal one involving the very soul of the movie industry.[83] Never again would Hollywood face such a fierce firestorm of public hostility, which began with the Arbuckle trials eight years earlier. It could be seen as a cleansing effort to finally banish the albatross that had hung around the movie industry from its inception—the public knowledge that the industry was a moral sewer and one that stood squarely against the very essence of decent, law-abiding America. In that sense, Pantages provided a valuable if unwelcome service to his business, but at great personal cost.

Examiner reporter Harry Lang provided a record of the events in the courtroom: "At 4:05 o'clock yesterday afternoon the Pantages jury was sworn in," he began in the October 3, 1929, edition; "six men and six women—after two solid days of picking."[84] The jury included several retirees, an oil man, several housewives, a bookkeeper and a former confectioner. The salt of the earth were about to try one of America's leading showmen. Lang introduced the lineup of prosecution witnesses in a manner normally reserved for sporting matches and mentioned that a "tremendous crowd" was expected to view the proceedings.

Pantages' attorney group had changed members, with new arrival Jerry Giesler taking an important role. Later the most famous criminal attorney in Hollywood, Giesler proved the attack dog Pantages needed to have any chance at justice. He grilled the prosecution's witnesses, beginning with Mrs. Pringle. The defense's strategy was to impugn Eunice with more than mere professional association with Dunaev; it tried to paint the two as lovers who hatched a scheme to divest Pantages of some of the money he made selling his theaters earlier that summer (usually reported as $15,000,000). Dunaev waited in the office of an attorney while Pringle was meeting with Pantages. The morning after Pantages' arrest, the same attorney announced a civil lawsuit for $500,000 against Pantages for sexual assault.

On the witness stand, Mrs. Pringle denied plans to file a civil lawsuit: "I have never thought about it."[85] When the jury visited the scene of the alleged crime later that day, its manager complained only to end up behind bars for 24 hours.

Two days after the start of the trial, Pringle went on the witness stand. Harry Lang was there to record the event. She was young (he often referred to her as a "child"), but for Lang she was indomitable in spirit. "They tried their mightiest [but Pantages' lawyers] failed to break down Eunice Pringle's story!"[86] An *Examiner* photo of Pringle on the witness stand revealed a primly dressed and boyishly coiffed young woman in a "characteristic pose" that may have reminded readers of the silent movie *The Passion of Joan of Arc*, released in the U.S. earlier that year, about the tragic story of a young woman accused of heresy in medieval France.[87] This movie portrayal may not have been Pringle's intent, but it certainly seemed the

Examiner's. "She had to tell before a crowded courtroom" about the attack, the *Examiner* caption noted, "in all its harrowing details."[88] This included D.A. Fitts showing her stained and ripped clothing to jury members. She left the witness stand with "her cheeks wet with tears."[89] One "white-haired" male juror cried.

Before leaving the stand, Pringle endured Giesler's "machine-gun" grilling, as the *Examiner* called it. He tried to establish her credentials as a student of drama, while also showing that she had visited Pantages several times previous in his office, sometimes being alone with him, but there was never any hint of impropriety in his behavior. By noting her dramatic skills, the implication was that she was capable of acting out, therefore her entire charges were part of an elaborate frame-up. He even asked Pringle to wear the dress on the day of the alleged attack "and then made her parade," the *Examiner* noted, "like a style mannequin" before the jury. It was effective theater, but it made no impression on the jury.[90] Similarly, he tried to break down her testimony—that Pantages had held her mouth shut with his right hand and had her arms pinned down while also leaving him one hand to remove her panties and and unzip his pants. Why didn't she scream? Her mouth was shut. Why didn't she use her arms to fight him off? They were pinned down. Why didn't she use her legs against him? She fainted shortly into the ordeal. Was she coached in her story by D.A. Fitts? "Nothing came of it," the *Examiner* declared.[91]

Throughout her testimony, Pantages "sucked a finger, sometimes he bit his thumb, more frequently he chewed his fingernails."[92] He also fidgeted in his chair, looked around and even "made noises in his throat."[93] But during her description of the attack, he stared straight at her. In his life, Pantages showed the strains of a man facing the truth. He did not live in a fantasy world, and despite spinning the details of his own past, he was remarkably honest about what he faced. That was part of the reason behind his stunning success: He was a practical man, living in the realities of everyday life. And despite his determination not to lose hope about his case, clearly his behavior in court indicates that he probably already had. He looked at the jury in "great wonderment," as the *Examiner* noted, but he could not have mistaken the message of the weeping and moist-eyed jurors.[94] Before leaving the stand, Fitts gave Pringle the red earrings that she had lost in the tiny room. It was Friday; the trial would resume at ten a.m. on Monday. While Pantages would return home to process the implications of Pringle's testimony, the jury would be treated to picnics.

When the trial resumed, Giesler cross-examined Pringle, who at times had difficulty remembering all the details of the events—"what she was doing with her own hands, what effort she made to get away"—on that tragic day.⁹⁵ "I was so excited, everything was so confused," she replied, "I just really can't remember little things like that!"⁹⁶ Yet, even as Giesler took one step forward, the defense fell two steps back with eyewitness after eyewitness describing details of the alleged assault that corroborated Pringle's version of events. Even a few of Pantages' former employees claimed the theater man asked them to change their testimony to help his case. Pringle's own eye doctor also testified, verifying that she came to him that Friday afternoon, and that after examining her eyes he told the court that her eyesight "was only one-third normal."⁹⁷

The evidence was building against Pantages as witness after witness testified: the police chemist who inspected Pringle's dress and testified for the prosecution; the policewoman who examined Pringle and found eight bite marks on her body (four more than Pringle had testified); and one of the police detectives who responded to the initial call and found "two broken bits of earring and the girl's purse on the floor."⁹⁸ Defense witnesses included the theater switchboard operator, that she had seen Pringle come to visit Pantages "at least ten times" and as "late as midnight." The suggestion was that if Pantages had lustful eyes on her, why didn't he choose those more opportune moments? The switchboard operator also told the court that on most of Pringle's visits to the theater, Dunaev accompanied her; Pringle frequently arrived in a red dress and "used rouge on her lips and some kind of dark powder which made her appear very Latin."⁹⁹

Then there was the strange case of Garland Biffle, former Arkansas attorney who never practiced law but who came to sell law books in California. He testified that in the Pantages theater lobby, he heard Duvaev telling Pringle not to get cold feet. Shortly after his testimony, Fitts charged him with perjury, arrested and jailed him.¹⁰⁰ Pantages' attorneys regarded Biffle's arrest as simply an attempt to hamstring the defense, yet when they asked Judge Fricke to intercede, he refused. He told them that Fitts perhaps had good reason to arrest Biffle.

Even the doctor who examined Pringle after Pantages' arrest, and who testified that she found none of the marks and bruises on her body that Pringle asserted, did not sway the jury. A doctor who ran an optical company in the Pantages theater building swore that Eunice and Pantages were in the tiny room for only a few minutes before the screaming started, but that seemed to have little effect in Pantages' favor. The "theatrical Croesus," as one *Examiner* reporter called Pantages, was in the worst fight of his life.¹⁰¹ In the third week of the trial, it was finally his turn to testify and the last hope for his defense.

On Tuesday, October 22, 1929, he strode to the witness stand. He went to great lengths to show in his verbal replies and physical re-enactments that Pringle had physically attacked him, rather than the opposite. He described a desperate Pringle who refused to take no for an answer in his refusal to book her play, which he found "too suggestive and vulgar."[102] "The custom in our business," he told the court, "when we don't want any act, we don't entirely throw them out of the office."[103] Perhaps Pringle was too young, too naïve, or simply too ambitious to understand the message he was sending her. In a style that the *Examiner* found theatrical ("Pantages himself is no mean actor—he achieved heights of dramaturgy"), he was forceful in his denials of the assault accusations.[104] "It was the role of the actor," crowed the *San Francisco Chronicle*, "rather than that of a multimillionaire theater magnate that Alexander Pantages assumed as he was finally given his opportunity to tell his own version of the attack. He held the center of the stage."[105]

If the testimony conveyed one message, it was of a helpless Pantages who, despite his power, business acumen and wealth, was not able to fend off a determined and clever young dancer. He ably outwitted greater foes in his day—the ruthless John Considine comes to mind—yet in the face of a teenage dancer, he was overmatched. On the face of it, this narrative simply seemed too incredible to swallow. When asked why he didn't push Pringle away and call for help, he countered, "There was no one to call."[106] He denied that he gave a statement to juvenile police that contradicted his court testimony, claiming that the earlier statement was false and made up by the police to trip him.

A sketch drawing of Pantages accompanying his transcribed testimony showed him with arms crossed, head tilted forward in an act of depressed supplication; it left the unmistakable impression of a man resigned to his fate. He had reached the point, the sketch implied, where he no longer cared to fight against what life threw at him. "Pantages, despite that he has made his millions here in America, speaks broken English. It's hard on the court stenographers."[107] His testimony revealed, likely for the first time in his life, his illiteracy. This must have devastated him; he had assiduously portrayed himself as a sophisticated businessman, yet here he was, in front of hundreds, revealing his inability to read. It came when the prosecutor asked him to read from the *Prince* play. "Can you read?" Fitts inquired. Pantages replied, "No, I can't. You read."

There was a finality to the proceedings that belied any suspense in the upcoming verdict. Pringle was returned to the witness to pointedly counter Pantages' entire testimony, and with a few loose ends the trial had come to an end. The only remaining excitement came when a male juror suddenly declared his unwillingness to hear any more of the case and asked to be dismissed. He was promptly replaced by a female alternate, the jury now numbering seven women and five men. In the closing arguments, the defense tried to show the improbability of a powerful theatrical magnate committing an assault at five o'clock in the afternoon surrounded by other offices, passersby in the street below and patrons in the theater. "Don't forget," urged Giesler, "that from time immemorial a man charged with this kind of offense has had prejudice against him because of the very nature of the charge and before a line of testimony is heard."[108]

The assistant prosecutor, on the other hand, no doubt with Fitts' approval, emphasized to the jury the reality of the crime upon Pringle's innocence: "Eunice Pringle will go through life forever bearing the stigma this man has forced upon her. The very thing that this child had to make her attractive has been stripped from her by the lust of this man, who has no bridle upon his passion."[109] Fitts provided his own dramatic gesture to end the case. During his closing argument, he abruptly wheeled around, pointed to a forlorn Pantages, and speaking to the jury declared, "This man, this very man who sits here before you this instant with a sneer on his face ... broke the body and the soul of this girl."[110]

It was expected that a verdict would be returned quickly. Harry Lang played up the drama of the wait, even noting that Judge Fricke ordered sheriff's guards to keep a watch over Pantages at his mansion. Jury deliberation continued through Saturday, with no end in sight. The jury asked to see more exhibits in the case. But by Sunday, after 53 hours of deliberation, at 9:27 p.m., the jury came to a decision. Lang in Monday's *Examiner* announced the verdict: "For what he did to Eunice Pringle, Alexander Pantages must forfeit everything." It was the opening sentence and no more needed to be added, except now the sentencing. The jury asked for clemency, but the judge made it clear that the law required Pantages be locked up, between one to 50 years in San Quentin prison. All his children present at the reading of the verdict—Rodney, Lloyd, Carmen and adopted daughter Dixie Martin—broke down crying, with Dixie fainting. Pantages remained blank-faced as the verdict was read. He turned to Giesler to asked what it meant.[111] "Pantages is Greek-born," the *Examiner* added, "he cannot yet speak English well; his understanding, too, is limited."[112] It was left to Giesler to explain the verdict. Within 30 minutes he would leave society and return to jail. "I got a raw deal," Pantages was reported saying on his way to prison.[113] "Of course we'll appeal the case," Giesler declared. "We'll fight it to the bitter end. We'll carry it to the highest court."

From the courtroom, Pantages bid goodbye to his family and was taken directly to the jail booking office. There he gave his particulars— "his age, 54; weight, 126 pounds and height, 5 feet 6½ inches"—and emptied his pockets, which contained $40 in cash, four packs of cigarettes, ten cigars and a small bottle of pills.[114] He also had with him "two religious tokens, a scapular and a medallion." Never known to be religious, Pantages asked to keep the tokens, and his wish was granted. He then gave up his gray suit for jail blue denims as well as his identity, no longer Alexander T. Pantages but prisoner number 119251. He was led to the tank for "high-power prisoners," which included a former chief deputy district attorney jailed for bribery, a dope peddler and a convicted murderer. Before entering the jail, while seated in the booking office, "he lowered his head and mumbled as if in prayer."[115] It was left to others to determine if this was a last refuge of a scoundrel or an act of real penitence.

The events that finally led Wall Street to lay its famous rotten egg in October, as *Daily Variety* memorably headlined it, still stumps experts. Probably there was not one factor, but many. An overheated market, unbridled manipulation, excessive levels of floating shares, an unstable world economy, a weak Federal Reserve Bank lacking leadership and resolve, and depressed commodities all contributed to the crash. However, it may have simply come down to the fact that "too many people held too much stock on borrowed money."[116] What began on Wednesday, October 23, was a convulsion of unprecedented proportions. As meticulously described in Maury Klein's *Rainbow's End: The Crash of 1929*, dark clouds had presaged the beginning of the crash, but the events that transpired in the last days of October cataclysmically swept over the market like a tsunami. It would not recover for 15 years. The liquidation of stocks began on that fateful mid-week after a sedate start to the trading day. The next day ("Black Thursday") the flooding worsened, as anxious speculators feverishly tried to unload the shares they had purchased on credit, which they would lose if the market tanked. On the New York Stock Exchange floor, there was pandemonium as wave upon wave of sell orders flooded the market with few buy orders. Huge crowds gathered outside the Exchange, along with police, including some on horseback. "One reporter," Klein noted, "expressed surprise at the number of women in the milling throng; he thought them mostly stenographers anxious about their small accounts in the market."[117]

Other minnows were equally stricken, their pale faces showing "not so much suffering as a sort of horrified incredulity—the dazed unbelief of men who have been robbed of all their by their dearest and most trusted friend."[118] Stock markets in other countries—including England, Canada and France—were also rattled. This was turning into a global financial rout. Meanwhile, the Fed observed events with studied aloofness but decided to do nothing. It was left to private bankers to inject funds into the market to calm it. Trading on Friday and the shortened Saturday session produced a relatively calm market. Newspapers headlines blared that the worst was over. If the minnows were wiped out during Black Thursday, on Monday it was the bigger fish that took a pounding. The Dow closed at 260.64 that day, 120 points off its high. Tuesday's trading confirmed that the shellacking that took place the previous day was no fluke; the selling reached pandemic proportions. More than 3.2 million shares changed hands just in the first 30 minutes of trading on the New York Stock Exchange. Before the day's end, and with some sudden unexpected buying in the last 15 minutes, the Dow had closed 30.57 points lower on volume of 16.4 million shares traded (not matched until April 1, 1968).[119] Dating to the previous Thursday, it had lost roughly 30 percent of its value in just five days of trading.[120]

The next few days brought some relief; buy orders resumed and by the weekend the Dow Jones had recouped some of its losses. But millions had lost money in the downfall, some of them their life savings. The New Era—as the fat seven years previous had been labeled with its "jazz economics"—was swept into the dustbin. According to Klein, "Belief in the rainbow itself, in a future where all was well, anything was possible, and endings were always happy, had suffered damage that might be irreparable."[121]

It was a belief that Pantages could share. He had assiduously built up an impressive chain with his own hands, without the help of family, education, connections or special insight. For over 25 years he labored to make his name a national brand, and succeeded beyond his wildest expectations. Like the stock market, Pantages for a time seemed invincible. Better financed competitors fell by the wayside, while his empire grew in stature, reach and economic muscle. Setbacks soon were left behind and his upward trajectory continued. Then suddenly it all fell apart. Hubris? Bad luck? Bad judgment? The victim of a set-up?

He was now left to pick up the pieces.

7. Aftermath

Theater owners came in a variety of backgrounds and temperaments. Most worked hard and built beautiful theaters; some treated their "performers scornfully and dismissively," as was the case with Edward Albee, who later had his head handed to him by Joe Kennedy.[1] Albee seemed to take delight in making life miserable for his actors. When they sought collective bargaining and fair treatment, he sabotaged those efforts.[2] Time may have mellowed him out, and toward the end of his career he reportedly took a more "angelic" attitude.[3]

Abraham Joseph "Abe" Balaban was at the opposite end of this extreme. He grew up in Chicago, one of eight children born to a Jewish family in 1890. In 1908 he lucked into taking over a nickelodeon, which he parlayed into one of the country's most spectacular theater chains. He built ever more elegant, grand theaters—even more spectacular than Pantages'—that combined both film and vaudeville. This "vaude-film" or "pic-vaude" policy was designed to "send his customers home feeling they had a grand time in a friendly environment."[4] In 1926, he sold his theaters to Paramount Studios, and three years later he retired. Here the resemblance to Pantages ends. *Variety* celebrated his retirement by devoting its February 27, 1929, issue to his accomplishments. Telegrams, letters and ads relating his accomplishments filled its pages. That August, he was given a farewell dinner in Chicago, with 1600 attendees.

Pantages received no testimonial dinners when he sold his theaters; no letters of support were sent in his behalf to the trades; there were no acts of love and respect by his associates.[5] The November 20, 1929, *Variety* did feature a lengthy piece that celebrated not his accomplishments but the end of his circuit. "Never Popular in Vaudeville," the headline blared, announcing the sale of his theaters, the shutting of his booking offices, and his "vaude swan song."[6] "Pantages was one of the most colorful executives in modern theatre annals," it opined. "Disliked for many causes by members of his own trade and creator of personal enemies for his business and other methods, yet he compiled a fortune."[7]

Pantages emerges from the piece as ruthless and stunningly cruel. The Pantages ethos, it said, was that he kept this own counsel, had an air of "righteousness" and believed that money "was the great fixer."[8] He laid down the law in his operations and brooked "no alibis, no apologies and no explanations."[9] This "lone wolf" had little time for partners; he insisted on being the boss and could not share credit. And it noted the many complaints against Pantages, which it claimed were the most received by any important theater owner in the country. In his many years in the business, it said, "there was a consistent line of charges of business abuse by actors ... alleging broken contracts, salary double crosses, illegal cancellations" and other complaints.[10] Office employees were accused of booking acts in which they held an interest; and when Pantages found out about the practice, rather than punishing the culprits, he split the fees with them. According to *Variety*, his cruelty was legendary. When a longtime former employee fell ill during his rape trial, friends wired Pantages seeking relief. His reply: "Wait 'till the trial is over."[11] The ex-employee died shortly after the trial ended.

On November 10, 1929, the day after his wife's sentencing, it was Pantages' turn after his guilty verdict. After his defense attorney's request for a new trial and a plea for leniency were denied by Judge Fricke, Pantages' sentencing came. Giesler whispered to Pantages to rise. "He lifted himself out of his chair at the counsel table with an air of tremendous reluctance."[12] Then Fricke made the pronouncement: six months to 50 years. Given that Pantages had to continue running his business, he would be allowed to serve his sentence in Los Angeles County Jail, not San Quentin. As he was led to his cell, "Pantages wiped tears away with a brusque swipe of his handkerchief."[13] On the other hand, Fitts celebrated a success rate of 74 percent of the 5200 cases he tried in 1929, and he expected the following year to be even better. On December 15, 1929, the *Examiner* noted Fitts' upcoming decision to run for governor.[14] It was left to pundits to determine if Fitts' passion in prosecuting Pantages was for political purposes.

For the first time in his life Pantages experienced conditions unlike any he could imagine. Prisoner 119251 in Tank 10-B-2 of the Los Angeles County Jail is not what he had envisioned for himself at the start of the year. Pantages woke up with a "long face for his first full day behind the bars. He looked on the prison fare, and forcing out of memory the delicacies always to be found in the refrigerator of his mansion, he ate a 7 o'clock breakfast of prunes, mush, bread and coffee."[15] Lunch was no less simple: "baked beans jutted with pork, a salad of various fresh vegetables and dried apples for desert."[16] One report noted dryly, "Probably not since early Alaskan days has this vaudeville king eaten three meals of such plain composition."[17]

Fittingly, while weary and unable to sleep (he was given a sleeping potion, which apparently did not work), his fighting spirit had not entirely vanished. "I got a raw deal," he told reporters. "The jury shouldn't have convicted a yellow dog on the evidence against me. But I'm going to ask for a new trial and I think I'll get it. If I don't, my attorneys are going to appeal. We will win with that."[18] If so, it would take extraordinary effort on the part of his legal counsel.

Giesler managed to get him a free evening out of jail to visit his stricken wife at their house, only to return to his prison home that night declaring to anyone who would listen that his wife was "going to die."[19] On top of that, he faced new lawsuits: Nicholas Dunaev sued Pantages in L.A. County Superior Court for slander and sought $500,000 in damages, and a witness in the trial sued Pantages for $250,000 for "making alleged false statements."[20] Most significantly, Eunice Pringle filed, on January 24, 1930, a civil suit against him seeking damages of $1,000,000.[21] This despite assurances to the contrary, both on the witness stand and after the guilty verdict was returned. "Pringle," the *Examiner* noted after the guilty decision, "made a written statement denying that a certain Los Angeles attorney was to file a million-dollar damage suit for her against Pantages."[22] Also in his in-box of troubles: Pantages faced another court case that resulted from a robbery at the Pantages Theater in Kansas City.[23]

Kate Rockwell briefly resurfaced during his trial, an old ghost returning to haunt him. She was part of the stock of state prosecution witnesses, but did not testify. She was startled at first to receive D.A. Fitts' summons, but "she secretly wanted to see Pantages again," her biographer attested.[24] There are different versions of the brief encounter; in one, she and Pantages ran into each in the hallway and briefly exchanged greetings. *The Los Angeles Times* described their past history, including how she financed the purchase of the Orpheum "because Pantages had promised to marry her."[25] In those days, "he used to climb over the bar of his dance hall to thrash drunken miners whose boisterous celebrations threatened to wreck the establishment."[26] Pantages admitted his "association with the woman but denied the promise of matrimony."[27] Pantages had seen her in the courtroom but did not acknowledge her; then one day he suddenly went to sit next to her in the anteroom of the court.

It was a remarkable moment that shows the depth of feeling that Rockwell still held for her former lover.

> "Hello, Kate, how are you?" he asked. His answer was a flood of tears from the middle-aged woman that once was a thing of beauty to Alaskan miners. Seeing that they were the cynosure of many eyes that knew that an unusual bit of human drama was being enacted, Pantages moved uncomfortably away.[28]

The press seems to have decided that Pantages had wronged Rockwell, and as such, the trial then could be regarded as his comeuppance. If true, it was a harsh verdict for the theater mogul, since neither party in the dysfunctional affair treated each other with decency. Rockwell's reputation was not utterly destroyed, nor was her name forever associated with a violent crime as happened to Pantages.

Rockwell's presence at the trial may have been ironic: It brought the past to Pantages, and provided a strange twist to the jury's deliberations. It was revealed after the trial ended that Rockwell was staying in the same hotel as the jury.[29] How this information got to the jury members was not revealed, yet during the jury's discussion of a verdict, it was discussed how "Pantages had secured his start in life while working in a house of ill fame and the woman who assisted him during that period was then present in court."[30] Is it possible that Kate's very presence, and the allusion to the past, helped convict Pantages?

The annus horribilis for the Pantages family drew to a close. The emotional, physical and psychological impact of the family's trials in 1929 took their toll. Both Lois and Alexander were physical wrecks. He complained of chest pains. The normally vigorous man, the one who had braved the treachery of the Yukon, was a shadow of his former self. His lawyers attempted to use his ailments as legal leverage to get their client released from prison, but their pleas fell on deaf ears. His legal team, led by Jerry Giesler, operated on two judicial tracks: one involving the civil lawsuits against Pantages placed by Dunaev and Pringle, and the other his client's appeals for a new trial.

The Dunaev and Pringle lawsuits were nuisances and intended to wound the already bleeding Pantages. During cross-examination, Pringle's mother strenuously denied any interest in filing a suit against Pantages seeking civil damages. When Giesler asked her about a visit that she, Pringle and Dunaev paid to a law office, she denied any interest in pressing a law judgment against Pantages. She claimed that they were "[n]ot over five minutes" in the office; and when asked about bringing a separate suit against Pantages, she replied, "I have never thought about it."[31] At the Garland Biffle trial, however, Pringle testified that while in the law office the day after Pantages' arrest, the matter of a civil lawsuit did come up, but she claimed she was not interested at the time.

What changed her mind? "'She was quoted as telling the press, "After the Pantages trial was over, I discovered that the publicity had wrecked my career as a dancer and stage performer and that I would have to begin training for another occupation." She put the blame on the bad publicity solely on Pantages, who should shoulder the responsibility and compensate her.[32] On January 4, 1930, Pringle, through her mother acting as her legal guardian, filed the suit against Pantages for a million dollars in damages.[33] After nearly two years of legal maneuvering, the case was finally settled on December 3, 1931, shortly after Pantages' retrial on the assault charges. Pringle accepted $3000 to settle the charges. She appeared in Superior Court with her mother at exactly ten p.m., but the judge refused to finalize the agreement until the father was present. When he finally arrived the judge asked them all if they understood that by signing the agreement, they were renouncing any further litigation against Pantages. They agreed and the matter was finally closed. Pringle's lawyers received $900 from the settlement, and Pringle pocketed the remaining $2100.[34]

The Dunaev suit seems to have fallen off the radar so far as the press was concerned. As for Garland Biffle, who testified in the first Pantages trial that he saw and heard Pringle and Dunaev in the lobby of the theater prior to her visit with the theater mogul, for which he was charged with perjury by D.A. Fitts, it took two trials (in the second one the jury favored his acquittal), but the matter was judged closed when both juries could not reach a final verdict. The state had planned to seek a third trial but seeing that "there appeared to be no chance of obtaining a conviction," it dropped the matter.[35] Biffle could go back to selling law books as he did prior to the Pantages case.

The convicted felon's lawyers wasted no time in seeking a new trial. Affidavits were filed immediately after the first trial's verdict. "What the contents of these affidavits are, defense attorneys refused to reveal," the *San Francisco Chronicle* explained, "but [they] would not deny that they were from jurors who served on the panel that ... found Pantages guilty."[36] It was left to the *Los Angeles Examiner* to state that there were threats ("terror" and "coerce" were the words used in the affidavits) made against those jurors who wanted to vote not guilty, that their names would be passed on to Reverend Shuler, who would denounce them on the radio.[37] Even as these machinations took place, a big concern for the *Examiner* was the length of women's skirts. In one December headline, "Farewell to Legs" it appears next to a picture of a shapely pair of female legs under a knee-high skirt.[38]

These appeals took place alongside attempts to get Pantages out of prison because "severe heart attacks are endangering his life."[39] Seven doctors gave testimony in Superior Court on Pantages' health struggles, indicating that the "convicted theater man is suffering from heart disease, known as 'true angina pectoris,' and that his incarceration is aggravating the malady."[40] To punctuate these claims, *The Los Angeles Times* conveniently showed a photo of the sick Pantages lying morosely and long-faced in the jail hospital.[41] One of his jailhouse doctors noted that Pantages had lost "four and one-half pounds" and "now weighs 114½ pounds."[42] A letter-writing campaign by Pantages' family and friends followed; these notes were delivered to Superior Judge Fricke, who presided over the original trial. Even Lois Pantages pleaded in a letter to Fricke to release her husband, "on the assertion that he was a 'very sick man' and that he 'was needed at home by his sick wife and his children.'"[43]

Fricke was pointed in his dismissal of the missive. "It was the usual type of sentimental letter," he stated. "I filed it in the wastebasket."[44] All similar written efforts landed in the same place.[45] There were also "visits from persons who were in touch with Pantages in jail," who got the same brush-off.[46] Hard-nosed Superior Judge Fricke, who had a "secret passion for orchids, magic tricks and chocolate cake" and rarely smiled in court, was impossible to move and refused to grant bail to Pantages and thus his freedom while his appeal case continued.[47] Instead of release, he was confined to a jail hospital for several more months, but he was permitted to visit his wife and complete the sale of his theaters at home on December 28, 1929.[48] Fricke allowed prison doctors to watch over him, claiming that while he was ill, he was not in life-threatening danger.[49]

As the effects of the stock market crash began to spread to the entire economy in 1930, Giesler worked feverishly to get his client a new start in life. The Pantages case established Giesler's reputation for mental swiftness and verbal dexterity. These qualities served him well in the retrial of the case. When he attempted in the first Pantages trial to highlight lurid details in Pringle's background, suggesting she and Dunaev were more than professionally involved, he was consistently swatted down by the presiding judge.[50] This laid the groundwork for the appeal to Pantages' conviction. Giesler was fortunate, he later said, that these objections were sustained in the opening trial. "The sustaining of those objections became the backbone of the brief I later submitted to the higher court of appeal."[51] The

7. Aftermath

brief landed at the California State Supreme Court and consisted of three volumes totaling "1200 printed pages" that Gielser claimed was "the most comprehensive treatise on statutory rape ever compiled."[52] "There were so many new elements in that brief," Giesler crowed, it "established precedent and authority not only in California but throughout the nation."[53] Because of his work, testimony about an underage accuser's past in an assault could now be introduced into evidence.

The brief detailed the improbability of Pringle's testimony. Here was an athletic young woman of about 115 pounds and five feet three inches who from the age of 11 had been "practicing the art of dancing," which included "toe and full-split dancing … acrobatic dancing, involving back flips, turns, side and back bends," which she practiced "several times weekly down to August ninth," and who during the attack claimed that "her arms and legs were free … who was kicking all the time"; yet throughout all this, "the defendant did not have a mark or scratch of any character or kind upon him after the act is alleged to have been consummated."[54]

Further, Pantages completed his violent act with only his free left hand (his right was over her mouth) while removing his clothes and undergarments, and her undergarments, even as her legs and arms were free to kick, shove, push, hit and prevent him from assaulting her. Lastly, in a recital of a theory he proposed in the first trial, he outlined the times Pringle had visited Pantages prior to August 9, 1929, and how these took place late in the evening yet without any "improper advance toward her" on these occasions when such attempts might have been easier to manage. He himself had never had any history of any such assaults in his life before. Yet, if her testimony is true, he chose "five o'clock in the afternoon on one of the busiest corners in the city of Los Angeles, in a room with a window looking down upon Seventh Street and only halfway between the street and the second story—a room only half a floor below the floor upon which were many offices occupied by numerous people and within hearing distance of many persons?"[55]

When Pantages was released on $100,000 bail on June 7, 1930, three days after the grand opening of the Hollywood Pantages, the wheels of justice finally were grinding on his behalf. He wept at the news.[56] A brass band played for him upon his release, and he was whisked home by his wife and children.[57] Other victories soon followed. More than four months after his release, his appeal for a retrial was finally granted by the California State Supreme Court on April 2, 1931. By a vote of five to two, the Court granted Pantages a new trial on the grounds of "prosecution misconduct"; as a result, the "defendant was not lawfully convicted."[58] The court further noted the "intemperate atmosphere in which the case was tried," adding that "the prosecution no doubt labored under the stress of public opinion and excitement, at times confronted with considerable provocation, but the testimony of the prosecutrix is so improbable as to challenge one's credulity and the jury should have been permitted to consider the evidence uninfluenced by the incidents and errors discussed in the main opinion."[59]

The day of his release from a prison hospital on June 7, 1930, Pantages was a sorry figure, drained of his former vitality. He is surrounded by his wife, Lois, daughter Carmen, and son Lloyd, in Los Angeles County Jail (*Marc Wanamaker, Bison Archives*).

The "stress of public opinion" was impossible to contain. While a jury could be sequestered, a judge could not. The outside world's thinking was bound to seep into a trial in one form or another, directly or indirectly. And after all, jury members and judges are human beings with their own emotions vulnerable to influence. As demonstrated in the Arbuckle trials, the press' role in judicial justice is not trifling. The *San Francisco Chronicle*, a competitor to Hearst's publications and not known for his brand of sensationalism, published a photo at the start of the first Pantages trial showing a smiling defendant while a forlorn Pringle is shown with her parents. Below the Pringle photo appeared one of Lois Pantages, flanked by her daughter Carmen and nurse. The unmistakable impression was of a man either in complete denial over his circumstances or simply an emotional cripple, oblivious to the misery around him, even that displayed by members of his own family.[60]

An opinion piece in an unnamed California newspaper, quoted by Giesler in his memoir, lays out the extent of the past vitriol against Pantages during the time of his second trial: "That a conviction was secured in the first instance was a surprise to many because of the prominence and wealth of Pantages."[61] It indicated that while he spent some time in the county jail, his "quick-witted and high-priced lawyers" would relieve him from further time spent behind bars.[62] "Some are of the opinion that he was already a well-known bad actor long the lines charged,"[63] referencing his reputation as a womanizer.

November 1931, when the second assault trial started, and October 1929 were separated by more than just 25 months. The nation had entered a catatonic stupor of the kind it had never before experienced. While many financial experts warned that the stock market crash would ripple into the nation's economy, no one really predicted the full impact of what turned out to be a full-on depression. In 1931, the nation's unemployment rate stood at 16 percent, consumer prices had dropped 17 percent, a massive drought was turning the Midwest into the Dust Bowl, and bank closures continued their upward trajectory, reaching 2500.[64] While the full effects of the Great Depression were yet to be completely felt, no one celebrated 1931 as a banner year for the nation's soul or its economy. The emotional and psychological toll of the financial meltdown on ordinary Americans would take years, if not decades, to erase. Pantages' assault charges was not on the nation's radar any longer. Yet in a cruel twist of fate, the American Newspaper Publishers' Association 1931 convention took place in October in Los Angeles at the same time as the Pantages retrial. In an act of severe myopia, the publishers declared that they would

> This is from some people who knew you years ago---It is a demand--
> Perhaps you can guess who it is---We do not care. We demand three
> things of you---The first is money---If you do not come across we
> strike at Carmen and then we take Lois---After you have suffered will
> come your turn. If you want to gamble the life of your wife and
> daughter and not pay us---go ahead----but remember----you will regret
> it.
>
> Collect ten thousand dollars in one hundred dollar bills. Do not
> try marked bills as we know money. We will collect it later in quite
> a safe way. Your first step will be to put an ad in the Los Angeles
> Evening Herald under Lost and Found---This is the ad-----"Lost bill-fold
> containing money, papers, and Elk Lodge Card, Liberal reward, Phone Tr
> 6321." This will let us know you are ready to do business. Have this
> in by Monday at the latest. We will carry out our threats---don't go
> wrong on that. Don't be a damn fool and risk your family's life.
> Your's isn't worth a damn and your family's wont be worth a plugged
> nickle if you think you can get away without coughing up.
>
> The Committe of Six

The assault trial brought Pantages death threats. While nothing came of the threat to kidnap Carmen and Lois Pantages, the notoriety of the trial strained the family's ties (*Marc Wanamaker, Bison Archives*).

no longer use the word "depression" to refer to the economic malaise then wrecking the nation. They found the term too harsh, perhaps injurious to the public's self-esteem. "Panic" and "hard times" were also on the list of rejected words. Instead, they would refer to the current economic crisis as a "period of stabilization." "And the sooner we forget that word 'depression,'" one publisher noted, "the sooner we'll return to normalcy."[65] It would take another decade before any semblance of normalcy returned to the American economy, and that was prompted by the onset of World War II. Meanwhile, publishers did their best to brighten the nation's mood with claims that the economy was improving, but they fell on deaf ears.[66]

The second Pantages trial, commencing on November 2, 1931, was presided over by Superior Judge Clair S. Tappaan, with eight men and four women selected for the jury, and opposing counsel repeating their main points of attack in exact replica from the first trial.[67] The state would show that Pantages assaulted Pringle, while Pantages' lawyers sought to portray their client as the victim of a frame-up. Unlike the first trial, the second gave the defense a chance to introduce into testimony Pringle's past private life. When Pringle was ready to testify, she was clad "in a plain black one-piece dress, with white lace trimming, her hair drawn demurely back from her brows," the *Los Angeles Times* reported. "[T]he girl again went through the sordid details of what she says occurred in Pantages' office on the afternoon of August 9, 1929."[68] The implication, at least according to the coverage, was an attempt on Pringle's part to portray herself as a complete innocent. If her comportment had any impact on the jury's final verdict, it was not revealed. Tellingly, the *Times* added that "she did not weep as much as she did at the first trial."[69] The same issue of the paper reported a $12,967 damages lawsuit against Rodney Pantages for "permitting a collision between his car and the one [the plaintiff] occupied."[70] The notice is less revealing of an accident, and more of the Pantages family lifestyle: Rodney was driven by a chauffeur when the accident occurred.

The task at hand for defense attorney Giesler was to put into the jury's mind that there was an ulterior motive to Pringle's actions, prior to and on the day of the alleged attack. He had to establish that there was something more than a professional relationship between Pringle and her supposed manager, Nicholas Dunaev ("attacking the chastity of the prosecutrix," as the *Times* noted) and that the two conspired together to blackmail Pantages.[71] The fact that she had filed a million-dollar lawsuit against Pantages helped Giesler, although when the lawyer sought to embellish this point in court, he was stopped by the judge.[72] Pringle was not helpful in this strategy. "When I tried to find out more about the link between them," Giesler indicated in his memoirs, "she slammed up."[73] Yet it may have been enough to plant the idea in the jury's minds. He also took care to repeat to the court that Dunaev was a 40-year-old bachelor, suggesting the life not of a steady family man but of a lothario.

Crucially, unlike the first trial, Dunaev became the unexpected star and focus of the second. Giesler kept hammering at Pringle about her relationship with him, asking whether it was not true that on "various occasions" she telephoned her mother to tell her she would not be returning to Garden Grove that night but would spend it at Dunaev's "apartment-house."[74] This information, according to Giesler, came directly from Dunaev's roommate as well as his landlady.[75] Pringle flatly denied this. When Mrs. Pringle came to the witness stand, Giesler's line of questioning regarding Dunaev continued. He asked her whether Pringle and Dunaev had become engaged, but the mother trashed the idea. Giesler, with this inquiry, was being the able courtroom strategist, painting a particular picture of her daughter and Dunaev that belied the innocent image Pringle had assiduously cultivated in both trials. Giesler, in effect, attempted to turn the tables on Pringle, putting *her* on trial rather than Pantages. It was an open question whether the jury would buy this line of reasoning.

"I called the Russian to the witness stand and questioned him," Giesler wrote, referring to Dunaev, "although I had a hard time getting him there."[76] It required subpoenaing the slippery character; but once on the witness stand, he didn't disappoint the defense. Once more, Giesler sought to play with the minds of the jury members. In his own words, he described how he managed to bring forth "certain bits of information which suggested that the Pantages episode was designed to advance their careers in the entertainment world."[77] This was a crucial point, since it meant that Dunaev and Pringle were not only bound professionally and likely personally, but in cahoots in using Pantages as a powerful foil to advance their showbiz paths, and presumably the fame and riches this would bring. This gave substance to the charge that they were romantically involved; but more than that, it created an image of the pair as clever schemers who would stop at nothing to push their careers. If the first trial could be summarized as *People v. Hollywood*, the second was *Hollywood v. Hollywood*, with the movie theater mogul now the victim of ruthless ambition. In a slip that weakened the state's case, Dunaev abruptly blurted out that he "'disliked Greeks,' glaring at Pantages."[78] With this comment, the blackmail theory now had a personal motive. Away from the intense public glare of the first trial, the focus on the personal motives of Pringle and Dunaev yielded points for the defense.

Yet the fact that this retrial was even occurring gave a further edge to the defense team. While retrials can be notoriously tricky and unpredictable, they also present challenges to the prosecuting team to dredge up past witnesses, some of whom may have moved or even passed away. While the testimony of dead witnesses can simply be read in court, it is not as effective as when the individual is sitting before the jury. Furthermore, memory can also get in the way of corroborating evidence; the passage of time can cloud recollections that were once fresh and vital. The net effect may be a less than credible witness. A star witness for the prosecution in the first trial, Frederick T. Wise, who had heard Pringle's scream from the street below and rushed into the theater, was "hesitant" and "vague" in the second.[79] If enough confusion could be sown in the jury, the "beyond a reasonable doubt" requirement to convict any defendant becomes a formidable barrier to conviction.

All that was left for Giesler was to put Pantages on the witness stand and hope he stuck to his previous testimony without any major surprises. In this regard, Pantages played his part well. If he appeared aloof and emotionless in his first trial, thus seemingly oblivious to the seriousness of the assault charges against him, the passage of time and nearly six months in jail, where he was very ill, changed him. "Pantages Weeps on Stand," the *Times* crowed, noting that he broke into tears and was "testifying always with much intense pantomime and gesticulation."[80] Comatose at the first trial, Pantages came alive at the second. What impact crying witnesses have on the jury is a matter of debate in legal circles. In a society of severe, stereotypical, if changing gender roles, a wealthy, middle-aged man crying during his testimony must have made an impact, particularly a man (Pantages) with a reputation as self-reliant, withdrawn and solipsistic.

There was nothing new in Pantages' testimony to suggest a different outcome to the trial's verdict from the first. He repeated his earlier story that he met Dunaev and Pringle in May 1929, watched the play performed, judged it unsuitable for his theaters, and tried to give her a polite rebuff, but that Pringle refused to abide by the rejection. It was on that basis that she came calling on him, as she had several times before, to change his opinion. It was an act of desperation on her part that she came to see him on August 9, and an act of charity that he took her to the balcony to watch the performance so he could continue his business. It was Pringle who then followed him and demanded a private audience, and he acceded. Why he did so, he did not explain. The publicity room door was locked, so he tried the mezzanine office and led her inside. Once there, she abruptly grabbed his necktie and slammed the door behind her. During his testimony, he arose to demonstrate how she held him and tugged on his shirt.[81] "I gave her a swift kick," he related, then struggled to usher her out the door as she started screaming.

The next day, the examining doctor to the case testified, claiming that the morning after the alleged events took place, she inspected Pringle and found no bruises or marks as the young dancer claimed. The doctor "also expressed disbelief in Miss Pringle's account of her life prior to this time."[82] A few popular sources claim that one last act by the defense helped Pantages' case. It involved bringing in the manager of the Moonbeam Glen Bungalow Court to testify that Pringle and Dunaev "lived as man and wife."[83]

Two days before Thanksgiving and three weeks after the trial started, at six p.m. on Tuesday, November 24, 1931, the case was sent to the jury—and they decided to have dinner before beginning deliberations. The next day, the jury asked to see prior testimony and even asked for a list of witnesses' names and a short "symposium" or summary of their testimony.[84] The judge provided the list of names but not the summary. On Thanksgiving Day, a special dinner was served to the jury members. Giesler claims that the jury had already reached a verdict by then, but "they wanted to

Victory at last: On November 27, 1931, Pantages was cleared of all assault charges. His look suggests both shock and relief at the verdict. From left his adopted daughter Dixie, Lloyd, Mrs. Rodney Pantages, son Rodney and daughter Carmen. He's seated next to Lois (*Marc Wanamaker, Bison Archives*).

have dinner as guests of the county, so they decided not to tell the judge about their decision until the next morning."[85] Out of guilt or gratitude, Giesler noted, the jury gave the judge flowers the next day.[86]

Finally, on Friday, November 28, 1931, came the verdict. "JURY ACQUITS PANTAGES AMID TUMULTUOUS SCENE," roared the *Los Angeles Times* headline the next day, capturing the wild cheers and yells that exploded in the courtroom.[87] Those cheering were asked to leave. Pantages' wife and three children were present. When Mrs. Pantages heard the verdict, she "half rose from her seat and fell back into the arms of [Giesler]."[88] It took the jury three days and four ballots to complete its job, but there was little doubt as to the outcome. One juror pointedly remarked on the unfavorable impression that Nicholas Dunaev had made on the jury, vindicating Giesler's strategy. "Despite my final vote my heart aches for this young girl," one juror attested. "I believe that she is the victim of a schemer."[89] No one could miss the reference to Dunaev.

Pringle was not magnanimous in defeat. She claimed to a reporter that seeking justice in California was an exercise in futility. The 12 jury members, she claimed, simply did not value "a girl's honor"; but with the verdict settled, she added disingenuously that she hoped to return to being "an ordinary American girl."[90] The contrast to Pantages is notable. He and his family were relieved; Mrs. Pantages wept copiously while Pantages planned a restful vacation. All he asked now of life was to be "forgotten" and to spend his "declining years in peace."[91] Interestingly, his desire to be forgotten echoed sentiments later uttered by Pringle.[92]

With Pringle's million-dollar suit to be settled about a week later, the events of August 9, 1929, mercifully came to a close. But could he truly live out his life in peace? In 1932, he sold the Hollywood Pantages to the Fox West Coast Theater chain. Twenty years after he started, Pantages was officially out of the theater business.

It is not entirely clear when the Kennedy myth began to take hold that he gave $10,000 to Pringle to accuse Pantages of rape in order to get hold of his theaters. In the tightly wound, passionate and intense atmosphere of the movie colony, gossip was a way of making sense of an often senseless and chaotic business. A chief feature of the movie industry is the unruly way that talent is treated; seemingly random events and whims could spell disaster or boon to a career. There was often little rhyme or reason to the life of actors, directors, writers and other creators in the business. Under all-powerful studio moguls, whose dictates tended toward megalomania and authoritarianism, gossip served as a way of leveling the uneven and unjust playing field.

The chief element behind the Kennedy myth is motive. Giesler asked in the second trial: Why would Pantages assault a teenager in broad daylight and risk being exposed when there were better opportunities? There was in Pantages, Giesler noted in his memoir, a "baffling combination of native common sense and imprudence ... imprudence bordering upon foolishness."[93] In this case, the lawyer alluded to Pantages granting a private audience to a desperate, star-struck young woman in a tiny office in a manner that invited trouble. Perhaps he thought he was being magnanimous—a sentiment that blinded him to the potential dangers of the act.

If so, it was not the first time Pantages exhibited such reckless magnanimity. In a 1922 letter he addressed to a member of his administrative staff in Seattle from his headquarters in Los Angeles, he complained about a "Mr. Earl Edmonson" whom he briefly employed as a bookkeeper and auditor but who turned out to be incompetent and a threat to his operation. He feared that Edmonson might sue him. "This is what I get from this man Edmonson," he stated ruefully in the letter. "I kept him and his wife here in my home for a year, fed him, housed him and entertained him for one year, and this is what I get out of the man."[94]

The episode reveals a social blindness on the part of Pantages, but not the thinking of a sexual predator. If the one juror in the second trial is correct, then Pantages is as much a victim as was Pringle, and the perpetrator behind the assault allegations was Dunaev. It is a neat and tidy theory, yet conspiracies of the kind that lay behind the Kennedy myth require more powerful personalities than an obscure writer and director such as Dunaev. It is here that Kennedy's name enters the discussion. Despite the contributions he made to the movie industry, such as his Harvard lectures and the creation of a respectable studio in RKO Pictures, the biggest bonus he brought was to his own bank account and not to the industry. He came, he saw and he enriched himself, at the expense of others. His assignation with Gloria Swanson was likely fairly well-known within the elite circles of Hollywood. The great white hope proved to be less a savior than a conqueror. Why not enter his name into the conspiracy? It certainly was believable; to many, Kennedy was capable of almost any transgression.

The movie industry has always been in a particularly advantageous position to shepherd rumors into cultural facts. As an industry it relies on publicity, which brings with it a whole ecology of communication channels that spread messages from inside the movie colony out into mainstream society. These channels include published books that cement rumors—in this case, Kenneth Anger's *Hollywood Babylon II*, which took the Kennedy myth circulating within Hollywood circles, both oral and written, and turned it into fact.[95] Cultural commentators and historians of one kind or another picked up the trail. So it was that Andy Edmonds, writing in *Los Angeles Magazine*, as well as Michael Parrish in his book recounting the history of the Los Angeles County District Attorney's Office, repeated the Kennedy myth.[96] The account was included in a Joseph Kennedy biography by Ronald Kessler as well as Marvin J. Wolf and Katherine Mader's *Fallen Angels: Chronicles of L.A. Crime and Mystery* (1986).[97]

Then in 2002 came the mea culpa. It began with a phone call from a writer to Marcy Worthington, whose mother was Eunice Pringle. In the Kennedy myth, after the assault charges against Pantages, when Pringle decided to tell all to the media in 1933, she abruptly and mysteriously died of poisoning. The writer told Worthington that her mother was involved in a sensational rape trial. "I knew she'd danced in Los Angeles," Worthington recalled. "When I asked why she'd stopped, she always said, 'Dancing was too corrupt.'"[98] Worthington didn't need proof that the poisoning account was wrong; she knew her mother had died of natural causes in 1996. She told Parrish that her mother gave up whatever life in show biz she had after the rape trials, taking up typing and shorthand on her way to becoming an executive secretary, later marrying, moving to San Diego and quietly starting a family. She also liked going to the ballet and theater. Worthington added that her mother was class valedictorian in high school and a Christian Scientist. As for any romantic liaison between Pringle and Dunaev, she flatly denied it. He was a friend and mentor to Eunice, but nothing more.[99] Worthington failed to mention the tremendous interest in Pringle unleashed by the first trial. Three theatrical agents sought her services—one involving Pringle's appearance at a nightclub "at a fancy price"—but the victorious prosecutrix nixed them all. "All I want is to be alone—to forget!" she cried.[100]

Parrish, who authored the 2002 piece in the *Los Angeles Times*, realized that the Kennedy story that had so long circulated was baseless. In the piece, Anger himself admitted that he had collected stories about Hollywood from as early as his high school days, ones that came from "entertainment-world families" that included the Kennedy tale.[101] "I researched it carefully," Anger claimed.[102] Anger did not know where the poisoning story came from, and Parrish asked if it might have come from the Pantages camp. Marvin Wolf admitted that anything was possible in Hollywood. "It's the sort of thing that a guy like Pantages would have known to do," Wolf admitted. "He was no sweetheart."[103]

8. Wrap-Up

It is unlikely that Alexander Pantages went to bed on the night of August 8, 1929, with the idea that he would wake up and in 24 hours be arrested and spend a night in jail. Like other Angelenos, he may have thought about his weekend plans, how he might further push his two sons, Rodney and Lloyd, into the theater business, and what lay in store for him in his now apparent move toward retirement. In the space of a few minutes during the next afternoon, his entire world was upended, and he would never completely recover. If any photo captures the "new" Pantages during this trying period, it is of the prisoner in his blue denims sitting next to a doctor who feels his pulse. It is Christmas Day 1929, and while many Americans enjoyed the holiday, Pantages stared gloomily into space, lost in a miasma of worry and dejection. To come back to normalcy from such a miserable condition required a superhuman act that might have been possible once but in the present reality was beyond his capacities. The man who was always in charge of his destiny was now ruled by it.

The fighting, ruthless, vibrant machine that was Pantages had broken down and was replaced by a thin, beaten, frail man who, at the moment his "not guilty" verdict was read in 1931, could not even muster a smile. While surrounded by his family, as captured in a photo in the *Los Angeles Times*—with Lois Pantages staring brightly into the camera, beaming, his daughter kissing him on his left temple, and son Lloyd standing above him—Pantages, with one hand tenderly cupped toward his wife's shoulder, looks ashen-faced at the camera, as nearly complete a death-mask on a live human being as possible. He had been in a relentless battle, consumed by lawyers, legal maneuverings and testimony for the past 29 months; but now free at last, with the freedom that he could barely dream about before him, the question was what to do with it.

He did not sit idle. "In recent years," *Variety* wrote in his obituary, "Pantages had been concerned mostly with his stable of race horses, with

Rodney handling the theatre and also running the small booking office in Los Angeles, in which he and his father were partnered with Harry Rogers. The elder Pantages also was lately reported to have cleaned up handsomely in oil investments."[1]

Apparently Pantages had enjoyed going to the Santa Anita races, so owning a few horses could be something to while away his time, since he had so much of it now. And there was always his family. On February 14, 1932, Jr., after a three-year engagement (no doubt because of the rape trials), Carmen Pantages married John W. Considine.[2] Irony heaped upon irony: The offspring of two bitter rivals became husband and wife, and one of the matrons of honor was none other than Marion Davies, permanent mistress to William Randolph Hearst. Even Harry Lang could not have written that script.

Pantages missed the stage. In 1933, if *Variety* is to be believed, he made plans to return to theater in a big way, not with movies but with vaudeville. He envisioned not merely a West Coast operation, like his previous circuit, but a "coast-to-coast chain," and to that end he "leased theaters in Hollywood, Seattle and Salt Lake from the bondholders" and entered into agreements with other show business executives.[3] It was never his style to announce a project before it happened; he preferred to do the planning and then spring it on the public. "This was a definite aboutface for Pantages. When he was at the height of his success, he acted first, achieved his successes, and later talked of it. Now he was announcing his plans first and never acting on them."[4]

Pantages spoke of grandiose theaters, as if willing himself to erect them. He made reference to a "great new chain of vaudeville houses bearing his name ... two to five hundred vaudeville theaters.... He even began to talk of producing films in Europe and he talked of opening musical theaters."[5] None of these extravagant plans came to fruition. How could they? They seemed hopelessly outlandish, even desperate. Pantages appeared like an actor in search of a character; unsure of himself and relying on bragging rights rather than the meticulous planning that was once his trademark. He still had wealth, although it had shrunk considerably from the dizzying heights of the 1920s; and life, at least as far as his family was concerned, settled into a kind of Hallmark card fuzziness.

An August 5, 1934, report indicated he may have been the victim of extortion, along with four other wealthy Southern Californians. The note demanded money or there would be "grave danger" to their families.[6] According to the article, "Mr. Pantages said that he tore up his note and disregarded it."[7]

Accusations targeting him also arose, one surfacing just several months after his release from prison and a year before his retrial. In a bizarre case that hints at District Attorney Buron Fitts' unorthodox tactics and power plays, Pantages found himself entangled in a situation involving a "Hollywood Love Market" (in today's parlance, an escort service). He was accused of being involved with underage girls at a "party" at the El Cortez Hotel in San Diego on October 30, 1930.

His former publicity man, William Jobelmann, was said to be working with a female partner, Olive Clark Day, in operating a Hollywood Love Market using underage girls to "entertain" wealthy businessmen in Southern California. In the process, Pantages and four others faced felony charges for "conspiracy and contributing to the delinquency of minors."[8] Conviction involved serving time in San Quentin and a fine. Escort services were already an established fact in the movie industry; with so many attractive actresses hovering on the fringes of the film colony and relatively few achieving steady employment, such services helped the less successful pay the rent and put food on the table.

Two 16-year-old girls (later amended to 17 in the press coverage) accused three businessmen, Pantages among them, and the two organizers behind the "love market" of criminal offenses resulting from the hotel party. Pantages again turned to Jerry Giesler to defend him. Since the escort service was run out of Los Angeles, this brought Fitts into uncomfortable alliance with the district attorney of the city of San Diego, where the resultant trial took place (Fitts preferred to be the star in such proceedings). Prior to the May 25, 1931, start of the trial, one of the five defendants pleaded guilty and became a state's witness. It took examining 100 potential jurors to finally select nine men and three women.[9]

The relationship between Jobelmann and Pantages added to the oddity of the case. In his first trial, press agent Jobelmann initially held his boss' contention that the Pringle matter was a frame-up. Yet he suddenly disappeared and when he re-emerged, he changed his story, backing up Pringle's version of events.[10] In that sense, his former employee help convict Pantages. But by 1931, the past seems to have been forgiven. The mercurial Jobelmann appears to have had some success as a press agent, yet his past was not altogether pristine. In 1922, his wife, an actress and wealthy former widow, won a divorce judgment against him on charges that he slapped her, had been rude to her, and was addicted to intoxicants.[11] "This is terrible," an exasperated Pantages told the press when hearing of the charges filed against him.[12] "I don't know anything at all about the charges. And the girls—I've never heard of them," a reference that echoed his denials of knowing Kate Rockwell in her lawsuit against him.[13] "I was a sick man at the time they say all this occurred."[14] And then he added his version of a conspiracy theory: "I think this is a lot of dirt dished up by my enemies to injure my appeal in the Pringle girl case."[15]

Yet, during the trial Pantages' eccentric antics only further provoked the public's unfavorable opinion of him. He arrived to be arraigned and dashed from his car "on a dead run with his coat over his head" into the court as his car circled outside the court waiting for his return.[16] "That formality being over, he again took up his athletic activities, chasing down the street the automobile which he brought with him ... the last seen of him was his automobile disappearing up the street, while three bail-bondsmen hung on the running board."[17] For a man who appeared near death a year earlier, it was a stunning recovery. Even Lois, who accompanied him throughout the San Diego trial, looked weary but chipper in one press photo.[18]

What emerged during the trial was a real estate deal gone wrong and attempts by two of the defendants to sort out with Pantages an $80,000 note held by a fourth party. There was no party in the Arbuckle sense, and any festivities would have been subdued. (Pantages on occasion smoked cigars, but he was not known as a drinker.) Prior to the trial, Pantages and his two partners (one now a trial defendant and the other a state witness) had engaged in civil lawsuits against one another, and the actions that led to the present criminal action may have also been intended to remove any past hard feelings.[19]

It was a clear case of overreach on the part of the politicized Fitts. It was built on flimsy accusations with less than stellar witnesses to back up the state's contentions. The prosecution alleged that Jobelmann drove the two teenagers to San Diego ostensibly to be with the three businessmen, while his partner Day checked into the hotel with the two young ladies under aliases. Day contacted Pantages and another businessman on another floor. The hotel, the state contented, got wind of the liaisons with the underage girls and ordered the festivities to cease. Evidence backed up the party claims, but missing were solid details to support asserted attacks against the girls. Soon it emerged that one of the key state witnesses, the Italian-born Lydia Nitto, may not have been 17 as claimed but several years older.

As in the first rape trial, spectators packed the courtroom, and despite the repetitive and often monotonous reality of courtroom drama, many "refused to leave their seats during the noon recess."[20] They witnessed the assembly-line quality of justice being served, and nothing could stop it

His theater years behind him, Pantages became an avid race horse owner and horse-track aficionado. Here he shares a trophy with Lois after a race (*Marc Wanamaker, Bison Archives*).

once it was set into motion. Even a car smashing into one driven by Fitts (he escaped unscathed) could not slow it down.[21] Except the prosecution's own incompetence. Under cross-examination, it emerged that Lydia Nitto's original testimony indicated no mistreatment by Pantages, but after she was jailed in Los Angeles Juvenile Hall for three days, she suddenly changed her testimony.[22]

Nitto also admitted that Pantages knew nothing about underage girls coming to visit the hotel during his stay there.[23] In fact, under intense grilling by a defense attorney, Nitto admitted that Pantages "treated me very nice," then added, "but I don't know why."[24] She also casually stated that she received "gifts of silk stockings" from the Los Angeles District Attorney's office.[25] Not only had she received the silk stockings but she and the other minors "were entertained with auto rides and shows while they were waiting to give testimony."[26] While the revelation did not stop the case, it did put the prosecution on the defensive and gave credence to the theory, amplified during closing arguments, that the state was not playing fair and was shaping the testimony of witnesses.[27] This, coupled with the revelation that Nitto might be older than claimed, brought the state case near collapse. That it continued was primarily due to the presiding judge, who carried the case along and denied dismissal petitions by the defense. The wheels of justice would grind on, but with deflated tire pressure.

On the witness stand, Pantages claimed the appearance of the young girls was nothing more than an intrusion on an otherwise boring business meeting.[28] "The little multimillionaire," it was reported, "animated his testimony with expressive gestures" and described the meeting with the women as being "casual" and he didn't even know their names.[29] Pantages admitted that his two partners in the real estate deal had tried several times to get him to come to San Diego. He was introduced to the young ladies as friends of one of his business partners. "This Nitto girl came over and sat in a chair beside me ... and began talking about how sick I looked."[30] After the chitchat, Pantages turned to her and suggested she leave to join her friends, who had already gone. That was the extent of the encounter.

In Los Angeles the same month as the trial, minister Billy Sunday told his listeners at the Bible Institute that it was not the economic depression that doomed the nation but its moral and spiritual depression. The country, he declared, "will not return to material prosperity until America is on its knees. We have been handing the hot end of the poker to God for too long. No nation ever survived the death of its religion."[31] It was the nativist voice from the past culture wars come back to strike against the modernizers. He inveighed against Hollywood and progressives like the novelist Sinclair Lewis.

A few days after notorious underworld leader Al Capone pleaded guilty to charges of violating the nation's liquor laws and evading income taxes, Pantages' "love market" trial was suspended due to a hung jury.[32] Nine of the 12 voted to exonerate Pantages and the others, but three jurors held out. After 18 days of sheer boredom punctuated by fits of tension and suspense and 24 hours of jury deliberation, the case ended in a mistrial. Eleven jury ballots produced no conclusive verdict. The state immediately announced a new trial for the following month, but prior to its start the prosecution decided to withdraw the case. The prosecuting attorney announced that "a retrial of the sensational 'girl market' case will be a 'hopeless gesture and an unwarranted expense on the county.'"[33] Perhaps the state no longer could afford silk stocking gifts to help in its efforts. Even justice was feeling the terrible effects of the Great Depression.

Assuming that Pantages *was* innocent, did the case reveal the real Pantages—the one whom his second trial exonerated? Did it show that he was not capable of raping a minor? A revealing point about all his trials is that there were no heroes. Pringle in one moment denied any financial interest in filing a civil lawsuit, in another doing so on the presumption that Pantages destroyed a showbiz career that only existed in her mind. Nicholas Dunaev may have used Pringle as a weapon to advance his own cause in an industry that relegated him to its fringes. Buron Fitts used all the tools at his disposal, including bullying, to build a reputation that he could ultimately run for high political office. Joseph P. Kennedy, a bit player in the assault trial, arrived in Hollywood, rearranged a few of its institutions, and left a wealthy and sexually satisfied man. William Randolph Hearst made his fortune by destroying the careers of others, doing so as a sport.

As for Pantages, he swam in a swamp of ruthless, cunning schemers, but by the end he was a toothless caricature of his old self. The man who once outwitted his enemies with ferocious mental energy and verve could now only comically run into a courthouse with his coat over his head, devoid of the dignity and gravitas he deserved from a long, pioneering career in the theater business. In the court of public opinion, subjected to gossip and innuendo, he emerged as the victim of rape, not its perpetrator.[34] Since institutionalized justice brought out only a tie (one conviction, one exoneration), does this outcome perhaps represent the closest approximation to truth? In the messy world of human reality, it may be the best explanation of events that offer none.

Hearst would have his own financial troubles in the 1930s that weakened his publishing empire. Kennedy chaired the newly created Securities and Exchange Commission under President Franklin D. Roosevelt in 1934: The former fox in the henhouse was asked to clean up the foxhole. Fitts ended his life committing suicide, Dunaev died in poverty, and Pringle lived out her years the nearest to what can be described as normalcy.

Pantages went to bed on Monday night, February 16, 1936, and never woke up. He was found by his maid, who knocked on his door at eight a.m. and got no response. She called the Pantages' gardener, who tried to revive him. An autopsy done the next day determined that he died from complications due to "hardening of the coronary arteries."[35]

His obituaries reflected the confusion about his age but were remarkably similar in condensing his life to its key points: born in Greece, working in Cairo and aboard steamships in the Mediterranean, his time in San Francisco and the Yukon, later the start of his empire in Seattle. Of course, there was the rape trial, his exoneration, and the fortune that he amassed along the way. He was called a "shrewd financier" with "surprising foresight" who sold his theaters in 1929 before the stock market crash.[36] Another obituary dubbed him the "One-Time Czar of the Theater." "He was Greek," *The Washington Post* indicated, "or at least, he thought he was. 'My father told me I was born on an island off the mainland of Greece.... I guess I'm about 72.'"[37] Did he really forget where he was born but suddenly remember his actual age? It was pure Pantages, mendacious to the end. *The Seattle Times*, noting his age as 64, gave him front-page prominence and extensively quoted his architect Marcus Priteca. According to Priteca, "He was planning to start anew. He was going to build theaters in California. He loved to erect buildings."[38]

Priteca added, "He was a fine man, undaunted and always considered a genius in his field. I have lost my best friend."[39] *The Los Angeles Times*: "Alexander Pantages, the Greek immigrant boy who amassed a fortune in the theater business, died yesterday, ending one of the most spectacular careers of a vanished age."[40] The *Times* noted that at the end of his career, he "did his business in the Greek tongue."[41] Of the 80 theaters Pantages owned at the height of his empire, the paper wrongly attested, there was only the Hollywood Pantages left in his portfolio. Kate Rockwell wept at the announcement of his death.[42] "Thank God, I never had anything mean to say about Alec," she offered.[43] "Alec had brains or he couldn't have climbed the ladder. He was a fine man. I never heard him tell a dirty story."[44]

If he was a fine man, he also struggled. In a revealing piece written shortly after his conviction, his entire life is recounted with remarkable objectivity, perhaps even compassion. Seven comic strip panels show him as a deck hand, waiter and vaudevillian, and also depict his matrimony suit by Rockwell, his rise in the theater business, his arrest for assault and finally his incarceration. From a snapshot point of view, the comic strip captures the essence of his life; only two panels of the seven indicate any element of accomplishment and success (as a vaudevillian and theater owner) while the rest are moments of great physical and mental anguish. For his actions, he, and those closest to him, paid a great price.

The piece detailed how his wife, from "an estimable family of Oakland, California ... gave generously of time and money to charity."[45] Yet, by virtue of the fact that she was married to a man who once was involved with a dance girl, she was shunned by Seattle's "exclusive society." Pantages must have bristled at this and it likely led, as the article suggested at the insistence of Mrs. Pantages, to the family's permanent move to Los Angeles. Once there, matters might have improved, and probably they did (as for example, the family's association with William Randolph Hearst and Marion Davies). But her drunk driving and manslaughter charges, and his case of sexual assault of a minor, tore up whatever social reputations were built by living in the southland. But that did not stop Davies being a bridesmaid at Carmen Pantages' wedding to Considine. The pole that Pantages desperately sought to climb became a stake in his heart.

That in his last few years he rediscovered his Greek tongue and did business with it, presumably with other Greek-Americans, suggests he completed the circle, returning to the roots that marked the opening chapter of his life. Perhaps this came as a comfort to him; the Greek past that he had so long ago relinquished came back to soothe his wounded spirit. If so, it is fitting. Perhaps he never left home, at least not in his heart, but instead wandered the earth only to find that in the end, he came back to the beginning. In the waters around Andros there are many shipwrecks, and also many memories of those who survived and found on its rocky shores life unbroken and a chance to start again. Perhaps that was on his mind on the night of February 16, 1936, as he lay in bed for what turned out to be his final few hours on Earth.

Chapter Notes

Preface

1. Edwin Schallert, "Pantages Theater Opens," *Los Angeles Times*, June 6, 1930, Section II, 9. A note about the spelling of "Theatre" versus "Theater." Convention at the time required that "theatre" refer to the art form while "theater" meant the actual building. Thus the Hollywood Pantages should correctly have been called a "Theater," not "Theatre" as it was actually spelled. Today's convention uses "theater" for both art and building. I will use the original title whenever it appears as a direct reference but will stay with "theater" in the text when discussing it. (See Carolee Danz with David Wilma, *100 Sterling Years* [Bothell, WA: Book Publishers Network, 2011], 25.)
2. Schallert, "Pantages Theater," II:9.
3. Schallert, "Pantages Theater," II:9.
4. Sheldon S. Wolin, *Democracy, Inc.: Managed Democracy and the Specter of Inverted Totalitarianism* (Princeton, NJ: Princeton University Press, 2008), 21.
5. Kenneth Anger, *Hollywood Babylon II* (New York: E.P. Dutton, 1984), 29.
6. Anger, *Hollywood*, 40.
7. Victoria Wilson, *A Life of Barbara Stanwyck* (New York: Simon & Schuster, 2013), 367.
8. From a personal conversation with Marcy Worthington in Los Angeles, June 2004.
9. David B. Sachsman and David W. Bulla, eds., *Sensationalism: Murder, Mayhem, Mudslinging, Scandals, and Disasters in 19th-Century Reporting* (New Brunswick, NJ: Transaction Publishers, 2013), xxviii. The paper was promptly shut down.
10. Frank Trentmann, *Empire of Things: How We Became a World of Consumers, from the Fifteenth Century to the Twenty-first* (London: Allen Lane, 2016), 86.
11. See, for example, William E. Huntzicker, "Sex, Six, and Sensation: Two Major Crime Stories in Antebellum New York," in David B. Sachsman and David W. Bulla, eds., *Sensationalism: Murder, Mayhem, Mudslinging, Scandals, and Disasters in 19th Century Reporting* (New Brunswick, NJ: Transaction Publishers, 2013). The story of a murder in April 1836 in New York City "made James Gordon Bennett and his *New York Herald* a financial success" (202).
12. Robert Shuler, *"Fighting Bob" Shuler of Los Angeles* (Indianapolis, IN: Dog Ear Publishing, 2011), 93.
13. See for example Yiorgos Anagnostou, *The Contours of White Ethnicity: Popular Ethnography and the Making of Usable Past in Greek America* (Athens: Ohio University Press, 2009) and Matthew Frye Jacobson, *Whiteness of a Different Color: European Immigrants and the Alchemy of Race* (Cambridge, MA: Harvard University Press, 1999). Both offer detailed examples of the extent, scope, and nature of white ethnicity in America. For a definition of race, I use the one offered by Thomas Sowell, *Race and Economics* (New York: David McKay, 1975), v, cited in Sowell, *Race and Culture: A World View* (New York: Basic Books, 1994), xiii: "The term 'race' will be used here in the broad social sense in which it is applied to everyday life to designate ethnic groups of various sorts—by race, religion, or nationality."
14. Krishnendu Ray, *The Ethnic Restaurateur* (London: Bloomsbury, 2016), 1.
15. Anagnostou, *The Contours of White Ethnicity*, 48.
16. Gregory D. Black, *Hollywood Censored: Morality Codes, Catholics, and the Movies* (Cambridge: Cambridge University Press, 1994), 3.
17. George Rodman, *Mass Media in a Changing World: History, Industry, Controversy* (New York: McGraw-Hill, 2008), 38.
18. Black, *Hollywood Censored*, 153.

19. Black, *Hollywood Censored*, 154.
20. Alexander Walker, *Sex in the Movies: The Celluloid Sacrifice* (Baltimore: Penguin Books, 1966), 23.
21. Even great silent-era film stars like Charlie Chaplin (an immigrant from England who refused American citizenship) felt the stings of the press: "Chaplin's appearance in the headlines as everything from an income tax evader, a leftist and a defiler of young women" made him "exceedingly unpopular" (Gene Fernett, *American Film Studios: An Historical Encyclopedia* [Jefferson, NC: McFarland & Company], 40). Eventually he was deported and settled in self-imposed exile in Switzerland.
22. For a fuller discussion on work and leisure dichotomy, please see Roy Rosenzweig, *Eight Hours for What We Will: Workers and Leisure in an Industrial City, 1870–1920* (Cambridge: Cambridge University Press, 1983).
23. "Grauman Quits Theater Field; Will Produce," *Los Angeles Times*, June 17, 1929, 5.
24. Daniel Yergin, *The Prize: The Epic Quest for Oil, Money and Power* (London: Free Press, 2009), 19–39.
25. This was vertical integration and monopolistic behavior of the kind that in 1948 was declared illegal by the United States Supreme Court under the Paramount Consent Decrees.
26. "Pantages Drops Plea for Visit to New Theater," *Los Angeles Times*, June 5, 1930, Sec. II, 3.
27. Schallert, "Pantages Theater," II:9.
28. Schallert, "Pantages Theater," II:9.
29. Schallert, "Pantages Theater," II:9.

Introduction

1. Theodore Saloutos, "Alexander Pantages, Theater Magnate of the West," *Pacific Northwest Quarterly*, October 1966, 137.
2. Carlo Curti, *Skouras: King of Fox Studios* (Los Angeles: Holloway House, 1967), 48.
3. Curti, *Skouras*, 52.
4. Dean Arthur Tarrach, "Alexander Pantages: The Seattle Pantages and His Vaudeville Circuit" (M.A. thesis: University of Washington, 1973), 22.
5. Tarrach, "Alexander Pantages," 22.
6. Tarrach, "Alexander Pantages," 22.
7. Tarrach, "Alexander Pantages," 27.
8. The name change likely took place sometime during his stay in San Francisco in the 1890s.
9. Erika Lee, "A Nation of Immigrants and a Gatekeeping Nation: American Immigration Law and Policy," in Reed Ueda, ed., *A Companion to American Immigration* (Malden, MA: Blackwell, 2006), 12.
10. U.S. Census Bureau, http://www.census.gov/population/www/documentation/twps0029/tab01.html.
11. John A. Koumoulides, "Greece and the Greek Diaspora: The Greek American Community at the Dawn of the Twenty-First Century, and the Twilight of the Twentieth," in John A. Koumoulides, ed., *Greece: The Legacy: Essays on the History of Greece, Ancient, Byzantine, and Modern* (Bethesda: University Press of Maryland, 1998), 161. Koumoulides notes (162) that more than 200,000 of the 450,000 Greek immigrants in the U.S. returned to Greece to live. This was certainly not the case with Pantages, who apparently never returned to Greece in his entire lifetime.
12. Reed Ueda, *Postwar Immigrant America* (Boston: Bedford Books, 1994), 5.
13. Ueda, *Immigrant America*, 4.
14. Dorothy M. Brown, *Setting a Course: American Women in the 1920s* (Boston: Twayne, 1987), 18.
15. Tyler Anbinder, "Nativism and Prejudice Against Immigrants," in Ueda, *Immigrant America*, 177.
16. See Robert Sklar, *Movie-Made America* (New York: Vintage, 1994), 3, for a discussion on its impact on movies.
17. Maria Christina Chatziioannou, "Greek Merchants in Victorian England," in Dimitris Tziovas, ed., *Greek Diaspora and Migration Since 1700* (Surrey, UK: Ashgate, 2009), 49.
18. Andre R. Fellow, *American Media History* (Belmont, CA: 2005: Thomson Wadsworth, 2005), 231.
19. Brown, *Setting a Course*, 31.
20. Kathy Peiss, *Cheap Amusements: Working Women and Leisure in the Turn-of-the-Century New York* (Philadelphia: Temple University Press, 1986) cited in Krishnendu Ray, *The Ethnic Restaurateur* (London and New York: Bloomsbury, 2016), 90.
21. Brown, *Setting a Course*, 19.
22. Brown, *Setting a Course*, 20.
23. I refer here to the scandals that rocked Hollywood in the 1920s, such as those involving the apparent wild party that led to the death of Virginia Rappe, perhaps at the hands of superstar film comedian Fatty Arbuckle, or the still-unsolved death of film director William Desmond Taylor. These scandals led to the formation of the Hays Office to instigate self-censorship on the part of the movie industry but really to sanitize the industry in the eyes of the public. All around were calls for moral upbraiding of the movie

industry that clearly should have revealed to Pantages the social quicksand he was navigating during his rape trial. It was not an era to step into a locked side-office with an attractive teenager without expecting repercussions.

24. Brown, *Setting a Course*, 20.
25. Maury Klein, *Rainbow's End: The Crash of 1929* (New York: Oxford University Press, 2001), 114.
26. Klein, *Crash*, 114.
27. *Los Angles Times*, August 10, 1929, 1.
28. *Seattle Times*, August 10, 1929, 1.
29. *San Francisco Chronicle*, August 10, 1929, 1.
30. *New York Times*, August 10, 1929, 11. Most reports of the Pantages affair in the *New York Times* were Associated Press stories.
31. Yiorgios Anagnostou, *Contours of White Ethnicity* (Athens: Ohio University Press, 2009), 3.
32. Kenneth Whyte, *The Uncrowned King: The Sensational Rise of William Randolph Hearst* (Berkeley, CA: Counterpoint, 2009), 223.
33. Gerald J. Baldasty, *Vigilante Newspapers* (Seattle: University of Washington Press, 2005), 6.
34. "Life of W.R. Hearst, Building of Publishing Empire," *Seattle Post-Intelligencer*, August 15, 1951, 2.
35. Ben Procter, *William Randolph Hearst: The Early Years, 1863–1910* (New York: Oxford University Press, 1998), 136.
36. John Higham, *Strangers in the Land: Patterns of American Nativism 1860–1925* (New Brunswick, NJ: Rutgers University Press, 1955), 127.
37. Roy Everett Littlefield III, *William Randolph Hearst: His Role in American Progressivism* (Lanham, MD: University Press of America, 1980), 39. As with many successful business people, the Hearst attitude toward Chinese immigrants did not come without irony: "Hearst family was then, and for many years, the biggest employer of cheap Chinese labor in California" (Ferdinand Lundberg, *Imperial Hearst: A Social Biography* [New York: Equinox Cooperative Press, 1936], 32).
38. Roger Daniels, *The Politics of Prejudice* (New York: Atheneum, 1970), 25. In this case, "Brown" refers to Japanese immigrants.
39. Cited in David Nasaw, *The Chief: The Life of William Randolph Hearst* (Boston: Hougton Mifflin, 2000), 380.
40. Eric Rauchway, "How 'America First' Got Its Nationalistic Edge," *Atlantic*, May 6, 2016, found at http://www.theatlantic.com/politics/archive/2016/05/william-randolph-hearst-gave-america-first-its-nationalist-edge/481497/.
41. Rockwell Hunt, ed., *California and Californians* (Chicago: Lewis Publishing Company, 1932), 429.
42. Ben Procter, *William Randolph Hearst: The Early Years, 1863–1910* (New York: Oxford University Press, 1998), 101.
43. Nasaw, *The Chief*, 80.
44. Taso G. Lagos, "Poor Greek to 'Scandalous' Hollywood Mogul: Alexander Pantages and the Anti-Immigrant Narratives of William Randolph Hearst's *Los Angeles Examiner*," *Journal of Modern Greek Studies*, 30:1 (Spring 2012), 55.
45. Fernett, *American Film Studios*, 47. As Fernett points out on the same page, Hearst purchased *Cosmopolitan* magazine, and his news bureau was called the International News Service.
46. William Randolph Hearst letter to the *New York American* (August 2, 1919), cited in Nasaw, *The Chief*, 271.
47. Alice Kessler-Harris, *In Pursuit of Equity: Women, Men, and the Quest for Economic Citizenship in 20th-Century America* (Oxford, UK: Oxford University Press, 2001), 5–6.
48. Marion Davies, *The Times We Had: Life with William Randolph Hearst* (Indianapolis, IN: Bobbs-Merrill, 1975), 18. There is an element of rebelliousness in Davies (born Marion Cecilia Douras). As a youngster in New York she once threw vegetables at a butler in a stately home; she was caught and arrested by police (4–5).
49. From Oscar Wilde's "A Women of No Importance," Act III. Found at: http://genius.com/Oscar-wilde-a-woman-of-no-importance-act-3-annotated.
50. Davies, *The Times We Had*, 66.
51. Victoria Wilson, *A Life of Barbara Stanwyck* (New York: Simon & Schuster, 2013), 81.
52. John Belton, *American Cinema/American Culture* (New York: McGraw-Hill, 1994), 8.
53. Andre R. Fellow, *American Media History* (Belmont, CA: Thomson Wadsworth, 2005), 222.
54. Sklar, *Movie-Made*, 4.
55. Sklar, *Movie-Made*, 4.
56. Belton, *Americana Cinema*, 9.

Chapter 1

1. Harold B. Franklin, *Motion Picture Theater Management* (New York: George H. Doran Co., 1927), 18.

2. Franklin, *Motion Picture Theater Management*, 18.
3. Personal correspondence between Rodney A. Pantages and Dean Arthur Tarrach, cited in Dean Arthur Tarrach, "Alexander Pantages: The Seattle Pantages and His Vaudeville Circuit" (M.A. thesis: University of Washington, 1973), 3.
4. Many popular accounts (such as Kenneth Anger's *Hollywood Babylon II*, 29) have him born in Athens but more historically minded ones say he hailed from Andros.
5. For the record here is the list of the chroniclers and their dates: Theodore Saloutos offers 1864, 1865, 1871, and 1872; Eugene Clinton Crane indicates 1876; Bernard Berelson and Howard Grant claim 1864; Joe Laurie, Jr., lists 1871; Edward W. Knappman shows 1875, and Dean Arthur Tarrach 1876.
6. Tarrach, "Alexander Pantages," 5.
7. Growing up in a tiny village on the Greek island of Euboea myself, I am intimately familiar with economic, social and cultural disparities between the hinterland and urban Greece.
8. Population figure for 1870 from http://dlib.statistics.gr/Book/GRESYE_02_0101_00100.pdf.
9. Keith R. Legg and John M. Roberts, *Modern Greece: A Civilization on the Periphery* (Boulder, CO: Westview Press, 1997), 30.
10. In another account ("Pantages Career Launched Here," *Seattle Post-Intelligencer*, February 18, 1936, 3), the father is a "cognac maker." The inaccuracies and improbabilities in the *P-I* account suggests this information may be suspect.
11. Population figure from www.populstat.info/Africa/egyptc.htm. By way of comparison, the population of New York City in 1860 was 800,000, thus making Cairo one of the largest cities in the world. NYC population statistic from Gergely Baies, *Feeding Gotham: The Political Economy and Geography of Food in New York, 1790–1860* (Princeton, NJ: Princeton University Press, 2016), 12.
12. Theodore Saloutos, "Alexander Pantages, Theater Magnate of the West," *Pacific Northwest Quarterly*, October 1966, 147.
13. Ellis Lucia, *Klondike Kate: The Life & Legend of Kitty Rockwell, the Queen of the Yukon* (New York: Hastings House Publishers, 1962), 102.
14. "Pantages Career Launched Here," *Seattle Post-Intelligencer*, February 18, 1936, 3. The various versions suggest that young Alexander Pantages spent a great deal of time in Egypt, which begs the question: did he attend elementary school on Andros?

15. Lucia, *Klondike Kate*, 102.
16. Edwin Schallert, "Boy's Dream Now Reality," *Los Angeles Times*, August 15, 1920, 1.
17. Theodore Saloutos, *The Greeks in the United States* (Cambridge, MA: Harvard University Press, 1964), 274.
18. Schallert, "Boy's Dream Now Reality," 1.
19. Saloutos, *Greeks in the United States*, 274.
20. Schallert, "Boy's Dream Now Reality," 1.
21. Saloutos, *Greeks in the United States*, 274.
22. Saloutos, *Greeks in the United States*, 274.
23. Schallert, "Boy's Dream Now Reality," 1.
24. Murray Morgan, *Skid Road: An Informal Portrait of Seattle* (Seattle: University of Washington Press, 1982), 151.
25. David McCullough, *The Path Between the Seas: The Creation of the Panama Canal, 1870–1914* (New York: Simon & Schuster, 1977), 49, and Ervan Garrison, *A History of Engineering and Technology: Artful Methods* (Boca Raton, FL: CRC Press, 1991), 182.
26. McCullough, *Path Between the Seas*, 52.
27. Pudney, *Suez*, 44.
28. Zachary Karabell, *Parting the Desert: The Creation of the Suez Canal* (New York: Alfred A. Knopf, 2003), 262.
29. Karabell, *Parting the Desert*, 262.
30. McCullough, *Path Between the Seas*, 55.
31. McCullough, *Path Between the Seas*, 101.
32. McCullough, *Path Between the Seas*, 101.
33. Gustave Anguizola, *Philippe Bunau-Varilla: The Man Behind the Panama Canal* (Chicago: Nelson-Hall, 1980), 17.
34. Anguizola, *Philippe Bunau-Varilla*, 17.
35. Anguizola, *Philippe Bunau-Varilla*, 17.
36. Anguizola, *Philippe Bunau-Varilla*, 18.
37. McCullough, *Path Between the Seas*, 11.
38. Dwight Carroll Miner, *The Fight for the Panama Route* (New York: Octagon Books, 1971), 24.
39. Anguizola, *Philippe Bunau-Varilla*, 20. Italics in the original.
40. Matthew Parker, *Panama Fever: The Epic Story of One of the Greatest Human Achievements of All Time—Building of the*

Panama Canal (New York: Doubleday, 2007), xxii.
41. Both quotations from Parker, *Panama Fever*, xxii, citing Austin Harrigan and J.T. Hughes, *Competition for the Best True Stories of Life and Work on the Isthmus of Panama During the Construction of the Panama Canal* (Balboa, Panama: Isthmian Historical Society, 1963), n.p.
42. Anguizola, *Philippe Bunau-Varilla*, 35.
43. James Burke, *Connections* (Boston: Little, Brown & Co., 1978), 239. The doctor who made the suggestion, John Gorrie, didn't take it further, but opted to investigate the disease as resulting from "volatile oil, rising from the swamps and marshes" (Burke, *Connections*, 239). He cooled the temperature in the room for malaria patients and in so doing accidentally created ice-making machines and may have laid the basis for refrigeration.
44. Parker, *Panama Fever*, xxii.
45. Anguizola, *Philippe Bunau-Varilla*, 46.
46. McCullough, *Path Between the Seas*, 95.
47. McCullough, *Path Between the Seas*, 89.
48. Parker, *Panama Fever*, xxiii.
49. Parker, *Panama Fever*, xxiii.
50. Tarrach, "Alexander Pantages," 5.
51. Morgan, *Skid Road*, 151.
52. Morgan, *Skid Road*, 151.
53. Morgan, *Skid Road*, 151.
54. Rockwell D. Hunt, ed., *California and Californians* (San Francisco: Lewis Publishing, 1932), 3.
55. Ben Procter, *William Randolph Hearst: The Early Years, 1863–1910*, 37.
56. W.A. Swanberg, *Citizen Hearst: A Biography of William Randolph Hearst* (New York: Charles Scribner's Sons, 1961), 18.
57. Jules Tygiel, *Workingmen in San Francisco, 1880–1901* (New York: Garland Publishing, 1992), xi.
58. Louis Pizzitola, *Hearst Over Hollywood* (New York: Columbia University Press, 2002), 8.
59. Procter, *William Randolph Hearst*, 37–8.
60. Procter, *William Randolph Hearst*, 37.
61. Procter, *William Randolph Hearst*, 38.
62. Swanberg, *Citizen Hearst*, 18.
63. Pizzitola, *Hearst Over Hollywood*, 8.
64. Swanberg, *Citizen Hearst*, 18.
65. Many Second Wave immigrants between 1880 and 1924 were single men, in contrast to the families that arrived to the American colonies in earlier centuries. For more on this point, please see Edmund S. Morgan, *The Genuine Article: A Historian Looks at Early America* (New York: W.W. Norton, 2004), 47.
66. Morgan, *Skid Road*, 151.
67. Schallert, "Boy's Dream Now Reality," 1.
68. Saloutos, *The Greeks in the United States*, 11.
69. Morgan, *Skid Road*, 151.
70. Morgan, *Skid Road*, 151.
71. Morgan, *Skid Road*, 151.
72. Saloutos, *The Greeks in the United States*, 274–75.
73. Morgan, *Skid Road*, 153–54.
74. Saloutos, *The Greeks in the United States*, 274–75.
75. Tarrach, "Alexander Pantages," 6.
76. Morgan, *Skid Road*, 151.
77. From www.cyberboxingzone.com/boxing/smith-mb.htm.
78. From www.rootsweb.com/~nsdigby/famous/billysmith.htm.
79. Morgan, *Skid Road*, 151–2.
80. Morgan, *Skid Road*, 151–2.
81. "Opium Case on Trial," *San Francisco Examiner*, December 23, 1896, 7.
82. "Pantages to Have a Hearing," *San Francisco Examiner*, December 3, 1896, 16.
83. "Local News Notes," *San Francisco Examiner*, December 8, 1896, 8, and "Opium Case on Trial," *San Francisco Examiner*, December 23, 1896, 7.
84. "Brown Was Guilty," *San Francisco Examiner*, December 24, 1896, 8.
85. "Brown Was Guilty," *San Francisco Examiner*, December 24, 1896, 8.
86. William Randolph Hearst, Jr., with Jack Casserly, *The Hearsts: Father and Son* (Niwot, CO: Roberts Rinehart Publishers, 1991), 12.
87. Judith Robinson, *The Hearsts: An American Dynasty* (Newark, NJ: University of Delaware Press, 1991), 174.
88. Hearst with Casserly, *The Hearsts*, 13.
89. Pizzitola, *Hearst Over Hollywood*, 8.
90. Pizzitola, *Hearst Over Hollywood*, x.
91. Hearst with Casserly, *The Hearsts*, 25. For an example of these college pranks, see Marion Davies, *The Times We Had: Life with William Randolph Hearst* (New York: Ballantine Books, 1975), 11.
92. Hearst with Casserly, *The Hearsts*, 25.
93. Procter, *William Randolph Hearst*, 34.
94. W.A. Swanberg, *Citizen Hearst*, 11.
95. John K. Winkler, *William Randolph Hearst: A New Appraisal* (New York: Hastings House, 1955), from photo caption, n.p.
96. Swanberg, *Citizen Hearst*, 11.
97. Hearst with Casserly, *The Hearsts*, 24. In a calculated act of cruelty for which he

gained a reputation, Hearst made Pulitzer suffer for being his competitor by raiding the other man's reporting staff at a time when the *World*'s publisher was going blind. He had no intention of keeping the reporters he hired, but soon fired them and left them without jobs and unable to go back to their former posts at the *World*. From Ferdinand Lundberg, *Imperial Hearst: A Social Biography* (New York: Equinox Cooperative Press, 1936), 52.

98. Hearst with Casserly, *The Hearsts*, 14.
99. Swanberg, *Citizen Hearst*, 43.
100. "Life of W.R. Hearst, Building of Publishing Empire," *Seattle Post-Intelligencer*, August 15, 1951, 2.
101. Edmund D. Coblentz, ed., *William Randolph Hearst: A Portrait in His Own Words* (New York: Simon & Schuster, 1952), 263.
102. Coblentz, *William Randolph Hearst*, 264.
103. Pizzitola, *Hearst Over Hollywood*, xiii.
104. John Evangelist Walsh, *Walking Shadows: Orson Welles, William Randolph Hearst, and* Citizen Kane (Madison: University Wisconsin Press, 2004), 39.
105. Mrs. Fremont Older, *William Randolph Hearst: American* (New York: D. Appleton-Century Co., 1936), 70.
106. Lundberg, *Imperial Hearst*, 34.
107. Pizzitola, *Hearst Over Hollywood*, 16.
108. Piers Brendon, *The Life and Death of the Press Barons* (New York: Athenaeum, 1983), 134.
109. David Nasaw, *The Chief: The Life of William Randolph Hearst* (Boston: Houghton Mifflin, 2000), 102–3.
110. Marc Norman, *What Happens Next: A History of American Screenwriting* (New York: Harmony Books, 2007), 87.
111. Coblentz, *William Randolph Hearst*, 257.
112. Coblentz, *William Randolph Hearst*, 34.
113. Lundberg, *Imperial Hearst*, 32. Even as the Hearst family used "cheap Chinese labor," Hearst's mother or a family friend could be photographed in a Chinese robe. See Judith Robinson, *The Hearsts*, photographs on 282 and 279.
114. In 1938, Hearst ordered all his newspapers to follow a set of principles that included keeping them free of racial prejudice. From Coblentz, *William Randolph Hearst*, 273.
115. Lundberg, *Imperial Hearst*, 32.
116. Swanberg, *Citizen Hearst*, 45–46.
117. Coblentz, *William Randolph Hearst*, 260.
118. Roy Everett Littlefield, III, *William Randolph Hearst: His Role in American Progressivism* (Lanham, MD: University Press of America, 1980), 6. Hearst was likely a "radical democrat" at the time of his takeover of the *Examiner*, but in his later years he became more staunchly conservative, perhaps even reactionary. This may reflect changing popular public opinion, or it may simply be his developing political outlook that changed as his business empire grew—or likely some combination of both. Hearst was always a skillful self-promoter and his politics reflected this. His radical youth served his newspapers well, since it brought him status and a following among many working-class readers, but later when the tone changed it might have damaged his standing with the working class and probably contributed to his newspapers' difficulties during the Great Depression years.
119. Coblentz, *William Randolph Hearst*, 35.
120. Walsh, *Walking Shadows*, 40.
121. Littlefield, *William Randolph Hearst*, 6.
122. Coblentz, *William Randolph Hearst*, 255.
123. Coblentz, *William Randolph Hearst*, 256.
124. David B. Sachsman, ed., *A Press Divided: Newspaper Coverage of the Civil War* (New Brunswick, NJ: Transaction Publishers, 2014), xi.
125. Littlefield, *William Randolph Hearst*, 115–16.
126. Coblentz, *William Randolph Hearst*, ix.
127. Douglas Fairbanks, Jr., interview, from the documentary "The Battle Over *Citizen Kane*," *The American Experience*, Public Broadcasting System broadcast on January 29, 1996. The irony is that he and/or his lieutenants tried to suppress Orson Welles's *Citizen Kane*, a film that no doubt sought to criticize his career.
128. Pierre Berton, *The Klondike Fever: The Life and Death of the Last Great Gold Rush* (New York: MJF Books, 1958), 104.
129. Berton, *The Klondike Fever*, 104.
130. "Return Laden with Wealth," *San Francisco Examiner*, July 15, 1897, 7. Most other historical accounts peg the arrival of the *Excelsior* on July 15, 1897, but the *Examiner* indicates July 14.
131. "Return Laden," *San Francisco Examiner*, July 15, 1897, 7.
132. Berton, *The Klondike Fever*, 104.
133. "El Dorado in the Icy Yukon Fields," *San Francisco Examiner*, July 16, 1897, 1.

134. The miner with $43,000 worth of gold in the Thursday edition of the *Examiner* now was reappraised at $65,000 on Friday's copy.
135. "El Dorado," *San Francisco Examiner*, July 16, 1897, 1.
136. "El Dorado," *San Francisco Examiner*, July 16, 1897, 1.
137. "El Dorado," *San Francisco Examiner*, July 16, 1897, 1.
138. Alexander Orr, "What the Miners Say," *San Francisco Examiner*, July 16, 1897, 2.
139. Berton, *The Klondike Fever*, 101.
140. Berton, *The Klondike Fever*, 101.
141. Lael Morgan, *Good Time Girls of the Alaska-Yukon Gold Rush* (Fairbanks, AK: Epicenter Press, 1998), 13.
142. David B. Wharton, *The Alaska Gold Rush* (Bloomington: Indiana University Press), 86.
143. Berton, *The Klondike Fever*, 100.
144. Morgan, *Skid Road*, 152.
145. Lucia, *Klondike Kate*, 103.

Chapter 2

1. Pierre Berton, *The Klondike Fever: The Life and Death of the Last Great Gold Rush* (New York: MJF Books, 1958), 96.
2. Berton, *The Klondike Fever*, 96.
3. Berton, *The Klondike Fever*, 96.
4. John Dobson, *Bulls, Bears, Boom, and Bust: A Historical Encyclopedia of American Business Concepts* (Santa Barbara, CA: ABC-CLIO, 2007), 81.
5. Berton, *The Klondike Fever*, 100.
6. Murray Morgan, *Skid Road: An Informal Portrait of Seattle* (Seattle: University of Washington Press, 1982), 152.
7. Alice Scourby, *The Greek Americans* (Boston: Twayne, 1984), 117.
8. David Wharton, *The Alaska Gold Rush* (Bloomington: Indiana University Press, 1972), 8.
9. Stan Cohen, *The Streets Were Paved with Gold* (Missoula, MT: Pictorial Histories Publishing, 2005), 44.
10. Dean Littlepage, *Gold Fever in the North: The Alaska-Yukon Gold Rush Era* (Anchorage, AK: Anchorage Museum of History and Art & Municipality of Anchorage, 1997), 6.
11. Wharton, *Gold Rush*, 8.
12. Wharton, *Gold Rush*, 8.
13. Quote from Littlepage, *Gold Fever in the North*, 5.
14. Wharton, *Gold Rush*, 11.
15. Lael Morgan, *Good Times Girls of the Alaska-Yukon Gold Rush* (Fairbanks, AK: Epicenter Press, 1998), 13.
16. L.E. Bragg, *More Than Petticoats: Remarkable Washington Women* (Guilford, CT: Globe Pequot Press, 1999), 92.
17. Littlepage, *Gold Fever in the North*, 5.
18. Cohen, *The Streets*, 188.
19. Lucia, *Klondike Kate*, 101.
20. Lucia, *Klondike Kate*, 100.
21. William M. Stanley, *A Mile of Gold: Strange Adventures on the Yukon* (Chicago: Laird & Lee, 1898), 199–200.
22. Littlepage, *Gold Fever*, viii.
23. Littlepage, *Gold Fever*, 5.
24. Wharton, *Gold Rush*, 68.
25. Morgan, *Skid Road*, 152.
26. "Month Old P.I. Gave Pantages His Start," *Seattle Post-Intelligencer* (April 9, 1926), from the Fonda WC Scrapbook #1, Suzzallo Special Collections, University of Washington, 173; cited in Dean Arthur Tarrach, "Alexander Pantages: The Seattle Pantages and His Vaudeville Circuit" (M.A. thesis: University of Washington, 1973), 6.
27. Tarrach, "Alexander Pantages," 6. What makes the story improbable is that there would probably have been other passengers besides Pantages who came with newspapers. Why he was chosen to sell his copy is not explained, probably because the story didn't happen.
28. Lucia, *Klondike Kate*, 101.
29. Claire Rudolf Murphy and Jane G. Haigh, *Gold Rush Women* (Anchorage: Alaska Northwest Books, 1997), 40.
30. Morgan, *Skid Road*, 152.
31. Wharton, *Gold Rush*, 87.
32. Murphy and Haigh, *Gold Rush Women*, 53.
33. Morgan, *Skid Road*, 152.
34. Lucia, *Klondike Kate*, 98. See also Morgan, *Good Time Girls*, 146, for reference to Pantages's "swarthy complexion."
35. Kenneth Anger, *Hollywood Babylon II* (New York: E.P. Dutton, 1984), 39.
36. David E. Koskoff, *Joseph P. Kennedy: A Life and Times* (Englewood Cliffs, NJ: Prentice-Hall, 1974), 14.
37. Ronald Kessler, *The Sins of the Father: Joseph P. Kennedy and the Dynasty He Founded* (New York: Warner Books, 1996), 16.
38. Koskoff, *Joseph P. Kennedy*, 14–15.
39. David Nasaw, *The Patriarch: The Remarkable Life and Turbulent Times of Joseph P. Kennedy* (New York: Penguin, 2012), 13.
40. Koskoff, *Joseph P. Kennedy*, 13.
41. Rose Fitzgerald Kennedy, *Times to Remember* (Garden City, NY: Doubleday, 1974), 57.

42. Cari Beauchamp, *Joseph P. Kennedy Presents: His Hollywood Years* (New York: Alfred A. Knopf, 2009), 5.
43. Nasaw, *The Patriarch,* 14.
44. Kessler, *The Sins of the Father,* 14.
45. Laurence Leamer, *The Kennedy Men* (New York: William Morrow, 2001), 9.
46. Leamer, *The Kennedy Men,* 9.
47. Kessler, *The Sins of the Father,* 14.
48. Beauchamp, *Joseph P. Kennedy Presents,* 5.
49. Beauchamp, *Joseph P. Kennedy Presents,* 5.
50. Swanberg, *Citizen Hearst,* 125.
51. Swanberg, *Citizen Hearst,* photo caption, 238–39.
52. Kenneth Whyte, *The Uncrowned King: The Sensational Rise of William Randolph Hearst* (Berkeley, CA: Counterpoint, 2009), 92.
53. Whyte, *The Uncrowned King,* 314.
54. David S. Sachsman and David W. Bulla, eds. *Sensationalism: Murder, Mayhem, Mudslinging, Scandals, and Disasters in 19th-Century Reporting* (New Brunswick, NJ: Transaction Publishers, 2013), xx.
55. Ben Procter, *William Randolph Hearst: The Early Years, 1863–1910* (New York: Oxford University Press, 1998),74.
56. Piers Brendon, *The Life and Death of the Press Barons* (New York: Athenaeum, 1983), 134.
57. Procter, *William Randolph Hearst,* 99–100.
58. David Nasaw, *The Chief: The Life of William Randolph Hearst* (Boston: Houghton Mifflin, 2000), 102–3.
59. Marc Norman, *What Happens Next: A History of American Screenwriting* (New York: Harmony Books, 2007), 87.
60. Ambrose Bierce quote cited in Philip J. Ethington, *The Public City: The Political Construction of Urban Life in San Francisco, 1850–1900* (Cambridge, UK: Cambridge University Press, 1994), 317.
61. Oliver Carlson and Ernest Sutherland Bates, *Hearst: Lord of San Simeon* (New York: Viking Press, 1936), 94.
62. Procter, *William Randolph Hearst,* 102.
63. Procter, *William Randolph Hearst,* 102.
64. Procter, *William Randolph Hearst,* 102.
65. W.A. Swanberg, *Citizen Hearst: A Biography of William Randolph Hearst* (New York: Charles Scribner's Sons, 1961), 119.
66. Kristin L. Hoganson, *Fighting for American Manhood: How Gender Politics Provoked the Spanish-American and Philippine-American Wars* (New Haven, CT: Yale University Press, 1998), 4.
67. Swanberg, *Citizen Hearst,* 117.
68. Hoganson, *Fighting for American Manhood,* 11.
69. William Randolph Hearst, Jr., with Jack Casserly, *The Hearsts: Father and Son* (Niwot, CO: Robert Rinehart, 1991), 42.
70. Carlson and Bates, *Hearst,* 92.
71. Nasaw, *The Chief,* 126.
72. Swanberg, *Citizen Hearst,* 117.
73. Procter, *William Randolph Hearst,* 104.
74. Hearst, Jr., with Jack Casserly, *The Hearsts,* 37.
75. Hoganson, *Fighting for American Manhood,* 10.
76. Hoganson, *Fighting for American Manhood,* 11.
77. Hoganson, *Fighting for American Manhood,* 11.
78. Roger Daniels, *The Politics of Prejudice* (New York: Atheneum, 1970), 66.
79. Hoganson, *Fighting for American Manhood,* 3.
80. Hearst, Jr., with Casserly, *The Hearsts,* 38.
81. Swanberg, *Citizen Hearst,* 120.
82. Swanberg, *Citizen Hearst,* 120.
83. Swanberg, *Citizen Hearst,* 124.
84. Judith Robinson, *The Hearsts: An American Dynasty* (Newark: University of Delaware Press, 1991), 324.
85. *New York Journal* (August 17, 1897), cited in Swanberg, *Citizen Hearst,* 120.
86. Swanberg, *Citizen Hearst,* 124.
87. Willis Abbot, *Watching the World Go By* (Boston: Little, Brown, 1933), 216, cited in Roy Everett Littlefield III, *William Randolph Hearst: His Role in American Progressivism* (Lanham, MD: University Press of America, 1980), 45.
88. Abbot, cited in Littlefield, *William Randolph Hearst,* 45.
89. Helen MacGill Hughes, *News and the Human Interest Story* (Chicago: University of Chicago Press, 1940), 269.
90. Swanberg, *Citizen Hearst,* 122.
91. Cited in Swanberg, *Citizen Hearst,* 120.
92. Swanberg, *Citizen Hearst,* 123.
93. Mrs. Fremont Older, *William Randolph Hearst: American* (New York: D. Appleton-Century Co., 1936), 182.
94. W. Joseph Campbell, "Not a Hoax: New Evidence in the *New York Journal's* Rescue of Evangelina Cisneros," in *American Journalism,* 2002, 19:4, 71 and 75.
95. Littlefield, *William Randolph Hearst,* 46.
96. Campbell, *American Journalism,* 68. "This article's conclusions," the author states, "also make clear that the Cisneros case was

far more complex, and far more important to U.S. diplomatic officials in Cuba, than previously understood" (70).
97. Edmond D. Coblentz, *William Randolph Hearst: A Portrait in His Own Words* (New York: Simon & Schuster, 1952), 58.
98. Littlefield, *William Randolph Hearst*, 43.
99. Hearst, Jr., with Casserly, *The Hearsts*, 37.
100. Ferdinand Lundberg, *Imperial Hearst: A Social Biography* (New York: Equinox Cooperative Press, 1936), 66.
101. W. Joseph Campbell, *The Year That Defined American Journalism: 1897 and the Clash of Paradigms* (New York: Routledge, 2006), xiii.
102. Littlefield, *William Randolph Hearst*, 48.
103. Coblentz, *William Randolph Hearst*, 54–57.
104. Robinson, *The Hearsts*, 325–26.
105. *New York World*, June 9, 1898, cited in Littlefield, *William Randolph Hearst*, 50.
106. Littlefield, *William Randolph Hearst*, 50.
107. Littlefield, *William Randolph Hearst*, 52.
108. Littlefield, *William Randolph Hearst*, 52–53.
109. "The Journal's Rescue of Evangelina Cisneros," *New York Journal* (October 11, 1897): 6, cited in Campbell, *American Journalism*, 74.
110. "Beyond Weyler's Reach," *New York Journal* (October 12, 1897): 6, cited in Campbell, *American Journalism*, 74.
111. Lindsay Chaney and Michael Cieply, *The Hearsts: Family and Empire: The Later Years* (New York: Simon & Schuster, 1981), 37.
112. *San Francisco Examiner* (March 1, 1987), 1, cited in Hearst, Jr., with Casserly, *The Hearsts*, inside front jacket.
113. Chaney and Cieply, *The Hearsts*, 35.
114. Morgan, *Skid Road*, 152.
115. Lucia, *Klondike Kate*, 104.
116. Saloutos, *The Greeks*, 275.
117. Morgan *Skid Road*, 153.
118. Morgan, *Skid Road*, 153.
119. Morgan, *Skid Road*, 153.
120. Morgan, *Skid Road*, 153.
121. Lucia, *Klondike Kate*, 104.
122. Morgan, *Skid Road*, 153.
123. Morgan, *Skid Road*, 153.
124. Lucia, *Klondike Kate*, 105.
125. Morgan, *Skid Road*, 153.
126. Morgan, *Good Time Girls*, 148.
127. Morgan, *Good Time Girls*, 148.
128. Morgan, *Good Time Girls*, 148.
129. Cohen, *The Streets Were Paved with Gold*, 185.
130. Lucia, *Klondike Kate*, 28.
131. Val Dumond and Babe Lehrer, *Mush On and Smile* (Tacoma, WA: Muddy Puddle Press, 2002), 282.
132. Lucia, *Klondike Kate*, 31.
133. Lucia, *Klondike Kate*, 33.
134. The story varies according to the source, but this version is from Bragg, *More Than Petticoats*, 85.
135. Murphy and Haigh, *Gold Rush Women*, 75.
136. Bragg, *More Than Petticoats*, 93.
137. Murphy and Haigh, *Gold Rush Women*, 75.
138. Morgan, *Good Time Girls*, 148.
139. Lucia, *Klondike Kate*, 101, and Bragg, *More than Petticoats*, 97.
140. "Pantages Rose from Klondike Dive to Riches," *Seattle Times*, October 28, 1929, 8.
141. "Pantages Rose," *Seattle Times*, October 28, 1929, 8.
142. Lucia, *Klondike Kate*, 107.
143. Lucia, *Klondike Kate*, 107.
144. Morgan, *Good Time Girls*, 149.
145. Lucia, *Klondike Kate*, 108.
146. Lucia, *Klondike Kate*, 122.
147. See T. Ann Brennan, *The Real Klondike Kate* (Fredericton, Canada: Goose Lane, 1990).
148. Lucia, *Klondike Kate*, 94.
149. Trav S.D., *No Applause—Just Throw Money; or the Book That Made Vaudeville Famous* (New York: Faber & Faber, 2005), 4. The book is amusing, even whimsical, yet informative.
150. Frank Cullen, with Florence Hackman and Donald McNeilly, *Vaudeville, Old and New: An Encyclopedia of Variety Performers in America, Volume 1* (New York: Routledge, 2007), xi.
151. Cullen et al., *Vaudeville*, xiv.
152. Cullen et al., *Vaudeville*, xxxvii.
153. S.D. Trav, *No Applause*, 6.
154. S.D. Trav, *No Applause*, 7.
155. S.D. Trav, *No Applause*, 11.
156. Cullen, *Vaudeville, Old and New*, 717.
157. Cullen, *Vaudeville, Old and New*, 1051.
158. Lucia, *Klondike Kate*, 19.
159. Dumond and Lehrer, *Mush On*, 2.
160. Murphy and Haigh, *Gold Rush Women*, 75.
161. "Pantages Rose," *Seattle Times*, October 28, 1929, 8.
162. "Pantages Rose," *Seattle Times*, October 28, 1929, 8.

163. "Pantages Rose," *Seattle Times*, October 28, 1929, 8.
164. Murphy and Haigh, *Gold Rush Women*, 75.
165. Murphy and Haigh, *Gold Rush Women*, 75.
166. Cullen et al. have Pantages's first theater called the "Klondyke Theater." In *Vaudeville*, xvii.
167. Morgan, *Good Time Girls*, 149.
168. Murphy and Haigh, *Gold Rush Women*, 75.
169. Morgan, *Good Time Girls*, 149.
170. "Pantages Rose," *Seattle Times*, October 28, 1929, 8.

Chapter 3

1. It was not by coincidence that after her vaudeville career ended, Rockwell spent considerable time in a lonely cabin in a barren part of eastern Oregon.
2. Lael Morgan, *Good Time Girls of the Alaska-Yukon Gold Rush* (Fairbanks, AK: Epicenter Press, 1998), 149.
3. Morgan, *Good Time Girls*, 150.
4. Morgan, *Good Time Girls*, 149.
5. Morgan, *Good Time Girls*, 150.
6. Ellis Lucia, *Klondike Kate: The Life and Legend of Kitty Rockwell, the Queen of the Yukon* (New York: Hastings House Publishers, 1962), 136.
7. Lucia, *Klondike Kate*, 136.
8. Interestingly, the Crystal does not appear in Polk's *City Directory* until the 1904 edition (1423).
9. Lucia, *Klondike Kate*, 135.
10. Morgan, *Good Time Girls*, 150.
11. Morgan, *Good Time Girls*, 150.
12. Lucia, *Klondike Kate*, 136.
13. Morgan, *Good Time Girls*, 149.
14. Morgan, *Good Time Girls*, 152.
15. Morgan, *Good Time Girls*, 150–51.
16. Lucia, *Klondike Kate*, 138.
17. Morgan, *Good Time Girls*, 151.
18. Morgan, *Good Time Girls*, 151.
19. Morgan, *Good Time Girls*, 151.
20. T. Ann Brennan, *The Real Klondike Kate* (Fredericton, Canada: Goose Lane Editions, 1990), 141.
21. Lucia, *Klondike Kate*, 138.
22. Morgan, *Good Time Girls*, 152.
23. Lucia, *Klondike Kate*, 141.
24. Lucia, *Klondike Kate*, 141.
25. "Uses Her Money, Then Jilts the Girl," *Seattle Times*, May 26, 1905, 1.
26. "Uses Her Money, Then Jilts the Girl," *Seattle Times*, May 26, 1905, 2.
27. Brennan, *The Real Klondike Kate*, 141.
28. Morgan, *Good Time Girls*, 153. In Rockwell's biography, it was stated that the amount was "less than $5,000" (Lucia, *Klondike Kate*, 149).
29. Lucia, *Klondike Kate*, 149.
30. She homesteaded on property "forty miles east of Bend and three miles northeast of ... Brothers" (Lucia, *Klondike Kate*, 166).
31. Murray Morgan, *Skid Road: An Informal Portrait of Seattle* (Seattle: University of Washington Press, 1982), 79.
32. Morgan, *Skid Road*, 79.
33. Eugene Clinton Elliott, *A History of Variety-Vaudeville in Seattle: From the Beginning to 1914* (Seattle: University of Washington Press, 1944), 51.
34. Morgan, *Skid Road*, 154.
35. Don Duncan, "Meet Mr. Architect," *Seattle Times*, January 24, 1971, *Charmed Land Magazine*, 4.
36. Elliott, *A History of Variety-Vaudeville*, 45.
37. Elliott, *A History of Variety-Vaudeville* 58.
38. Elliott, *A History of Variety-Vaudeville*, 58.
39. Frank Lynch, "Seattle Scene: The Golf Date that Saved a Life," *Seattle Post-Intelligencer*, August 15, 1951, 15.
40. Lynch, "Seattle Scene," 15.
41. Taso G. Lagos, "Film Exhibition in Seattle, 1897–1912: Leisure Activity in a Scraggly, Smelly Frontier Town," *Historical Journal of Film, Radio and Television* 23, No. 2 (2003): 102.
42. William Arnold, "A Century of Movies in Seattle," *Seattle Post-Intelligencer*, November 16, 1998, D1.
43. Quote from Kenneth Clark, *Civilisation*, BBC-TV Series, 1969, Episode 13, 33:05.
44. "Edison's Vitascope Cheered," *New York Times*, April 24, 1896, 5.
45. David Puttnam, *Movies and Money* (New York: Alfred A. Knopf, 1998), 13.
46. Arnold, "A Century of Movies," November 16, 1998, D1.
47. Arnold, "A Century of Movies," November 16, 1998, D1.
48. Karla Stover, *Tacoma Curiosities: Geoduck Derbies, the Whistling Well of the North End, Alligators in Snake Lake and More* (Charleston, SC: The History Press, 2016), 41.
49. Stover, *Tacoma Curiosities*, 41.
50. Stover, *Tacoma Curiosities*, 41.
51. Polk's *City Directory* for 1911 lists, in the "Theatres—Motion Pictures" section, an operation under the name of "Glisa Tovanovitz" at 1408 Third Avenue, and "Mrs. Marie Marcello" for one at 408 Fifth Avenue

Notes—Chapter 3

South. Polk's City Directory (Seattle: Polk's Seattle Directory Co., 1911), 1999.

52. From http://www.pontchartrain.net/495433.

53. Stover, *Tacoma Curiosities*, 41.

54. Census figures from U.S. Census Bureau at www.census.gov/population/www/documentation/twps0027/tab13.txt.

55. Elliott, *A History of Variety-Vaudeville in Seattle*, 37.

56. Elliott, *A History of Variety-Vaudeville in Seattle*, 60.

57. Elliott, *A History of Variety-Vaudeville in Seattle*, 63.

58. Polk's City Directory (Seattle: Polk's Seattle Directory Co., 1911), 1423.

59. Frank Cullen with Florence Hackman and Donald McNeilly, *Vaudeville, Old and New: An Encyclopedia of Variety Performers in America* (New York: Routledge, 2007), V2,863.

60. "Opening of the New Pantages Theater," *Seattle Times*, October 8, 1907, 5.

61. "Opening of the New Pantages Theater," *Seattle Times*, October 8, 1907, 5.

62. See, for example, the real estate advertisement in the *Seattle Daily Times*, May 29, 1902, 8.

63. Elliott, *A History of Variety-Vaudeville in Seattle*, 63.

64. Elliott, *A History of Variety-Vaudeville in Seattle*, 63.

65. Daniel Czitrom, "Early Motion Pictures," in *Communication in History*, ed. David Crowley and David Heyer (Boston: Allyn & Bacon, 2007), 178.

66. Dean Arthur Tarrach, "Alexander Pantages: The Seattle Pantages and His Vaudeville Circuit" (M.A. thesis: University of Washington, 1973), 22–23.

67. Frank Cullen et al., *Vaudeville, Old and New*, V1, xxxix.

68. "Pantages Banquets Actors After Tiring Performances," *Los Angeles Times*, April 6, 1911, III:3.

69. "Pantages, His Warring Style," *Los Angeles Times*, March 13, 1912, III:4.

70. "Warring Style," *Los Angeles Times*, March 13, 1912, III:4.

71. "Warring Style," *Los Angeles Times*, March 13, 1912, III:4.

72. Lawrence Kreisman, "Curtain Up," *Seattle Post-Intelligencer*, May 6, 1990, *Pacific Magazine* insert, 25.

73. John Reddin, "'Benny' Priteca About to Lose Happy Home," *Seattle Times*, September 27, 1964, 33.

74. Reddin, *Seattle Times*, 33.

75. Duncan, *Seattle Times*, 4.

76. Reddin, *Seattle Times*, 33.

77. Reddin, *Seattle Times*, 33.

78. Clarence Bagley, "B. Marcus Priteca," in *The History of King County, Washington, Volume II* (Seattle: S.J. Clarke Publishing, 1929), 443.

79. Duncan, *Seattle Times*, 4.

80. Duncan, *Seattle Times*, 4.

81. Kreisman, *Seattle Post-Intelligencer*, 25.

82. Arnold, "A Century of Movies," November 16, 1998, D1.

83. Quote from Puget Sound Theater Organ Society site, www.pstos.org/instruments/wa/seattle/clemmer.htm.

84. Bagley, "B. Marcus Priteca," V2, 443.

85. Sally Dunstan, "Either Palomor and Pantages, She Was a Jewel," *Seattle Times* (March 23, 1965): *Charmed Land Magazine*, insert, 10.

86. Mariam Sutermeister, "B. Marcus Priteca," in *Shaping Seattle Architecture: A Historical Guide to the Architects*, ed. Jeffrey Karl Ochsner (Seattle: University of Washington Press, 1994), 181.

87. Duncan, *Seattle Times*, 4.

88. Duncan, *Seattle Times*, 4.

89. Duncan, *Seattle Times*, 4.

90. In Anderson vs. Pantages Theatre Company, 114 Washington 24 (1921), an African American attorney sued when he and two friends purchased box tickets to a Pantages theater but were refused seating in the box. Case found at: http://courts.mrsc.org/washreports/114WashReport/114WashReport0024.htm.

91. Eric L. Flom, "B. Marcus Priteca," Cyperpedia Library, www.historylink.org/index.cfm?DisplayPage=output.cfm&file_id=8815.

92. Sutermeister, "B. Marcus Priteca," 182.

93. Kenneth Anger, *Hollywood Babylon II* (New York: E.P. Hutton, 1984), 29.

94. "Starting Big New Theater," *Los Angeles Times*, January 24, 1919, II:1.

95. "New Theater," *Los Angeles Times*, January 24, 1919, II:1. Pantages's original plan to build the Salt Lake City theater were halted at the request of the War Industries Board on account of World War I. It was built after the war ("Pantages Asked to Halt Big Theater Job," *Los Angeles Times*, September 7, 1918, II:1).

96. Sutermeister, "B. Marcus Priteca," 182.

97. Sutermeister, "B. Marcus Priteca," 182.

98. Sutermeister, "B. Marcus Priteca," 182.

99. Jackie McDermott, "Priteca," in *Intermission: Featuring Original Drawings of B. Marcus Priteca*, program for the Architectural Secretaries Association Annual Fundraiser, November 29, 1973.

100. McDermott, *Intermission*.

101. McDermott, *Intermission*.
102. Roger Daniels, *Coming to America: A History of Immigration and Ethnicity in American Life* (New York: Perennial, 2002), 3.
103. Edward J. Erler, Thomas G. West, and John Marini, *The Founders on Citizenship and Immigration: Principles and Challenges in America* (Lanham, MD: Rowman & Littlefield, 2007), 108.
104. Daniels, *Coming to America*, 275.
105. Michael Schudson and Susan E. Tifft, "American Journalism in Historical Perspective," in *The Press*, ed. Geneva Overholser and Kathleen Hall Jamieson (Oxford: Oxford University Press, 2005), 22.
106. Al Sandine, *The Taming of the American Crowd* (New York: Monthly Review Press, 2009), 52.
107. Martin B. Gold, *Forbidden Citizens: Chinese Exclusion and the U.S. Congress: A Legislative History* (Alexandria, VA: The Capitol.Net, 2012), 8.
108. Gold, *Forbidden Citizens*, 11.
109. Michael Schudson and Susan E. Tifft, "American Journalism in Historical Perspective," in *The Press*, ed. Geneva Overholser and Kathleen Hall Jamieson (Oxford: Oxford University Press, 2005), 20, 22.
110. Carola Suárez-Orozco, "Identities Under Siege: Immigration Stress and Social Mirroring among the Children of Immigrants," in *The New Immigration: An Interdisciplinary Reader*, ed. Marcelo M. Suárez-Orozco, Carola Suárez-Orozco, and Desiree Qin-Hilliard (New York: Routledge, 2005), 144–45. Note the capitalization of "Northern" Europe unlike its southern and eastern counterparts.
111. Suárez-Orozco, "Identities Under Siege," 145.
112. Erika Lee, "A Nation of Immigrants and a Gatekeeping Nation: American Immigration Law and Policy," in *A Companion to American Immigration*, ed. Reed Ueda (Malden, MA: Blackwell), 11–12.
113. Lee, "Immigrants," 20.
114. Lee, "Immigrants," 20.
115. Lee, "Immigrants," 20.
116. Daniels, *Coming to America*, 122.
117. It should be noted that the heaviest amount of immigration on a per capita basis in the United States was in 1854 when a million foreigners entered the country at a time when the nation's population was 25 million, or roughly at a rate of twenty per thousand, or 2 percent of the total population. See Daniels, *Coming to America*, 124.
118. Dan Georgakas, "Greek American Radicalism: The Twentieth Century," *Journal of Hellenic Diaspora* 20 (1994): 9.
119. Zeese Papanikolas, *Buried Unsung* (Lincoln: University of Nebraska Press, 1991), 9.
120. Papanikolas, *Buried*, 9. See also Charles Moskos, *Greek Americans: Struggle and Success* (New Brunswick, NJ: Transaction Publishers, 2002), 6.
121. Papanikolas, *Buried*, 9.
122. E.D. Karampetsos, "Nativism in Nevada: Greek Immigrants in White Pine County," *Journal of the Hellenic Diaspora* 24 (1998): 62.
123. Karampetsos, "Nativism in Nevada," 66.
124. Karampetsos, "Nativism in Nevada," 62.
125. Helen Zeese Papanikolas, *Toil and Rage in a New Land: The Greek Immigrants in Utah* (Salt Lake City: Utah Historical Society, 1974) 138, quoted in Moskos, *Greek Americans*, 16.
126. Helen Z. Papanikolas, "Magerou: The Greek Midwife," *Utah Historical Quarterly*, 38, No. 1 (Winter 1950): 59.
127. Daniels, *Coming to America*, 276.
128. Prescott F. Hall cited in Daniels, *Coming to America*, 276.
129. Michael R. Olneck, "Americanization and the Education of Immigrants, 1900–1925: An Analysis of Symbolic Action," *American Journal of Education* 97 (August 1989): 402.
130. Georgakas, "Greek American Radicalism," 8.
131. Daniels, *Coming to America*, 276.
132. Kristin L. Hoganson, *Fighting for American Manhood: How Gender Politics Provoked the Spanish-American and Philippine-American Wars* (New Haven, CT: Yale University Press, 1998), 10.
133. Krishnendu Ray, *The Ethnic Restaurateur* (London and New York: Bloomsbury, 2016), p. 108.
134. Matthew Frye Jacobson, *Whiteness of a Different Color: European Immigrants and the Alchemy of Race* (Cambridge, MA: Harvard University Press, 1999), 5.
135. Ray, *Restaurateur*, 109.
136. Taso G. Lagos, "Poor Greek to 'Scandalous' Hollywood Mogul: Alexander Pantages and the Anti-Immigrant Narratives of William Randolph Hearst's *Los Angeles Examiner*," *Journal of Modern Greek Studies* 30 (May 2012): 46.
137. Lagos, "Poor Greek," 46.
138. Yiorgos Anagnostou, *The Contours of White Ethnicity: Popular Ethnography and the Making of Usable Past in Greek America* (Athens: Ohio University Press, 2009), 10–11.
139. Anagnostou, *White Ethnicity*, 48.
140. Moskos, *Greek Americans*, 6.

Chapter 4

1. That monopoly control, in which film studios owned the means of production, distribution, and exhibition, formally ended with the Paramount Consent Decrees in 1948. Under President Roland Reagan in the 1980s, the prohibition against movie theater ownership of movie theaters was relaxed and once more Hollywood came to exert monopoly control over film production.
2. It is now part of an apartment complex, the Pantages Apartments. The house was designated a historical landmark in 2004 by the Seattle Landmarks Board.
3. Dean Arthur Tarrach, "Alexander Pantages: The Seattle Pantages and His Vaudeville Circuit" (M.A. thesis: University of Washington, 1973), 12.
4. Dorothea Mootafes, Theodora Dracopoulos Argue, Paul Plumis, Perry Scarlatos, and Peggy Falangus Tramountanas, eds., *A History of Saint Demetrios Greek Orthodox Church and Her People, 1882–1999* (Seattle: Saint Demetrios Greek Orthodox Church, 2007), 60.
5. Mootafes et al., *Saint Demetrios*, 41.
6. Mootafes et al., *Saint Demetrios*, 60 and 64.
7. Mootafes et al., *Saint Demetrios*, 60–61.
8. Warren Eugene Crane, "Alexander Pantages," *System: The Magazine of Business* (March 1920): 502.
9. Crane, "Alexander Pantages," 502.
10. Crane, "Alexander Pantages," 503.
11. Tarrach, "Alexander Pantages," 12–13.
12. Tarrach, "Alexander Pantages," 18.
13. "Alex Pantages Here Planning Film Conquest," *Seattle Post-Intelligencer*, August 18, 1925, 1.
14. "That New Templar Speedster," *Los Angeles Times*, October 26, 1919, VI:6.
15. Eugene Clinton Elliott, *A History of Variety-Vaudeville in Seattle: From the Beginning to 1914* (Seattle: University of Washington Press, 1944), 53.
16. "Mrs. Pantages Sought Divorce," *Los Angeles Examiner*, Friday, September 20, 1929, 4.
17. Tarrach, "Alexander Pantages," 61–62.
18. Dan Georgakas, "Greek-American Radicalism: The Twentieth Century," *Journal of Hellenic Diaspora* 20, No. 1 (1994): 7.
19. Joseph H. Pleck, "American Fathering in Historical Perspective," in *Families in the U.S.: Kinship and Domestic Politics* (Philadelphia: Temple University Press, 1998), 354.
20. Pleck, "American Fathering," 354.
21. Maury Klein, *Rainbow's End: The Crash of 1929* (New York: Oxford University Press, 2001), 119.
22. Klein, *Crash*, 119.
23. Klein, *Crash*, 104.
24. Klein, *Crash*, 104.
25. Klein, *Crash*, 102.
26. Tarrach, "Alexander Pantages," 49. Washington became the 42nd state on November 11, 1889.
27. Tarrach, "Alexander Pantages," 50.
28. "The United States was rapidly becoming a more urban nation; the proportion of Americans living in large cities of one hundred thousand or more people climbed from 20 to 25 percent between 1900 and 1920" (Kathryn H. Fuller, *At the Picture Show* [Washington, DC: Smithsonian Institution Press, 1996], 3).
29. Fuller, *At the Picture Show*, x.
30. Fuller, *At the Picture Show*, xiii.
31. Fuller, *At the Picture Show*, 3.
32. Terry Ramsaye, *A Million and One Nights* (New York: Simon & Schuster, 1926), 483.
33. Marc Norman, *What Happens Next: A History of American Screenwriting* (New York: Harmony Books, 2007), 92.
34. Kirsten Ostherr, *Cinematic Prophylaxis: Globalization and the Contagion in the Discourse of World Health* (Durham, NC: Duke University Press, 2005), 29.
35. Ostherr, *Cinematic Prophylaxis*, 29.
36. David A. Yallop, *The Day the Laughter Stopped: The True Story of Fatty Arbuckle* (New York: St. Martin's Press, 1976), 94.
37. Robert Sklar, *Movie-Made America* (New York: Vintage Books, 1994), 137.
38. Alexander Walker, *Sex in the Movies: The Celluloid Sacrifice* (Baltimore: Penguin Books, 1966), 23.
39. Klein, *Crash*, 114.
40. Yallop, *the Day the Laughter Stopped*, 94.
41. Greg Merritt, *Room 1219: The Life of Fatty Arbuckle, the Mysterious Death of Virginia Rappe, and the Scandal That Changed Hollywood* (Chicago: Chicago Review Press, 2013), 1.
42. Merritt, *Room 1219*, 2.
43. Quoted in Merritt, *Room 1219*, 5.
44. Rappe's age is given in most accounts as being around twenty-six; Merritt claims she had turned thirty that summer. Merritt, *Room 1219*, 9.
45. "Arbuckle Is Charged with Murder of Girl; Actress' Dying Words Cause Star's Arrest," *San Francisco Examiner*, September 11, 1921, 1.
46. "Arbuckle Is Charged," *San Francisco Examiner*, September 11, 1921, 1.

47. "Arbuckle Is Charged," *San Francisco Examiner*, September 11, 1921, 1.
48. Yallop, *The Day the Laughter Stopped*, 85.
49. "Arbuckle Always Keen for Parties, Say Friends," *San Francisco Examiner*, September 11, 1921, 3.
50. "Arbuckle Always Keen," *San Francisco Examiner*, September 11, 1921, 3.
51. "Arbuckle Always Keen," *San Francisco Examiner*, September 11, 1921, 3.
52. "Miss Rappe Was Designer, Film Actress," *San Francisco Examiner*, September 11, 1921, 3.
53. "Girl Rational When She Named Actor, Says Nurse," *San Francisco Examiner*, September 11, 1921, 1.
54. "Girl Rational," *San Francisco Examiner*, September 11, 1921, 1.
55. "Girl Rational," *San Francisco Examiner*, September 11, 1921, 1.
56. "Girl Rational," *San Francisco Examiner*, September 11, 1921, 1.
57. "Film Star Is Firm in Refusal to Break Silence to Police," *San Francisco Examiner*, September 11, 1921, 2.
58. "Remains of Miss Rappe at Morgue," *San Francisco Examiner*, September 11, 1921, 3.
59. "Arbuckle Film Withdrawn at Two Theaters," *San Francisco Examiner*, September 11, 1921, 3.
60. "Palace Hotel Bars Arbuckle as Guest," *San Francisco Examiner*, September 11, 1921, 3.
61. "Brady Asks Arbuckle Indictment Today; Witnesses Guarded, Intimidation Feared," *San Francisco Examiner*, September 12, 1921, 1.
62. "Brady Asks Arbuckle," *San Francisco Examiner*, September 12, 1921, 1.
63. "Brady Asks Arbuckle," *San Francisco Examiner*, September 12, 1921, 1.
64. "Brady Asks Arbuckle," *San Francisco Examiner*, September 12, 1921, 1.
65. "Dead Girl's Fiance Calls, He Says," *San Francisco Examiner*, September 12, 1921, 1.
66. "Dead Girl's Fiance," *San Francisco Examiner*, September 12, 1921, 1.
67. "Day in Jail Is Blue Sunday for Arbuckle," *San Francisco Examiner*, Monday, September 12, 1921, 1.
68. "Day in Jail," *San Francisco Examiner*, September 12, 1921, 1.
69. "Day in Jail," *San Francisco Examiner*, September 12, 1921, 1.
70. "'Mystery Girl' Defends Film Star 'He Has Always Been a Gentleman,'" *San Francisco Examiner*, Monday, September 12, 1921, 2.
71. "Woman's Vigilant Committee," *San Francisco Examiner*, September 13, 1921, 3.
72. "They Walked Into His Parlor," *San Francisco Examiner*, September 15, 1921, 1.
73. "Manslaughter Laid to Arbuckle at Inquest," *San Francisco Examiner*, September 15, 1921, 1.
74. "Vigilant Women Condemn Wild Orgy of Arbuckle," *San Francisco Examiner*, Thursday, September 15, 1921, 1.
75. "Beauty Linked with Tragedy," *San Francisco Examiner*, September 15, 1921, 1.
76. "'Fatty's Movie Days Over,' Says Film Man," *San Francisco Examiner*, September 15, 1921, 3.
77. "Before the Fatal Trip," photograph, *San Francisco Examiner*, September 15, 1921, 3.
78. "Cowboys Mob Arbuckle Film," *San Francisco Examiner*, September 18, 3.
79. "Arbuckle Gives Bail for Manslaughter," *San Francisco Examiner*, Thursday, September 29, 2.
80. "Warrant for Maud Delmont," *San Francisco Examiner*, November 19, 1921, 5.
81. Oscar H. Fernbach, "Arbuckle to Face Trial in Court Today," *San Francisco Examiner*, Thursday, November 14, 1921, 1.
82. Walter Vogdes, "Actor Least Conspicuous at His Trial," *San Francisco Examiner*, Wednesday, November 16, 1921, 6.
83. Walter Vogdes, "'Pawns' Move in Arbuckle Case Slowly," *San Francisco Examiner*, Friday, November 18, 1921, 4.
84. Oscar H. Fernbach, "Zey Prevost, Alice Blake in Witness Chair," *San Francisco Examiner*, Friday, November 18, 1921, 4.
85. Walter Vodges, "By the House They Listen to Zey Prevost," *San Francisco Examiner*, Tuesday, November 22, 1921, 4.
86. Oscar H. Fernbach, "Miss Rappe's Actions Told by Companions," *San Francisco Examiner*, Saturday, November 24, 1921, 4.
87. Fernbach, "Miss Rappe's Actions," *San Francisco Examiner*, November 24, 1921, 4.
88. Oscar H. Fernbach, "Defense Ends with Arbuckle on Stand," *San Francisco Examiner*, Tuesday, November 29, 1921, 1.
89. Fernbach, "Defense Ends," *San Francisco Examiner*, November 29, 1921, 1.
90. Fernbach, "Defense Ends," *San Francisco Examiner*, November 29, 1921, 1.
91. "Comedian Gets Handshake," photo, *San Francisco Examiner*, December 1, 1921, 6.
92. Oscar H. Fernbach, "11 Arbuckle Jurors Await Challenges," *San Francisco Examiner*, January 13, 1922, 1.
93. Oscar H. Fernbach, "Zey Prevost Up-

sets Trial of Arbuckle," *San Francisco Examiner*, January 29, 1922, 1.
94. "Chronological History of Actor's Case," *San Francisco Examiner*, April 13, 1922, 1.
95. "Jurors Write Exoneration," *San Francisco Examiner*, April 13, 1922, 1.
96. "Ratification of the Verdict," photo, *San Francisco Examiner*, April 13, 1922, 3.
97. Stuart Oderman, *Roscoe "Fatty" Arbuckle: A Biography of the Silent Film Comedian, 1887–1933* (Jefferson, NC: McFarland, 2005), 43.

Chapter 5

1. Edwin Schallert, "Boy's Dream Now Reality," *Los Angeles Times*, August 15, 1920, III:1.
2. Schallert, "Boy's Dream," *Los Angeles Times*, August 15, 1920, III:1.
3. Schallert, "Boy's Dream," *Los Angeles Times*, August 15, 1920, III:14.
4. Schallert, "Boy's Dream," *Los Angeles Times*, August 15, 1920, III:14.
5. Maury Klein, *The Crash of 1929* (New York: Oxford University Press, 2001), 83.
6. Klein, *Crash*, 103.
7. Robert Shuler, *"Fighting Bob" Shuler of Los Angeles* (Indianapolis, IN: Dog Ear Press, 2011), 89.
8. "Champion 'Aginner' of Universe is Shuler," *Los Angeles Times*, Sunday, June 1, 1930, II:1.
9. "Champion 'Aginner,'" *Los Angeles Times*, June 1, 1930, II:1.
10. Klein, *Crash*, 122.
11. Klein, *Crash*, 122.
12. Jules Tygiel, *The Great Los Angeles Swindle* (New York: Oxford University Press, 1994), 248.
13. "Waiting to Testify," photo, *Los Angeles Examiner*, December 10, 1029, 3.
14. Schallert, "Boy's Dream," *Los Angeles Times*, August 15, 1920, III:14.
15. Klein, *Crash*, 119.
16. "Pantages Banquets Actors After Tiring Performances," *Los Angeles Times*, III:3.
17. Schallert, "Boy's Dream," *Los Angeles Times*, August 15, 1920, III:14.
18. Grace Kingsley, "Alex Pantages Is Christopher Columbus of New Talent," *Los Angeles Times*, August 31, 1914, III:4.
19. "To Aid Boys' Home Fund," *Los Angeles Times*, December 9, 1919, II:2.
20. "Pantages Asked to Halt Big Theater Job," *Los Angeles Times*, September 7, 1918, II:1.
21. "Pastors Accuse Mrs. McPherson of Fund Theft; Evangelist Is Shown as Friend of Pantages," *New York Times*, October 12, 1929, 40.
22. "Washington Next," *Los Angeles Times*, September 10, 1920, III:4.
23. *Los Angeles Times*, September 10, 1920, III:4.
24. "R-K-O's Purchase of Pantages Circuit Reported Closing at $8,000,000," *Variety*, April 3, 1929, 36.
25. *Los Angeles Times*, September 10, 1920, III:4.
26. Joe Bigelow, "Pantages Vet Vaudeville Showman, Dies at 65; Had a Colorful Career," *Variety*, February 19, 1936, 63.
27. "Hollywood Showshouse Is Planned," *Los Angeles Times*, October 6, 1923, II:18.
28. Bigelow, "Pantages Vet," 63.
29. "Pan's Name on Circuit Will Pass Out at New Year's; Never Popular in Vaudeville," *Variety*, November 20, 1929, 33.
30. Bigelow, "Pantages Vet," 63.
31. "Pan's Name," *Variety*, November 20, 1929, 33.
32. Bigelow, "Pantages Vet," 63.
33. Bigelow, "Pantages Vet," 63.
34. "Pan's Name," *Variety*, November 20, 1929, 33.
35. "Pantages Faces Suit by Kearns," *Los Angeles Times*, February 17, 1924, A2.
36. "Answer to Dempsey's Suit Filed," *Los Angeles Times*, April 16, 1924, 24.
37. "Dempsey Defers Suit," *New York Times*, November 29, 1929, p. 16. Dempsey's own manager filed a cross-complaint against Dempsey for failure to repay a personal loan of $312.
38. "Pan's Name," *Variety*, November 20, 1929, 33.
39. "Pan's Name," *Variety*, November 20, 1929, 33.
40. "Pan's Name," *Variety*, November 20, 1929, 33.
41. "Pan's Name," *Variety*, November 20, 1929, 33.
42. Bigelow, "Pantages Vet," 63.
43. "Pan's Name," *Variety*, November 20, 1929, 33.
44. Bigelow, "Pantages Vet," 63.
45. Bigelow, "Pantages Vet," 63.
46. Bigelow, "Pantages Vet," 63.
47. "Pan's Name," *Variety*, November 20, 1929, 33.
48. "Pan's Name," *Variety*, November 20, 1929, 33.
49. "Pan's Name," *Variety*, November 20, 1929, 33.
50. Found at www.los-angeles-theatre.com/theaters/pantages-theater/history.php.
51. Bigelow, "Pantages Vet," 63.

52. "Pan's Name," *Variety*, November 20, 1929, 33.
53. "Ora Carew Asks Guard," *Los Angeles Times*, July 18, 1924, 1.
54. "Ora Carew," *Los Angeles Times*, July 18, 1924, 1.
55. "Pantages Driver Held," *Los Angeles Times*, February 22, 1924, 14.
56. Dean Arthur Tarrach, "Alexander Pantages: The Seattle Pantages and His Vaudeville Circuit" (M.A. thesis: University of Washington, 1973), 62.
57. "Mrs. Pantages Sued for $1893," *San Francisco Chronicle*, September 20, 1929, 5.
58. "Pantages Switches to Films in 100 Per Cent Deal with Fox," *Film Daily*, July 28, 1927, 1.
59. *Film Daily*, July 28, 1927, 4.
60. David Nasaw, *The Patriarch: The Remarkable Life and Turbulent Times of Joseph P. Kennedy* (New York: Penguin Press, 2012), xx.
61. Nasaw, *The Patriarch*, 3.
62. Nasaw, *The Patriarch*, 5.
63. Nasaw, *The Patriarch*, 7.
64. Nasaw, *The Patriarch*, 11.
65. Ronald Kessler, *The Sins of the Father: Joseph P. Kennedy and the Dynasty He Founded* (New York: Warner Books, 1996), 11–12.
66. Kenneth Anger, *Hollywood Babylon II* (New York: E.P. Dutton, 1984), 39.
67. Kessler, *Sins of the Father*, 15.
68. Koskoff, David E., *Joseph P. Kennedy: A Life and Times* (Englewood Cliffs, NJ: Prentice-Hall, 1974), 37.
69. Kessler, *Sins of the Father*, 17.
70. Cari Beauchamp, "The Mogul in Mr. Kennedy," in *Vanity Fair*, March 31, 2002 from www.vanityfair.com/news/2002/04/joekennedy200204, n.p.
71. Koskoff, *Joseph P. Kennedy*, 25.
72. Koskoff, *Joseph P. Kennedy*, 25.
73. Kessler, *Sins of the Father*, 31.
74. Kessler, *Sins of the Father*, 31.
75. Kenneth Anger, *Hollywood Babylon II* (New York: E.P. Dutton, 1984), 40.
76. Koskoff, *Joseph P. Kennedy,*, 25.
77. Kessler, *Sins of the Father*, 54.
78. Anger, *Hollywood*, 41- 42.
79. Anger, *Hollywood*, 42.
80. Anger, *Hollywood*, 42.
81. Koskoff, *Sins of the Father*, 29.
82. Cari Beauchamp, *Vanity Fair*, 2002, np.
83. Cari Beauchamp, *Vanity Fair*, 2002, np.
84. Koskoff, *Joseph P. Kennedy*, 30.
85. Koskoff, *Joseph P. Kennedy*, 28.
86. Koskoff, *Joseph P. Kennedy*, 32.
87. Kessler, *Sins of the Father*, 55.
88. Koskoff, *Joseph P. Kennedy*, 34.
89. Koskoff, *Joseph P. Kennedy*, 34.
90. Kessler, *Sins of the Father*, 56.
91. Koskoff, *Joseph P. Kennedy*, 36.
92. Kessler, *Sins of the Father*, 57.
93. Kessler, *Sins of the Father*, 57, 59.
94. Kessler, *Sins of the Father*, 57.
95. Kessler, *Sins of the Father*, 57. It should be noted that the theater was known as "Pantages Theater" in the drawings and newspaper accounts of its grand opening, so it seems odd that Kessler refers to it as "Pantages Hill Street" house. Also, it is located on the northeast corner of Seventh and Hill streets, not the northwest corner (this from a personal visit to the theater in downtown Los Angeles).
96. Anger, *Hollywood*, 45.
97. "RKO-Pathe Merger Talk Is Renewed on Coast" and "Pantages Reiterates His Denial of Deal for Chain," *The Film Daily*, 18 February 1929, 1, 8.
98. "Negotiations Reported on for Pantages and Interstate Houses," *The Film Daily*, March 25, 1929, 1, 2.
99. "Kennedy Stays," *Variety*, April 3, 1929, 5.
100. "R-K-O-Pantages Merger Reported Progressing," *The Film Daily*, March 31, 1929, 1.
101. "R-K-O-Pantages Merger," *The Film Daily*, March 31, 1929, 1.
102. "R-K-O-Pantages Merger," *The Film Daily*, March 31, 1929, 29.
103. "Kennedy Stays," *Variety*, April 3, 1929, 36.
104. "Kennedy Stays," *Variety*, April 3, 1929, 36.
105. "Kennedy Stays," *Variety*, April 3, 1929, 36.
106. "Keith-Pan Hitch," *Variety*, April 17, 1929, 4.
107. "Keith-Pan Hitch," *Variety*, 17 April 1929, 4.
108. "$14,000,000 Theatre Deal," *New York Times*, April 18, 1929, 37.
109. "$14,000,000 Theatre Deal," *New York Times*, April 18, 1929, 37.
110. "Keith's Buys Proctor, *Variety*, May 15, 1929, 1.
111. "Keith and Pan Deal Closing," *Variety*, May 15, 1929, 28.
112. "Grauman Out," *Variety*, May 29, 1929 20.
113. "Pantages Merger Near," *New York Times*, June 7, 1929, 32.
114. "Western R.-K.-O. Buys Pantages Theaters," *New York Times*, July 26, 1929, 21.
115. Klein, *Crash*, 126.

116. Klein, *Crash*, 148.
117. Klein, *Crash*, 134.
118. Klein, *Crash*, 152.
119. Klein, *Crash*, 152.
120. Klein, *Crash*, 152.
121. Klein, *Crash*, 133.
122. From www.pbs.org/wgbh/americanexperience/features/timeline/crash/.
123. Harold Bierman, Jr., *The Causes of the 1929 Stock Market Crash* (Westport, CT: Greenwood Press, 1998), 50.
124. Klein, *Crash*, 183.
125. Bierman, *Stock Market Crash*, 50.
126. The Seventh and Hill Theater was sold to RKO pictures by Pantages, but it later became the Warner Brothers Downtown Theater.
127. Megan A. Wagner, "Spectacular Los Angeles Trials," *Los Angeles Lawyer*, March 2003, 72.
128. "Annuls Jail Term for Mrs. Pantages," *New York Times*, November 9, 1929, 15.
129. There was confusion about the correct spelling of the driver of the other vehicle. At first he was mentioned as "Joe Rokomoto," later replaced by Juro Rokumoto. Is this a case of reverse "white ethnicity"? I retain the latter spelling as it appeared during the Lois Pantages trial.
130. "Doctor Denies Mrs. Pantages Intoxicated," *San Francisco Chronicle*, September 13, 1929, 3.
131. It was a Stutz automobile.
132. "Pantages Case Death Charge," *Los Angeles Examiner*, June 25, 1929, 5.
133. "Mrs. Pantages Arraigned on Death Charge," *Los Angeles Examiner*, July 19, 1929, 3.
134. "Witness in Pantages Prosecution Tells of Death Threats," *Los Angeles Examiner*, August 1, 1929, 3.
135. "Steuer Plays Waiting Role," *Los Angeles Examiner*, September 4, 1929, 9. According to the *Washington Hellenic Review* 6, February 1929, 9, the engagement between Carmen Pantages and John Considine, Jr., was announced six months prior to the start of the first rape trial. The marriage did not take place until February 1932 after the Pringle cases ended completely.
136. "Mrs. Pantages Tried Today in Murder Case," *Los Angeles Examiner*, September 3, 1929, 1.
137. "Mrs. Pantages 'Persecuted,' Says Lawyer," *San Francisco Chronicle*, September 24, 1929, 16.
138. Discroll, "Theater Man's Wife," *Los Angeles Examiner*, September 4, 1929, 9.
139. Discroll, "Theater Man's Wife," *Los Angeles Examiner*, September 4, 1929, 9.

140. Discroll, "Theater Man's Wife," *Los Angeles Examiner*, September 4, 1929, 9.
141. Harry Lang, "State Alienists Watch Mrs. Pantages," *Los Angeles Examiner*, September 5, 1929, 1.
142. "Champion 'Aginner' of Universe Is Shuler," *Los Angeles Times*, June 1, 1930, Part II, 2.
143. McPherson and Shuler hated each other and did their best to castigate the other as evil. The theatrics that this tension sparked made for good theater and likely helped to bring further attention on their ministries. For more on the rivalry, see for example Robert Shuler, *"Fighting Bob" Shuler of Los Angeles* (Indianapolis: Dog Ear Publishing, 2011), 89.
144. Jules Tygiel, *The Great Los Angeles Swindle* (New York: Oxford University Press, 1994), 277.
145. Mark Sumner Gill, "'Fighting Bob' Shuler: Fundamentalist and Reformer" (PhD diss., The Claremont Graduate School, 1988), 9.
146. Edmund Wilson, *The City of Our Lady the Queen of Angels*, cited in Tygiel, *Swindle*, 277.
147. Edmund Wilson, *The City of Our Lady the Queen of Angels*, cited in Tygiel, *Swindle*, 277.
148. Tygiel, *Swindle*, 277.
149. Robert Shuler, *"Fighting Bob,"* 94. Italics in the original.
150. "Champion 'Aginner,'" *Los Angeles Times*, June 1, 1930, II:2.
151. "Champion 'Aginner,'" *Los Angeles Times*, June 1, 1930, II:2.
152. Shuler, *"Fighting Bob,"* 92.
153. Shuler, *"Fighting Bob,"* 93.
154. Shuler, *"Fighting Bob,"* 99–100.
155. Shuler, *"Fighting Bob,"* 99.
156. "Shuler Bases Defense on Right to Prophecy," *Los Angeles Examiner*, October 3, 1929, 6. Shuler at first claimed that the radio station belonged to him, just as KSFG belonged to McPherson, but an examination revealed that it was owned by his church, Trinity Methodist. In theory the station could have barred Shuler from preaching and continued operating it, yet this did not happen and the station still lost its license.
157. "Secret Aimee Bank Account Investigated," *Los Angeles Examiner*, October 23, 1929, 5.
158. Harry Lang, "Mrs. Pantages Set Free," *Los Angeles Examiner*, November 9, 1929, 1.
159. Lang, "Pantages Free," *Los Angeles Examiner*, November 9, 1929, 1.
160. "Mrs. Rokumoto and $78,500 from

Mrs. Pantages," *Los Angeles Examiner*, November 9, 1929, 2.
161. *New York Times*, November 9, 1929, 15.
162. "Pantages on Trial; Jury Under Guard," *Seattle Times*, October 1, 1929, 1.
163. Procter, *William Randolph Hearst*, 104.

Chapter 6

1. This according to her mother's testimony at the Pantages rape trial. Most accounts have Pringle being born in Garden Grove, south of Los Angeles. See "Mother's Story Hits Defense," *Los Angeles Times*, October 4, 1929, 5.
2. "Eunice's Testimony Reveals How She First Met Producer," *Los Angeles Examiner*, Saturday, October 5, 1929, 4.
3. "'Justice, All I Ask,' Sobs Girl's Mother," *Los Angeles Examiner*, August 11, 1929, 3.
4. "'Justice, All I Ask,'" *Los Angeles Examiner*, August 11, 1929, 3.
5. Jerry Giesler and Pete Martin, *The Jerry Giesler Story* (New York: Simon & Schuster, 1960), 34.
6. "'Justice, All I Ask,'" *Los Angeles Examiner*, August 11, 1929, 3.
7. "Nick Dunaev Enters Trial," *Los Angeles Examiner*, October 12, 1929, 5. The *Examiner* provided no information about Dunaev's background. The site http://househistoryman.blogspot.com/2013/03/the-man-who-could-bend-dime-with-his.html lists a Nicholas A. Dunaev as born to a nobleman and Lord Mayor of Moscow in 1884. He graduated from the University of Moscow Law School, but chose acting, writing, and directing as his profession. He moved to the United States in 1919 to work at the Vitagraph studios in New York, and is said to have appeared in 34 films in the 1910s and 1920s on two continents. He worked to elect Franklin D. Roosevelt, delivering thousands of votes, but after moving to Washington, D.C., he found himself with little employment. By 1947 he was broke yet continued to write. He published a novel, *Seven Doors to Sin*, in 1954 under the imprint of Vantage Press (a vanity press). A couple took him into their home where he died of illness in 1963. He lies buried in an unmarked grave at the Congressional Cemetery in Washington, D.C.
8. "Here's Text of the Playlet," *Los Angeles Examiner*, October 17, 1929, 6.
9. Giesler and Martin, *Jerry Giesler*, 27.
10. "'Crime on Minor,' Fitts Tells Jury; 'Frameup' Cries Gilbert in Reply," *Los Angeles Examiner*, October 4, 1929, 5.
11. According to testimony, the mother, Mrs. Pringle, had an "apartment" that she shared with Eunice at 1116 South Mariposa, near downtown Los Angeles. In Pringle's own court testimony, she also indicated that Garden Grove was her home, 417 East Acacia Street, described in one *Examiner* account as a "cottage" (October 17, 1929, 7). The relationship between the two addresses is not clear, nor is it evident from the testimony on the morning of August 9, 1929, whether she drove from Garden Grove or from South Mariposa to downtown. It is known from the *Examiner* coverage of the trial that Eunice spent time both with her father and mother. Where Dr. Pringle lived is not indicated in the *Examiner*. It is possible that the Garden Grove address was the main Pringle residence while the Mariposa apartment was an addition to accommodate Eunice's professional acting career.
12. "Eyewitness Corroborates Pringle Girl," *Los Angeles Examiner*, October 8, 1929, 8.
13. Giesler and Martin, *Jerry Giesler*, 26.
14. "Eunice Pringle Again in Court," *Los Angeles Times*, January 22, 1930, II:7.
15. "Eunice's Testimony," *Los Angeles Examiner*, October 5, 1929, 4.
16. Room's dimensions from "Actor's Testimony Describes Girl's Hysterical Flight," *Los Angeles Examiner*, August 17, 1929, 5; and quotation from "Pantages Accuser's," *Los Angeles Examiner*, August 15 1929, 10.
17. "Eunice's Testimony," *Los Angeles Examiner*, October 5, 1929, 5.
18. "Eunice's Testimony," *Los Angeles Examiner*, October 5, 1929, 5.
19. Michael Parrish, *For the People: Inside the Los Angeles County District Attorney's Office, 1850–2000* (Los Angeles: Angel City Press, 2001), 92.
20. "Pantages Freed on $25,000 Bail," *Los Angeles Examiner*, August 11, 1929, 3.
21. "Pantages Held on Girl's Charges," *Los Angeles Examiner*, August 10, 1929, 5.
22. "Pantages Freed," *Los Angeles Examiner*, August 11, 1929, 3.
23. "Girl's Mother Hits Pantages' Defense," *Los Angeles Examiner*, October 4, 1929, 5.
24. "Pantages Freed," *Los Angeles Examiner*, August 11, 1929, 3.
25. "Pantages Held," *Los Angeles Examiner*, August 10, 1929, 5.
26. "Pantages Held," *Los Angeles Examiner*, August 10, 1929, 1.
27. "A. Pantages in Jail on Complaint of Girl, 16," *Seattle Times*, August 10, 1929, 1.
28. *Seattle Times*, August 10, 1929, 1, and

"Dancer Who Accused Pantages Receives Threats Over Phone," *Seattle Times*, August 12, 1929, 7.
29. *Seattle Times*, August 10, 1929, 1.
30. "Pantages Held," *Los Angeles Examiner*, August 10, 1929, 5.
31. "Pantages Held," *Los Angeles Examiner*, August 10, 1929, 5.
32. Megan A. Wagner, "Spectacular Los Angeles Trials," *Los Angeles Lawyer*, March 2003, 74.
33. "Pantages Held," *Los Angeles Examiner*, August 10, 1929, 5.
34. "Pantages Held," *Los Angeles Examiner*, August 10, 1929, 5.
35. "Pantages Freed," *Los Angeles Examiner*, August 11, 1929, 3.
36. "Pantages Freed," *Los Angeles Examiner*, August 11, 1929, 3.
37. "Pantages Freed," *Los Angeles Examiner*, August 11, 1929, 3.
38. "'Say Nothing,' Lawyer Warns," *Los Angeles Examiner*, August 17, 1929, 4.
39. "'Say Nothing,' Lawyer Warns," *Los Angeles Examiner*, August 17, 1929, 4.
40. "'Justice, All I Ask,'" *Los Angeles Examiner*, August 11, 1929, 3.
41. "'Justice, All I Ask,'" *Los Angeles Examiner*, August 11, 1929, 3.
42. "'Justice, All I Ask,'" *Los Angeles Examiner*, August 11, 1929, 3.
43. "'Justice, All I Ask,'" *Los Angeles Examiner*, August 11, 1929, 3.
44. "'Justice, All I Ask,'" *Los Angeles Examiner*, August 11, 1929, 3.
45. "Guard for Pantages Case Girl Asked," *Los Angeles Examiner*, August 12, 1929, 1.
46. "Pantages Staff Grilled in Girl Case," *Los Angeles Examiner*, August 13, 1929, 5.
47. All files related to the 1929 court case are apparently lost, so it is impossible to verify this.
48. "Pantages Accuser's Story Unshaken," *Los Angeles Examiner*, August 15, 1929, 1.
49. "Pantages Accuser's," *Los Angeles Examiner*, August 15, 1929, 1.
50. "Pantages Accuser's," *Los Angeles Examiner*, August 15, 1929, 1.
51. "Pantages Accuser's," *Los Angeles Examiner*, August 15, 1929, 10.
52. "Pantages Accuser's," *Los Angeles Examiner*, August 15, 1929, 10.
53. "Pantages Accuser's," *Los Angeles Examiner*, August 15, 1929, 10.
54. "Pantages Accuser's," *Los Angeles Examiner*, August 15, 1929, 10.
55. "Pantages Accuser's," *Los Angeles Examiner*, August 15, 1929, 10.
56. "Pantages Accuser's," *Los Angeles Examiner*, August 15, 1929, 10.
57. "Surprise Witness Blow to Pantages," *Los Angeles Examiner*, August 16, 1929, 10.
58. "District Attorney Properly Takes Personal Charge in Grave Prosecution," *Los Angeles Examiner*, August 14, 1929, n.p.
59. "District Attorney Takes Charge," *Los Angeles Examiner*, August 14, 1929, n.p.
60. "District Attorney Takes Charge," *Los Angeles Examiner*, August 14, 1929, n.p.
61. "District Attorney Takes Charge," *Los Angeles Examiner*, August 14, 1929, n.p.
62. "Trial Expected by Accused," *Los Angeles Examiner*, August 16, 1929, 10.
63. Jules Tygiel, *The Great Los Angeles Swindle* (New York: Oxford University Press, 1994), 261.
64. "Pantages Aide Seized in Witness Tampering," *New York Times*, August 18, 1929, 21.
65. "Girl Usher Extends Charges on Pantages," *New York Times*, August 19, 1929, 19.
66. "Pantages Wins Delay," *New York Times*, August 20, 1929, 28.
67. "Pantages Bolsters Lines," *Los Angeles Times*, August 29, 1929, I:10.
68. "Pantages Bolsters," *Los Angeles Times*, August 29, 1929, I:10.
69. "Stock Market Breaks; Shares Drop Billion," *Los Angeles Examiner*, August 10, 1929, 1.
70. "'It Seems Like a Nightmare,'" *Los Angeles Examiner*, August 11, 1929, 3.
71. "Alleged Victim, as Camera Records Her Moods," *Los Angeles Examiner*, August 16, 1929, 10.
72. "District Attorney Properly Takes Personal Charge in Grave Prosecution," *Los Angeles Examiner*, August 14, 1929.
73. "District Attorney," *Los Angeles Examiner*, August 14, 1929.
74. "District Attorney," *Los Angeles Examiner*, August 14, 1929.
75. "Sorrow Ends Separation of Parents," *Los Angeles Examiner*, August 16, 1929, 10.
76. "Sorrow Ends," *Los Angeles Examiner*, August 16, 1929, 10.
77. "Taking No Chances," *Los Angeles Examiner*, August 22, 1929, 5.
78. "Fitts Removes Pantages Case Girl from City," *Los Angeles Examiner*, August 28, 1929, 5.
79. "Fitts Removes," *Los Angeles Examiner*, August 28, 1929, 5.
80. "Fitts Removes," *Los Angeles Examiner*, August 28, 1929, 5.
81. "Both Pantages and Wife Face Courts Today," *Los Angeles Examiner*, September 30, 1929, 4.
82. "Pantages Attack Trial Starts Today," *Los Angeles Examiner*, October 1, 1929, 5.

83. The Roman Polanski rape case in the 1970s and O.J. Simpson murder trial in the 1990s stand out as two more recent examples.
84. "Pantages Testimony Today," *Los Angeles Examiner*, October 3, 1929, 1.
85. "Mother's Story," *Los Angeles Examiner*, October 4, 1929, 5.
86. "Pringle Girl Tells Attack," *Los Angeles Examiner*, October 5, 1929, 1.
87. "Telling Pitiful Story," *Los Angeles Examiner*, October 5, 1929, 5.
88. "Telling Pitiful Story," *Los Angeles Examiner*, October 5, 1929, 5.
89. "Telling Pitiful Story," *Los Angeles Examiner*, October 5, 1929, 5.
90. "Pringle Attack," *Los Angeles Examiner*, October 5, 1929, 5.
91. "Pringle Attack," *Los Angeles Examiner*, October 5, 1929, 5.
92. "Pringle Attack," *Los Angeles Examiner*, October 5, 1929, 5.
93. "Pringle Attack," *Los Angeles Examiner*, October 5, 1929, 5.
94. "Pringle Attack," *Los Angeles Examiner*, October 5, 1929, 5.
95. "Eyewitness Corroborates," *Los Angeles Examiner*, October 8, 1929, 8.
96. "Eyewitness Corroborates," *Los Angeles Examiner*, October 8, 1929, 8.
97. "Pantages Alibi Shattered," *Los Angeles Examiner*, October 12, 1929, 5.
98. "Testimony of Chemist Hits Pantages," *Los Angeles Examiner*, October 15, 1929, 2.
99. "Court Bars Pantages' Frameup Evidence," *San Francisco Chronicle*, October 22, 1929, 1.
100. "Pantages Witness Jailed," *Los Angeles Examiner*, October 16, 1929, 1.
101. "Pantages Expected on Stand Tomorrow, Closing Defense," *Los Angeles Examiner*, October 29, 1929, 3.
102. "Pantages Enacts 'Attack,'" *Los Angeles Examiner*, October 23, 1929, 2.
103. "Here's Showman's Story to Court," *Los Angeles Examiner*, October 23, 1929, 2.
104. "Testimony Presented in Stage Style," *Los Angeles Examiner*, October 23, 1929, 2.
105. "'Girl attacked me,' Swears Pantages," *San Francisco Chronicle*, October 23, 1929, 1.
106. "Pantages Enacts 'Attack,'" *Los Angeles Examiner*, October 23, 1929, 2.
107. "Testimony Presented in Stage Style," *Los Angeles Examiner*, October 23, 1929, 2.
108. "State Demands Prison for Pantages," *San Francisco Chronicle*, October 25, 1929, 1–2.
109. "State Demands Prison," *San Francisco Chronicle*, October 25, 1929, 2.
110. "Pantages Jury Locked Up," *Los Angeles Examiner*, October 26, 1929, 2.
111. "Pantages Guilty!" *Los Angeles Examiner*, October 28, 1929, 2.
112. "Pantages Guilty!" *Los Angeles Examiner*, October 28, 1929, 2.
113. "Pantages Guilty!" *Los Angeles Examiner*, October 28, 1929, 1.
114. "'I Got Raw Deal,' Says Convicted Showman," *Los Angeles Examiner*, October 28, 1929, 2.
115. "'I Got Raw Deal,' Says Convicted Showman," *Los Angeles Examiner*, October 28, 1929, 2.
116. Klein, *Crash*, 204.
117. Klein, *Crash*, 212.
118. Klein, *Crash*, 212.
119. Klein, *Crash*, 229.
120. Klein, *Crash*, 229.
121. Klein, *Crash*, 241.

Chapter 7

1. Frank Cullen with Florence Hackman and Donald McNeilly, *Vaudeville, Old and New: An Encyclopedia of Variety Performers in America, Volume 1* (New York: Routledge, 2007), 15, 60.
2. Cullen, *Vaudeville*, 15.
3. "Pan's Name on Circuit Will Pass Out at New Years; Never Popular in Vaudeville," *Variety*, November 20, 1929, 38.
4. Cullen, *Vaudeville*, 2007, 60.
5. Cullen, *Vaudeville*, 2007, 60.
6. "Pan's Name," *Variety*, November 20, 1929, 38.
7. "Pan's Name," *Variety*, November 20, 1929, 38.
8. "Pan's Name," *Variety*, November 20, 1929, 38.
9. "Pan's Name," *Variety*, November 20, 1929, 38.
10. "Pan's Name," *Variety*, November 20, 1929, 38.
11. "Pan's Name," *Variety*, November 20, 1929, 38.
12. "Pantages Sentenced," *Los Angeles Examiner*, November 10, 1929, 1.
13. "Pantages Sentenced," *Los Angeles Examiner*, November 10, 1929, 3.
14. "Fitts Reveals His Political Plans Shortly," *Los Angeles Examiner*, December 15, 1929, 17.
15. "Pantages to Make New Prison Fight," *San Francisco Chronicle*, October 29, 1929, 2.
16. "Pantages to Make," *San Francisco Chronicle*, October 29, 1929, 2.

Notes—Chapter 7

17. "Pantages to Make," *San Francisco Chronicle*, October 29, 1929, 2.
18. "Pantages Charges He Was Made Victim of 'Raw Deal,'" *San Francisco Chronicle*, October 29, 1929, 2.
19. "Pantages Sees Wife During Brief Liberty," *San Francisco Chronicle*, October 30, 1929, 4.
20. "Russian Sues Pantages," *New York Times*, November 15, 1929, 13.
21. "Girl Sues Pantages for $1,000,000," *New York Times*, January 25, 1930, 13.
22. "Fitts Will Get Affidavits in Pantages Case," *New York Times*, November 5, 1929, 13.
23. "Suit Delay Asked by Pantages," *Los Angeles Times*, November 28, 1929, II:9.
24. Ellis Lucia, *Klondike Kate: The Life & Legend of Kitty Rockwell, the Queen of the Yukon* (New York: Hastings House, 1962), 216.
25. "Dance 'Queen' May Aid State," *Los Angeles Times*, October 4, 1929, A5.
26. "Dance 'Queen,'" *Los Angeles Times*, October 4, 1929, A5.
27. "Dance 'Queen,'" *Los Angeles Times*, October 4, 1929, A5.
28. "Pantages Meets Old Yukon Pal," *Los Angeles Times*, October 5, 1929, A2.
29. "'Jurors Feared Shuler,' Says Pantages' Plea," *Los Angeles Examiner*, November 7, 1929, II:1.
30. "'Jurors Feared Shuler,'" *Los Angeles Examiner*, November 7, 1929, II:6.
31. "Girl's Mother Hits Pantages' Defense," *Los Angeles Examiner*, October 4, 1929, 5.
32. "Pringle Suit Quiz Blocked," *Los Angeles Times*, January 26, 1930, Part II, 2.
33. "Pringle Girl Asks Million," *Los Angeles Times*, January 25, 1930, II:1.
34. "Girls Settles Pantages Suit," *Los Angeles Times*, Friday, December 4, 1931, 12.
35. "Biffle Perjury Case Dismissed," *Los Angeles Times*, February 1, 1930, II:1.
36. "Pantages Battles to Win New Trial," *San Francisco Chronicle*, November 3, 1929, 3.
37. "'Jurors Fear Shuler,' Says Pantages' Plea," *Los Angeles Examiner*, November 7, 1929, II:1.
38. "Farewell to Legs," *Los Angeles Examiner*, December 10, 1929, 10. Three days later the *Examiner* profoundly asked in a headline, "Long Skirts vs. Short; Oh, What to Do?," *Los Angeles Examiner*, December 13, 1929, 3. Hearst's predilection for cheesecake, even as the nation started its long swoop toward the Great Depression, had no end in sight. Or was he trying to cheer his readers with distraction?
39. "Pantages Asks Release to Save Life," *New York Times*, December 24, 1929, 19.
40. "Pantages Decision Today," *Los Angeles Times*, January 30, 1930, II:1.
41. "Pantages in New Battle," *Los Angeles Times*, January 31, 1930, II:1.
42. "Pantages Decision Today," *Los Angeles Times*, January 30, 1930, II:5.
43. "Denounces Effort to Get Pantages Out," *New York Times*, January 31, 1930, 5.
44. "Pantages in New Battle," *Los Angeles Times*, January 31, 1930, II:1.
45. "Denounces Effort," *New York Times*, January 31, 1930, 15.
46. "Denounces Effort," *New York Times*, January 31, 1930, 15.
47. "Notorious Cases for a 'No-Nonsense' Judge," *Los Angeles Times*, August 20, 2006, B:2.
48. "Pantages Permitted to See Wife at Home," *Los Angeles Examiner*, December 19, 1929, 7.
49. "Theater Man Permitted to Have Doctors," *Los Angeles Examiner*, December 28, 1929, 1.
50. Interestingly, in his memoirs, Giesler spells Pringle's manager "Dunave" instead of Dunaev. Newspaper coverage of the first Pantages trial spelled Giesler as "Geisler."
51. Jerry Giesler and Pete Martin, *The Jerry Giesler Story* (New York: Simon & Schuster, 1960), 32.
52. Giesler and Martin, *Giesler*, 33.
53. Giesler and Martin, *Giesler*, 33.
54. Giesler and Martin, *Giesler*, 34.
55. Giesler and Martin, *Giesler*, 35.
56. "Pantages Freed on Bond," *Los Angeles Times*, June 7, 1931, II:1. The photo accompanying the article shows a man barely able to smile.
57. Brass band from Kenneth Anger, *Hollywood Babylon II* (New York: E.P. Dutton, 1984), 37, and his family taking him home from "Release," *New York Times*, June 7, 1930, 8.
58. "Pantages Conviction Upset by High Court," *New York Times*, April 3, 1931, 23.
59. "Pantages Conviction Upset," *New York Times*, April 3, 1931, 23.
60. "Pantages Loses in First Court Battle," *San Francisco Chronicle*, October 2, 1929, 5.
61. Giesler and Martin, *Giesler*, 36.
62. Giesler and Martin, *Giesler*, 36. The "quick-witted" lawyers to whom the opinion piece referred in the first trial were Earl M. Daniels, W.J. Ford, Jerry Giesler, and W.I. Gilbert.
63. Giesler and Martin, *Giesler*, 36.
64. Statistics from www.thepeoplehistory.com/1931.html.
65. "Word Depression Delted," *Los Angeles Times*, November 12, 1931, II:2.
66. "Southern California Business Begins

Upward Swing," sketch, *Los Angeles Times*, November 15, 1931, 1.
67. "Pantages Fight to Begin Today," *Los Angeles Times*, November 4, 1931, II:1.
68. "Row Halts Pringle Quiz," *Los Angeles Times*, November 5, 1931, II:1.
69. "Row Halts Pringle Quiz," *Los Angeles Times*, November 5, 1931, II:2.
70. "Damage Suit Filed Against Rodney Pantages," *Los Angeles Times*, November 5, 1931, II:2.
71. Quote from "Pantages Jury Still Debating," *Los Angeles Times*, November 26, 1931, II:1.
72. "Pantages Accuser Sticks to Story [unintelligible]," *Los Angeles Times*, November 6, 1931, II:2.
73. Giesler and Martin, *Giesler*, 37.
74. "Pantages Accuser Sticks," *Los Angeles Times*, November 6, 1931, II:2. The *Times* gives the residence as being "2032 Ivar street," but a search on Google Maps reveals no such street number and Ivar as being an avenue and not a street.
75. "Pantages Accuser Sticks," *Los Angeles Times*, November 6, 1931, II:2.
76. Giesler and Martin, *Giesler*, 37.
77. Giesler and Martin, *Giesler*, 37.
78. "Introduction of Enlivening Evidence in Pantages Trial Today Hinges on Court Decision," *Los Angeles Times*, November 19, 1931, II:2.
79. "Pantages Jury Hears Details," *Los Angeles Times*, November 11, 1931, II:2.
80. "Pantages Weeps on Stand," *Los Angeles Times*, November 20, 1931, II:1.
81. "Pantages Weeps on Stand," *Los Angeles Times*, November 20, 1931, II:2.
82. "Pringle Girl's Story Assailed," *Los Angeles Times*, November 21, 1931, II:1.
83. Anger, *Hollywood*, 33. In Anger's account, it is fellow defense attorney Jake Ehrlich who uncovered the lodging manager that helped to break open the case for Pantages's side.
84. "Pantages Jury Still Debating," *Los Angeles Times*, November 26, 1931, II:1.
85. Giesler and Martin, *Giesler*, 37.
86. Giesler and Martin, *Giesler*, 37.
87. "Jury Acquits Pantages Amid Tumultuous Scene," *Los Angeles Times*, November 28, 1931, II:1.
88. "Jury Acquits Pantages," *Los Angeles Times*, November 28, 1931, II:1.
89. "Jury Acquits Pantages," *Los Angeles Times*, November 28, 1931, II:1.
90. "Jury Acquits Pantages," *Los Angeles Times*, November 28, 1931, II:1.
91. "Jury Acquits Pantages," *Los Angeles Times*, November 28, 1931, II:1.

92. "Pringle Girl Plot Charged," *Los Angeles Examiner*, November 23, 1929, 5.
93. Giesler and Martin, *Giesler*, 14.
94. Pantages' letter dated May 29, 1922, from the Special Collections Division of the University of Washington Libraries.
95. Kenneth Anger, *Hollywood Babylon II* (New York: Dutton, 1984).
96. Andy Edmonds, "Showstopper," *Los Angeles Magazine*, December 1989, 128–36, and Michael Parrish, *For the People: Inside the Los Angeles County District Attorney's Office, 1850–2000* (Los Angeles: Angel City Press, 2001), 92–93.
97. Ronald Kessler, *The Sins of the Father: Joseph P. Kennedy and the Dynasty He Founded* (New York: Warner, 1996) and Marvin J. Wolf and Katherine Mader, *Fallen Angels: Chronicles of L.A. Crime and Mystery* (New York: Facts on File, 1986). According to Parrish, much of what Anger and Edmonds wrote entered Kessler's biography.
98. Michael Parrish, "A Myth Maker's Clarification," *Los Angeles Times Magazine*, June 12, 2002, 24.
99. Parrish, "A Myth Maker's Clarification," 32.
100. "Pringle Girl Plot Charged," *Los Angeles Examiner*, November 23, 1929, 5.
101. Parrish, "A Myth Maker's Clarification," 32.
102. Parrish, "A Myth Maker's Clarification," 32.
103. Parrish, "A Myth Maker's Clarification," 32.

Chapter 8

1. "Pantages, Vet Vaudeville Showman, Dies at 65; Had a Colorful Career," *Variety*, February 19, 1936, 63.
2. "Pantages Considine Wedding Set for Today," *Los Angeles Times*, February 14, 1932, 18.
3. "Pantages, Vet Vaudeville Showman," *Variety*, February 19, 1936, 63.
4. Dean Arthur Tarrach, "Alexander Pantages: The Seattle Pantages and His Vaudeville Circuit" (M.A. thesis: University of Washington, 1973), 26.
5. Tarrach, "Alexander Pantages," 26.
6. "Extortion Note Names 5 Rich Men," *New York Times*, August 5, 1934, 7.
7. "Extortion Note," *New York Times*, August 5, 1934, 7.
8. "Pantages Case Lags," *Los Angeles Times*, May 28, 1931, II:1.
9. "Pantages's Jury in Box," *Los Angeles Times*, June 6, 1931, II:1.

10. "Fitts' Star Pantages Witness Missing," August 14, 1929, 1, and "Pantages Aids Charge Perjury Plot," *Los Angeles Examiner*, August 18, 1929, 1.
11. "Movie Actress Wins Divorce," *New York Times*, May 14, 1922, 47.
12. "Pantages Accused," *Los Angeles Times*, March 11, 1931, II:1.
13. "Pantages Accused," *Los Angeles Times*, March 11, 1931, II:1.
14. "Pantages Accused," *Los Angeles Times*, March 11, 1931, II:1.
15. "Pantages Accused," *Los Angeles Times*, March 11, 1931, II:1.
16. "Love Mart Quiz Shifts," *Los Angeles Times*, March 12, 1931, II:2.
17. "Love Mart Quiz Shifts," *Los Angeles Times*, March 12, 1931, II:2.
18. "Little Concern Shown Over Trial," *Los Angeles Times*, June 9, 1931, II:2.
19. "Love Mart Quiz Shifts," *Los Angeles Times*, March 12, 1931, II:2.
20. "Pantages Case Lags," *Los Angeles Times*, May 28, 1931, II:2.
21. "Fitts Has Close Call in Smash," *Los Angeles Times*, March 12, 1931, II:12.
22. "Quiz Helps Pantages," *Los Angeles Times*, June 6, 1931, II:1.
23. "Quiz Helps Pantages," *Los Angeles Times*, June 6, 1931, II:2.
24. "Gifts Sent Party Girl," *Los Angeles Times*, June 9, 1931, II:2.
25. "Gifts Sent Party Girl," *Los Angeles Times*, June 9, 1931, II:1.
26. "Gifts Sent Party Girl," *Los Angeles Times*, June 9, 1931, II:1.
27. "Pantages Case Nearing Close," *Los Angeles Times*, June 17, 1931, II:3.
28. "Pantages on Stand," *Los Angeles Times*, June 12, 1931, II:1.
29. "Pantages on Stand," *Los Angeles Times*, June 12, 1931, II:1.
30. "Pantages on Stand," *Los Angeles Times*, June 12, 1931, II:2.
31. "America Going Crazy, Billy Sunday Asserts," *Los Angeles Times*, June 14, 1931, II:8.
32. "Jurors Fail to Agree," *Los Angeles Times*, June 19, 1931, II:1.
33. "Pantages Trial Off," *Los Angeles Times*, July 13, 1931, II:1.
34. See "Why Be Good?" in Kenneth Anger, *Hollywood Babylon II* (New York: E.P. Dutton, 1984), 28–37. The breezy chapter reveals the extent of Kennedy's perfidy (as does the chapter that follows on Joseph P. Kennedy, "Bootlegger Joe," 38–47). The main issue with such accounts, besides the lack of direct evidence to support the contention, is that it borrows on the same sensational elements that Hearst famously used without any attempt of objectivity. Anger believes Kennedy poisoned Eunice Pringle when she planned to speak up about the plot to the press, when a little more investigation might have revealed the baselessness of this charge. It satisfied some desire in the movie industry to get back at Kennedy for his carpetbagging ways in Hollywood, but it did nothing for journalistic truth. Kennedy, like Pantages and Hearst, was no angel but he was not a poisoner.
35. "Pantages Rites to Be Tomorrow," *Seattle Times*, February 18, 1936, 4.
36. "A. Pantages Dead; Theater Magnate," *New York Times*, February 18, 1936, 23.
37. "Pantages Dies; One-Time Czar of the Theater," *Washington Post*, February 18, 1936, 12.
38. "Pantages Dies Unexpectedly in L.A. Home," *Seattle Times*, February 17, 1936, 2.
39. "Pantages Dies Unexpectedly in L.A. Home," *Seattle Times*, February 17, 1936, 2.
40. Unintelligible Headline, *Los Angeles Times*, February 18, 1936, II:1.
41. Unintelligible Headline, *Los Angeles Times*, February 18, 1936, II:1.
42. "Klondike Kate Sobs at News of Death," *Los Angeles Times*, February 18, 1936, II:13.
43. "He Was a 'Fine Man,' Says 'Klondike Kate,'" *Seattle Post-Intelligencer*, February 18, 1936, 3.
44. "He Was a 'Fine Man,' Says 'Klondike Kate,'" *Seattle Post-Intelligencer*, February 18, 1936, 3.
45. "Pantages Rose from Klondike Dive to Riches," *Seattle Times*, October 28, 1929, 8.

Bibliography

Abbot, Willis. *Watching the World Go By*. Boston: Little, Brown, 1933.

Anagnostou, Yiorgos. *The Contours of White Ethnicity: Popular Ethnography and the Making of Usable Past in Greek America*. Athens: Ohio University Press, 2009.

Anger, Kenneth. *Hollywood Babylon II*. New York: E.P. Dutton, 1984.

Anguizola, Gustave. *Philippe Bunau-Varilla: The Man Behind the Panama Canal*. Chicago: Nelson-Hall, 1980.

Bagley, Clarence. "B. Marcus Priteca." In *The History of King County, Washington, Volume II*. Seattle: S.J. Clarke Publishing, 1929.

Baies, Gergely. *Feeding Gotham: The Political Economy and Geography of Food in New York, 1790–1860*. Princeton, NJ: Princeton University Press, 2016.

Baldasty, Gerald J. *Vigilante Newspapers*. Seattle: University of Washington Press, 2005.

"The Battle Over *Citizen Kane*." *The American Experience*, Public Broadcasting System, broadcast on January 29, 1996.

Beauchamp, Cari. "The Mogul in Mr. Kennedy." *Vanity Fair*, March 31, 2002. www.vanityfair.com/news/2002/04/joekennedy200204.

Beauchamp, Cari. *Joseph P. Kennedy Presents: His Hollywood Years*. New York: Alfred A. Knopf, 2009.

Belton, John. *American Cinema/American Culture*. New York: McGraw-Hill, 1994.

Berton, Pierre. *The Klondike Fever: The Life and Death of the Last Great Gold Rush*. New York: MJF Books, 1958.

Bierman, Harold, Jr. *The Causes of the 1929 Stock Market Crash*. Westport, CT: Greenwood Press, 1998.

Black, Gregory D. *Hollywood Censored: Morality Codes, Catholics, and the Movies*. Cambridge: Cambridge University Press, 1994.

Bragg, L.E. *More Than Petticoats: Remarkable Washington Women*. Guilford, CT: Globe Pequot Press, 1999.

Brendon, Piers. *The Life and Death of the Press Barons*. New York: Athenaeum, 1983.

Brennan, T. Ann. *The Real Klondike Kate*. Fredericton, Canada: Goose Lane Editions, 1990.

Brown, Dorothy M. *Setting a Course: American Women in the 1920s*. Boston: Twayne, 1987.

Burke, James. *Connections*. Boston: Little, Brown, 1978.

Campbell, W. Joseph. "Not a Hoax: New Evidence in the *New York Journal's* Rescue of Evangelina Cisneros." *American Journalism*, 19 (2002).

Campbell, W. Joseph. *The Year That Defined American Journalism: 1897 and the Clash of Paradigms*. New York: Routledge, 2006.

Carlson, Oliver, and Ernest Sutherland Bates. *Hearst: Lord of San Simeon*. New York: Viking Press, 1936.

Chaney, Lindsay, and Michael Cieply. *The Hearsts: Family and Empire: The Later Years*. New York: Simon & Schuster, 1981.

Chatziioannou, Maria Christina. "Greek Merchants in Victorian England." In *Greek Diaspora and Migration Since*

1700, Dimitris Tziovas, ed. Surrey, UK: Ashgate, 2009.

Coblentz, Edmond D. *William Randolph Hearst: A Portrait in His Own Words*. New York: Simon & Schuster, 1952.

Cohen, Stan. *The Streets Were Paved with Gold*. Missoula, MT: Pictorial Histories Publishing, 2005.

Crane, Warren Eugene. "Alexander Pantages." *System: The Magazine of Business* (March 1920).

Crowley, David, and David Heyer, eds. *Communication in History*. Boston: Allyn & Bacon, 2007.

Cullen, Frank, with Florence Hackman and Donald McNeilly. *Vaudeville, Old and New: An Encyclopedia of Variety Performers in America*. New York: Routledge, 2007.

Curti, Carlo. *Skouras: King of Fox Studios*. Los Angeles: Holloway House, 1967.

Czitrom, Daniel. "Early Motion Pictures" In *Communication in History*, David Crowley and David Heyer, eds. Boston: Allyn & Bacon, 2007.

Daniels, Roger. *Coming to America: A History of Immigration and Ethnicity in American Life*. New York: Perennial, 2002.

Daniels, Roger. *The Politics of Prejudice*. New York: Atheneum, 1970.

Danz, Carolee, with David Wilma. *100 Sterling Years*. Bothell, WA: Book Publishers Network, 2011.

Davies, Marion. *The Times We Had: Life with William Randolph Hearst*. Indianapolis, IN: Bobbs-Merrill, 1975.

Dobson, John. *Bulls, Bears, Boom, and Bust: A Historical Encyclopedia of American Business Concepts*. Santa Barbara, CA: ABC-CLIO, 2007.

Dumond, Val, and Babe Lehrer. *Mush On and Smile*. Tacoma, WA: Muddy Puddle Press, 2002.

Edmonds, Andy. "Showstopper." *Los Angeles Magazine*, December 1989.

Elliott, Eugene Clinton. *A History of Variety-Vaudeville in Seattle: From the Beginning to 1914*. Seattle: University of Washington Press, 1944.

Erler, Edward J., Thomas G. West, and John Marini. *The Founders on Citizenship and Immigration: Principles and Challenges in America*. Lanham, MD: Rowman & Littlefield, 2007.

Ethington, Philip J. *The Public City: The Political Construction of Urban Life in San Francisco, 1850–1900*. Cambridge, UK: Cambridge University Press, 1994.

Fellow, Andre R. *American Media History*. Belmont, CA: 2005: Thomson Wadsworth, 2005.

Fernett, Gene. *American Film Studios: An Historical Encyclopedia*. Jefferson, NC: McFarland, 2002.

Franklin, Harold B. *Motion Picture Theater Management*. New York: George H. Doran Co., 1927.

Fuller, Kathryn H. *At the Picture Show*. Washington, D.C.: Smithsonian Institution Press, 1996.

Garrison, Ervan. *A History of Engineering and Technology: Artful Methods*. Boca Raton, FL: CRC Press, 1991.

Georgakas, Dan. "Greek-American Radicalism: The Twentieth Century." *Journal of Hellenic Diaspora* 20, No. 1 (1994).

Giesler, Jerry, and Pete Martin. *The Jerry Giesler Story*. New York: Simon & Schuster, 1960.

Gill, Mark Sumner. "'Fighting Bob' Shuler: Fundamentalist and Reformer." PhD diss., The Claremont Graduate School, 1988.

Gold, Martin B. *Forbidden Citizens: Chinese Exclusion and the U.S. Congress: A Legislative History*. Alexandria, VA: The Capitol.Net, 2012.

Harrigan, Austin, and J.T. Hughes. *Competition for the Best True Stories of Life and Work on the Isthmus of Panama During the Construction of the Panama Canal*. Balboa, Panama: Isthmian Historical Society, 1963.

Hearst, William Randolph, Jr., with Jack Casserly. *The Hearsts: Father and Son*. Niwot, CO: Roberts Rinehart Publishers, 1991.

Higham, John. *Strangers in the Land: Patterns of American Nativism 1860–1925*. New Brunswick, NJ: Rutgers University Press, 1955.

Hoganson, Kristin L. *Fighting for American Manhood: How Gender Politics Provoked the Spanish-American and*

Philippine-American Wars. New Haven, CT: Yale University Press, 1998.

Hughes, Helen MacGill. *News and the Human Interest Story.* Chicago: University of Chicago Press, 1940.

Hunt, Rockwell D. ed. *California and Californians.* San Francisco: Lewis Publishing, 1932.

Huntzicker, William E. "Sex, Six, and Sensation: Two Major Crime Stories in Antebellum New York." In *Sensationalism: Murder, Mayhem, Mudslinging, Scandals, and Disasters in 19th Century Reporting,* David B. Sachsman and David W. Bulla, eds. New Brunswick, NJ: Transaction Publishers, 2013.

Jacobson, Matthew Frye. *Whiteness of a Different Color: European Immigrants and the Alchemy of Race.* Cambridge, MA: Harvard University Press, 1999.

Karabell, Zachary. *Parting the Desert: The Creation of the Suez Canal.* New York: Alfred A. Knopf, 2003.

Karampetsos, E.D. "Nativism in Nevada: Greek Immigrants in White Pine County." *Journal of the Hellenic Diaspora* 24 (1998).

Kennedy, Rose Fitzgerald. *Times to Remember.* Garden City, NY: Doubleday, 1974.

Kessler-Harris, Alice. *In Pursuit of Equity: Women, Men, and the Quest for Economic Citizenship in 20th-Century America.* Oxford, UK: Oxford University Press, 2001.

Kessler, Ronald. *The Sins of the Father: Joseph P. Kennedy and the Dynasty He Founded.* New York: Warner Books, 1996.

Klein, Maury. *Rainbow's End: The Crash of 1929.* New York: Oxford University Press, 2001.

Klein, Maury. *The Crash of 1929.* New York: Oxford University Press, 2001.

Koskoff, David E. *Joseph P. Kennedy: A Life and Times.* Englewood Cliffs, NJ: Prentice-Hall, 1974.

Koumoulides, John A., ed. *Greece: The Legacy: Essays on the History of Greece, Ancient, Byzantine, and Modern.* Bethesda: University Press of Maryland, 1998.

Lagos, Taso G. "Film Exhibition in Seattle, 1897–1912: Leisure Activity in a Scraggly, Smelly Frontier Town." *Historical Journal of Film, Radio and Television* 23, No. 2 (2003).

Lagos, Taso G. "Poor Greek to 'Scandalous' Hollywood Mogul: Alexander Pantages and the Anti-Immigrant Narratives of William Randolph Hearst's *Los Angeles Examiner.*" *Journal of Modern Greek Studies* 30 (May 2012).

Leamer, Laurence. *The Kennedy Men.* New York: William Morrow, 2001.

Lee, Erika. "A Nation of Immigrants and a Gatekeeping Nation: American Immigration Law and Policy." In *A Companion to American Immigration,* Reed Ueda, ed. Malden, MA: Blackwell, 2006.

Legg, Keith R., and John M. Roberts. *Modern Greece: A Civilization on the Periphery.* Boulder, CO: Westview Press, 1997.

Littlefield, Roy Everett III. *William Randolph Hearst: His Role in American Progressivism.* Lanham, MD: University Press of America, 1980.

Littlepage, Dean. *Gold Fever in the North: The Alaska-Yukon Gold Rush Era.* Anchorage, AK: Anchorage Museum of History and Art & Municipality of Anchorage, 1997.

Lucia, Ellis. *Klondike Kate: The Life & Legend of Kitty Rockwell, the Queen of the Yukon.* New York: Hastings House, 1962.

Lundberg, Ferdinand. *Imperial Hearst: A Social Biography.* New York: Equinox Cooperative Press, 1936.

McCullough, David. *The Path Between the Seas: The Creation of the Panama Canal, 1870–1914.* New York: Simon & Schuster, 1977.

Merritt, Greg. *Room 1219: The Life of Fatty Arbuckle, the Mysterious Death of Virginia Rappe, and the Scandal That Changed Hollywood.* Chicago: Chicago Review Press, 2013.

Miner, Dwight Carroll. *The Fight for the Panama Route.* New York: Octagon Books, 1971.

Mootafes, Dorothea, Theodora Dracopoulos Argue, Paul Plumis, Perry Scarlatos, and Peggy Falangus Tramountanas, eds. *A History of Saint Demetrios Greek Orthodox Church* and Her People, 1882–1999. Seattle: Saint Demetrios Greek Orthodox Church, 2007.

Morgan, Edmund S. *The Genuine Article: A Historian Looks at Early America.* New York: W.W. Norton, 2004.

Morgan, Lael. *Good Time Girls of the Alaska-Yukon Gold Rush.* Fairbanks, AK: Epicenter Press, 1998.

Morgan, Murray. *Skid Road: An Informal Portrait of Seattle.* Seattle: University of Washington Press, 1982.

Moskos, Charles. *Greek Americans: Struggle and Success.* New Brunswick, NJ: Transaction Publishers, 2002.

Murphy, Claire Rudolf, and Jane G. Haigh. *Gold Rush Women.* Anchorage, AK: Alaska Northwest Books, 1997.

Nasaw, David. *The Chief: The Life of William Randolph Hearst.* Boston: Houghton Mifflin, 2000.

Nasaw, David. *The Patriarch: The Remarkable Life and Turbulent Times of Joseph P. Kennedy.* New York: Penguin, 2012.

Norman, Marc. *What Happens Next: A History of American Screenwriting.* New York: Harmony Books, 2007.

Ochsner, Jeffrey Karl, ed. *Shaping Seattle Architecture: A Historical Guide to the Architects.* Seattle: University of Washington Press, 1994.

Older, Mrs. Fremont. *William Randolph Hearst: American.* New York: D. Appleton-Century Co., 1936.

Olneck, Michael R. "Americanization and the Education of Immigrants, 1900–1925: An Analysis of Symbolic Action." *American Journal of Education* 97 (August 1989).

Ostherr, Kirsten. *Cinematic Prophylaxis: Globalization and the Contagion in the Discourse of World Health.* Durham, NC: Duke University Press, 2005.

Overholser, Geneva, and Kathleen Hall Jamieson, eds. *The Press.* Oxford: Oxford University Press, 2005.

Papanikolas, Helen Z. "Magerou: The Greek Midwife." *Utah Historical Quarterly*, 38, No. 1 (Winter 1950).

Papanikolas, Helen Zeese. *Toil and Rage in a New Land: The Greek Immigrants in Utah.* Salt Lake City: Utah Historical Society, 1974.

Papanikolas, Zeese. *Buried Unsung.* Lincoln: University of Nebraska Press, 1991.

Parker, Matthew. *Panama Fever: The Epic Story of One of the Greatest Human Achievements of All Time—Building of the Panama Canal.* New York: Doubleday, 2007.

Parrish, Michael. "A Myth Maker's Clarification." *Los Angeles Times Magazine*, June 12, 2002.

Parrish, Michael. *For the People: Inside the Los Angeles County District Attorney's Office, 1850–2000.* Los Angeles: Angel City Press, 2001.

Peiss, Kathy. *Cheap Amusements: Working Women and Leisure in the Turn-of-the-Century New York.* Philadelphia: Temple University Press, 1986.

Pizzitola, Louis. *Hearst Over Hollywood.* New York: Columbia University Press, 2002.

Pleck, Joseph H. "American Fathering in Historical Perspective." In *Families in the U.S.: Kinship and Domestic Politics.* Philadelphia: Temple University Press, 1998.

Procter, Ben. *William Randolph Hearst: The Early Years, 1863–1910.* New York: Oxford University Press, 1998.

Puttnam, David. *Movies and Money.* New York: Alfred A. Knopf, 1998.

Ramsaye, Terry. *A Million and One Nights.* New York: Simon & Schuster, 1926.

Rauchway, Eric. "How 'America First' Got Its Nationalistic Edge." *Atlantic*, May 6, 2016. http://www.theatlantic.com/politics/archive/2016/05/william-randolph-hearst-gave-america-first-its-nationalist-edge/481497/.

Ray, Krishnendu. *The Ethnic Restaurateur.* London: Bloomsbury, 2016.

Robinson, Judith. *The Hearsts: An American Dynasty.* Newark, NJ: University of Delaware Press, 1991.

Rodman, George. *Mass Media in a Changing World: History, Industry, Controversy.* New York: McGraw-Hill, 2008.

Rosenzweig, Roy. *Eight Hours for What We Will: Workers and Leisure in an Industrial City, 1870–1920.* Cambridge: Cambridge University Press, 1983.

Sachsman, David B., ed. *A Press Divided:*

Newspaper Coverage of the Civil War. New Brunswick, NJ: Transaction Publishers, 2014.

Sachsman, David B., and David W. Bulla, eds. *Sensationalism: Murder, Mayhem, Mudslinging, Scandals, and Disasters in 19th Century Reporting.* New Brunswick, NJ: Transaction Publishers, 2013.

Saloutos, Theodore. "Alexander Pantages, Theater Magnate of the West." *Pacific Northwest Quarterly,* October 1966.

Saloutos, Theodore. *The Greeks in the United States.* Cambridge, MA: Harvard University Press, 1964.

Sandine, Al. *The Taming of the American Crowd.* New York: Monthly Review Press, 2009.

Schudson, Michael, and Susan E. Tifft. "American Journalism in Historical Perspective." In *The Press,* Geneva Overholser and Kathleen Hall Jamieson, eds. Oxford: Oxford University Press, 2005.

Scourby, Alice. *The Greek Americans.* Boston: Twayne, 1984.

Shuler, Robert. *"Fighting Bob" Shuler of Los Angeles.* Indianapolis, IN: Dog Ear Press, 2011.

Sklar, Robert. *Movie-Made America.* New York: Vintage, 1994.

Sowell, Thomas. *Race and Culture: A World View.* New York: Basic Books, 1994.

Sowell, Thomas. *Race and Economics.* New York: David McKay, 1975.

Stanley, William M. *A Mile of Gold: Strange Adventures on the Yukon.* Chicago: Laird & Lee, 1898.

Stover, Karla. *Tacoma Curiosities: Geoduck Derbies, the Whistling Well of the North End, Alligators in Snake Lake and More.* Charleston, SC: The History Press, 2016.

Suárez-Orozco, Carola. "Identities Under Siege: Immigration Stress and Social Mirroring among the Children of Immigrants." In *The New Immigration: An Interdisciplinary Reader,* ed. Marcelo M. Suárez-Orozco, Carola Suárez-Orozco, and Desiree Qin-Hilliard. New York: Routledge, 2005.

Suárez-Orozco, Marcelo M., Carola Suárez-Orozco, and Desiree Qin-Hilliard, eds. *The New Immigration: An Interdisciplinary Reader.* New York: Routledge, 2005.

Sutermeister, Mariam. "B. Marcus Priteca." In *Shaping Seattle Architecture: A Historical Guide to the Architects,* ed. Jeffrey Karl Ochsner. Seattle: University of Washington Press, 1994.

Swanberg, W.A. *Citizen Hearst: A Biography of William Randolph Hearst.* New York: Charles Scribner's Sons, 1961.

Tarrach, Dean Arthur. "Alexander Pantages: The Seattle Pantages and His Vaudeville Circuit." M.A. thesis: University of Washington, 1973.

Trav, S. *No Applause—Just Throw Money; or the Book That Made Vaudeville Famous.* New York: Faber & Faber, 2005.

Trentmann, Frank. *Empire of Things: How We Became a World of Consumers, from the Fifteenth Century to the Twenty-first.* London: Allen Lane, 2016.

Tygiel, Jules. *The Great Los Angeles Swindle.* New York: Oxford University Press, 1994.

Tygiel, Jules. *Workingmen in San Francisco, 1880–1901.* New York: Garland Publishing, 1992.

Tziovas, Dimitris, ed. *Greek Diaspora and Migration Since 1700.* Surrey, UK: Ashgate, 2009.

Ueda, Reed, ed. *A Companion to American Immigration.* Malden, MA: Blackwell, 2006.

Ueda, Reed. *Postwar Immigrant America.* Boston: Bedford Books, 1994.

Wagner, Megan A. "Spectacular Los Angeles Trials." *Los Angeles Lawyer,* March 2003.

Walker, Alexander. *Sex in the Movies: The Celluloid Sacrifice.* Baltimore: Penguin Books, 1966.

Walsh, John Evangelist. *Walking Shadows: Orson Welles, William Randolph Hearst, and* Citizen Kane. Madison: University of Wisconsin Press, 2004.

Wharton, David B. *The Alaska Gold Rush.* Bloomington: Indiana University Press, 1972.

Whyte, Kenneth. *The Uncrowned King: The Sensational Rise of William Randolph Hearst.* Berkeley, CA: Counterpoint, 2009.

Wilson, Victoria. *A Life of Barbara Stanwyck*. New York: Simon & Schuster, 2013.

Winkler, John K. *William Randolph Hearst: A New Appraisal*. New York: Hastings House, 1955.

Wolf, Marvin J., and Katherine Mader. *Fallen Angels: Chronicles of L.A. Crime and Mystery*. New York: Facts on File, 1986.

Wolin, Sheldon S. *Democracy, Inc.: Managed Democracy and the Specter of Inverted Totalitarianism*. Princeton, NJ: Princeton University Press, 2008.

Yallop, David A. *The Day the Laughter Stopped: The True Story of Fatty Arbuckle*. New York: St. Martin's Press, 1976.

Yergin, Daniel. *The Prize: The Epic Quest for Oil, Money and Power*. London: Free Press, 2009.

Newspapers

Film Daily
Los Angeles Examiner
Los Angeles Times
New York Journal
New York Times
New York World
San Francisco Chronicle
San Francisco Examiner
Seattle Post-Intelligencer
Seattle Times
Variety
Washington Post

Index

Numbers in bold italics indicate pages with illustrations

Academy Awards 1, *8*
Adams, Evangeline 123
Aegean Sea (Greece) 16
Agua Priesta (Mexico) 103
Alaska (state) 36–37, 40, 58, 59
Alaska-Yukon Gold Rush 1, 33, 36, 37, 52, 55, 60, 63
Alaska-Yukon Pacific Exposition 68
Albee, Edward 116, 153
American Dream 1, 109
American Newspaper Publisher's Association 161
American Revolution 84
Anagnostou, Yiorgos 1
Andros (Greece) 3, 9, 16, 17, 18, 19, 34, 178
Angelus Temple 102
Anger, Kenneth 169
Anopheles mosquito 22–23
Anti-Catholic Association 112
Anti-immigrant sentiment, United States 5, 9, 10
Arbuckle, Roscoe "Fatty": alcohol consumption 89, 90, 94, 86; automobile collection 87; birth 88; hotel party 90–91, 92, 96; manslaughter case 91, 127; movie career 87, 88; newspaper coverage of 91–94; residences 89; trials 1, 97, 98, *99*, 100, 115, 133, 143–45, 161
Arkansas 148
Associated Press 142
Athens (Greece) 9, 18
August 9, 1929 16, 17, 159, 167, 170
Automobile Club of Southern California 126

Babson, Roger 123
Balaban, Abraham Joseph 153
Balaban Brothers 5
Bank of England 143
Bara, Theda 10, 87
Battle of Argonne 141
Beatty, Dr. Hannah 136
Beauchamp, Cari 115
Belasco, David 26

Bernhardt, Sarah 30, 64
Bible 44, 84
Bible Institute 175
Biffle, Garland 148, 157
Birmingham (Alabama) 106
Birth of a Nation 75
Black Thursday 151–52; see also New York Stock Exchange
Blake, Alice 89
Blank, Dr. Benjamin 6
Blue Laws 10, 84–85
Bolero 54
Boston (Massachusetts) 42, 113–14, 116
Brady, District Attorney Matthew 98, 100
British colonialism 112
Broadway Pantages Theater 68, 103
Brooklyn Bridge 20–21
Brown, Sam 27
Bryan, William Jennings 34, 61
Bucharest (Romania) 88

Cairo (Egypt) 18, 19, 32, 73, 101, 177
Calgary (Canada) 105
California 126, 141, 144, 148, 167, 177
California Gold Rush 35
California Highway 101 88; see also El Camino Real
California State Supreme Court 6, 159–60
Camp Fire Girls 129
Canada 152
Canadian Northwest Mounted Police ("Mounties") 40–41, 49, 51
Cantor, Eddie 6
Capone, Al 175
Carmel (California) 103
Catalina Island (California) 88
Catholics 111–13
Chagres River (Panama) 22
Chaplin, Charlie 123, 127
Chatziioannou, Maria Christina 9
Chicago (Illinois) 8, 67, 70, 77, 106, 108, 153
Chicago Tribune 142
Chile 51
Chilkoot Pass (Alaska) 38

209

China 102, 126
Chinatown (San Francisco) 25, 30
Christian Science 169
Christianity 125
Cincinnati (Ohio) 87
Clark, Kenneth 62
Clemmer, James Q. 69
Clemmer Theater 69
Cleveland, Grover 28
Cole, Charlie 49
Colorado Fuel and Iron Company 74
Columbia Trust Bank 41, 114
Communist Party, United States 75
Considine, John W. 64–65, 68, 78, 149; rivalry with Pantages 64–65
Considine, John, Jr. 78, 104, 171, 178
Coolidge, President Calvin 102
Cooper & Levi 60; see also Levy, Eugene
Coughlin, Father Charles 125
Coxey's Army 34
Crafts, Dr. Wilbur 85
Crawford, Joan 2
Croesus 148
Crystal Theater 57, 58, 61, 63, 79; dimensions 60; films shown 65–66; location in Seattle 60; remodel 65; as storefront 60; "vaude-film" 60
Cuba 43–48, 91
Cuba libre campaign 43, 44
Cullen, Frank 53
Culture wars 83–85

Daniels, Roger 72, 73
Davies, Marion 14–15, 104, 171, 178
Dawson City (Canada) 33, 35–36, 39–40, 48–49, 51–52, 56, 59; Charlie Cole's Saloon 49; Cole's Opera House 50; colorful characters 50; dance halls 54; Savoy Theatrical Company 51
Dawson Daily News 50
Day, Olive Clark 172
Decker, Karl 46
Delaware 122
de Lesseps, Ferdinand 18, 20, 21
Delmont, Maude 89, 90, 97
Dempsey, Jack 106
"Devil's Church" 85; see also Motion Picture Industry, United States
Deyo, Solita 128, 130, 143; see also Pringle, Eunice Alice
Dickens, Charles 44
Dietrich, Marlene **82**
Dow Jones Industrial Average 123, 152
Dream Theater 69
Dunaev, Nicholas A. 129–30, 135, 146, 148, 155–58, 163–65, 167–69, 176
Dunganstown, County Wexford, Ireland 112
Durfee, Minta 88, 94, 95
Dust Bowl 161
Dyea (Alaska) 37–38

East Boston (Massachusetts) 41, 111–12
Eastern Europe 85
Edison, Thomas Alva 15, 61, 63, 78
Edison's Unique Theater 61
Edmonds, Andy 169
Edmonson, Earl 168
Edmonton (Canada) 7
El Camino Real 88; see also California Highway
El Cortez Hotel 172
Ellis Island (New York) 40
Empire Theater 66
England 152
Eunice Pringle 127
Europe 171
Excelsior 32, 35, 36

Fairbanks, Douglas 32
Fairchild, Policewoman 144–45
Fallen Angels: Chronicles of Los Angeles Crime and Mystery 169
Federal Radio Commission 127
Federal Reserve 122–23, 151
Fernadez, Amado 137
Fernbach, Oscar H. 97, 98
Film Booking Office (FBO) 116
Film Daily 117, 118
Financial panic of 1907 78
Fishback, Fred 88
Fitts, District Attorney Buron 124, 137, 141, 144, 147–48, 150, 155, 157, 172, 174, 176
Florida 43, 77
Ford, W. Joseph **134**
Forth Worth (Texas) 106
Fortlouis, Ira 89
Fox, William 5, 85
Fox (20th Century) film studios 85, 87, 118
Fox West Coast Theaters 167
France 146, 152
Free Public Library 47
Fresno Pantages Theater 130
Fricke, Superior Court Judge Charles W. 128, 145, 148, 150, 154, 158

Garden Grove (California) 129, 163
Garden Grove High School 135
Gasoline Gus 88
Giesler, Jerry 81, 110, 146–48, 150, 154–56, 158–59, 163–68, 172
Glasgow (Scotland) 68
Graf Zeppelin 133
Grauman, Sid 5, 119
Grauman's Chinese Theater 5, 119
Great Depression 1, 71, 73, 161, 176
Great Panic of 1893 34
Greece 3, 17, 18, 34, 79, 101, 104, 176
Greek American Political Club 79
Greek Americans in film exhibition 7
Greek Club 79
Greek Immigrants 9, 74, 77, 83, 164, 177,

Index   211

178; habits of 74; nativist antagonism 75, 76; radicalism 75; *see also* New Immigrants
Greek Orthodox Church 18, 77, 79, 104
Griffith, D.W. 75

Haines (Alaska) 38
Harding, President Warren G. 98
Harvard Lampoon 28
Harvard University 27, 28, 113–14, 115
Hasty Pudding Club 28
Havana (Cuba) 46, 47
Hawaii 48
Hayes, Will 98, 115
Hearst, George 27
Hearst, Phoebe 27, 43, 47
Hearst, William Randolph: "America First" 13; antics 27, 48; anti-feminism 14; and Arbuckle manslaughter case 88, 91, 100, 95; competition with Joseph Pulitzer 44; Cuba visit 47–48; and immigration 30; journalism style 14, 29, 31, 43, 45, 47, **105**, 128, 176, 133; nationalist philosophy 13; newspaper publisher 3, 43, 143, 161; and Pantages family 104, 171, 178; personality 46, 115; press attack on Pantages 12, 100; social influence 12, 144; Spanish-American War 42; start of press career 12–13
Herald Square (New York) 62
Heyden, Stone & Company 114
Hofstadter, Richard 73
Hollywood (California) 87, 91, 129, 171
Hollywood Babylon II 12, 169
Hollywood Pantages Theater 1, *2*, 6, 71, 85, 106, 108, 120, 159, 167, 177; stars at grand opening 1
Hungary 85

"Ideal ethnic" 76
Immigrants Restriction League 112
Immigration, United States 9, 13, 30, 72–75
Immigration Act of 1917 73
Inaugural movie screening, United States 61; *see also* Koster & Bial's Music Hall
Industrial Revolution 10, 83
Industrial Workers of the World ("Wobblies") 75
Influenza epidemic of 1918–19 78
"Introvert communities" 9
Irish immigration 112

Jacobson, Matthew Frye 76
Jeffries, Jim 61
Jews 113
Jews in Hollywood 5, 9, 85, 126, 139, 153
Jobelmann, William 172
The Journalist 47
Juneau (Alaska) 38
Justice, Dr. O.M. 109

Kafenia 74
Kansas 88
Kansas City (Missouri) 66, 106
Kansas City Pantages Theater 155
Keane, Roy 142
Kearney, Dennis 25
Keaton, Buster 88
Keith-Albee-Orpheum (KAO) Theaters 116
Kennedy, Joseph P.: alleged conspiracy 2, 12, 167–69, 111, 176; biography of 41, 111–13, 169; Boston Latin School 41; East Boston home 41; entrepreneurial spirit 41, 113; grandfather 112; Irish Catholics 42; movie industry involvement 115, 118–119, *120*, 153, 167; movie theaters 114, 116
Kennedy, Mary 42
Kennedy, P.J. 41, 111–12, 114
Kennedy, Ted 42
Kerasotes, Gus 7
Kessler, Ronald 117, 169
Kessler-Harris, Alice 14
Ketchikan (Alaska) 38
Keyes, Asa 141
Klein, Maury 122, 151–52
Klondicitis 33, 35
Klondike (Canada) 33, 34, 36, 40, 51, 52, 60
Know Nothing party 72
Koskoff, David E. 116
Koster & Bial's Music Hall 61, 62–63
Ku Klux Klan 127

La Petite Theater 61
Lake Bennett (Canada) 39, 40, 49
Lake Lindeman (Canada) 38
Lampmann, Dell 62
Lang, Harry 125, 127, 137, 139, 146, 150
Lasky, Jesse *120*
Lawler, Anne 116
Lazarus, Judge Sylvain 96
Leisure activities in the United States 83–84
Leonard, Eddie 130
Levy, Eugene 60
Lewis, Sinclair 175
Liverpool 112
Loew, Marcus 78, 115
Lois Theater 66
Los Angeles (California) 1, 6, 7–8, 66, 68, 80, 88, 94, 96, 100–01, 103, 105–06, 108, 117, 126, 130, 141, 155, 159, 161, 168–69, 171–72, 178
Los Angeles County 141
Los Angeles County District Attorney's Office 169, 174
Los Angeles County Health Department 127
Los Angeles County Jail 1, 71, 154
Los Angeles County Superior Court 10, 155, 158
Los Angeles Examiner 11, 14, 83, 125, 130,

132–34, 135–39, 140, 142–45, 146–47, 149–50, 155, 157
Los Angeles Magazine 169
Los Angeles Pantages Theater 71, *81*, 101, 117, 120, 130, 137, 159
Los Angeles Police Department 126–27, 132, 149
Los Angeles Public Library 126
Los Angeles Times 1, 10, 101–03, 106, 125, 142, 155, 158, 163, 165, 167, 169, 170, 175, 177
Louisiana 77
Loveless, Arthur Lamont 79
Lucia, Ellis 52
Ludlow (Colorado) 77
Lumiére projector 63

Mader, Katherine 169
USS *Maine* 47
Martin, Dixie 79, 150, *166*
Marysville (California) 129
McKinley, President William 47
McPherson, Aimée Semple 10, 102–03, 105, 125, 127
Mediterranean Sea 177
Mellon, Andrew 123
Melody Lane 130
Memphis (Tennessee) 66, 106
Merritt, Greg 88
Methodist Church 129
Mexico 81
Meyer, Walter 25–26
Middle Ages 53
Middle East 87
Million Dollar Theater 88
Millionaires and Hired Girls 127
Miltiades-Miller, Luca 77
Minneapolis (Minnesota) 105
Minority groups, United States 4
Monopolistic practices, movie industry 6; see also Vertical integration, movie industry
Moonbeam Glen Bungalow Court Apartments 165
Motion picture exhibition 60, 62–63
Motion picture industry, United States (Hollywood) 60, 80, 85, 86, 91, 92, 103, 111, 115, 117, 135, 145–46, 164, 167–69, 175–76; censorship codes 85; and immigrants 72; see also Culture wars; Relationship of film to human health 86
Murdock, J.J. 118

New England 77, 114
"New Immigrants" 9, 72–73, 75, 76, 83, 90
New Orleans (Louisiana) 106
New York (New York) 8, 20–21, 51, 57, 61, 63, 67, 70, 101, 106, 108, 129, 142
New York Journal 43, 44, 46, 47
New York Life Insurance Company 78

New York Stock Exchange 1, 110, 122–23, 151–52
New York Times 62, 118, 120, 142
New York World 28, 43, 44, 46–48
Newark (New Jersey) 47
Nitto, Lydia 173–75
Nome (Alaska) 57
Noodles Island 112
Norman, Marc 29, 43
North America 112

Oakland (California) 105, 177
"Old Immigrants" 9, 72–74, 75
Oregon 59
Orpheum Theater 55, 57, 155
Orthodox Jews 113
Ottoman Empire 18

Palace Hotel 93
Pan-Islam nationalism 19
Panama 20, 34, 59
Panama Canal 20–23; American development 22, 23; French development 20–23; politics of 22
Pantages, Alexander: actor contracts 8, 67; ambition 16, 18, 19, 20, 25–26, 32, 33, 68, 106; and American experience 16, 39; birth 9, 17, 79; business practices 17, 55, 69, 106, 107, 108; child with Rockwell 57; cultural biography 3; death 17, 178; drug arrest 27; and Greek American community 79, 104, 105; family 19, 124; infidelities 81, 83, 109–10; :Hollywood Love Market" case 172, 175; illiteracy 2, 8, 149; *immigrant-ness* 2, 4, 7, 40, 178; ingenuity 40; Jim Crow seating in theaters 70, 80; Kennedy conspiracy 117; lawsuits 70–71, 80; malaria 23–24; menial jobs 20, 26, 49, 50; *model ethnic* 5; movie theater development 2, 7, 68, 70, 104; nervous breakdown 80; nicknames 102, 107, 108, 118, 148; as *Pantazis* 9, 18; personality 23, 79, 80, 168, 173; physical aspects 151; press coverage of, 12, 125, 127, 136–39, *140*, 143, 146, 154, *160*, *166*; prisoner 72, 151, 154–55, 158, 170; recreation 79; relationship with Kate Rockwell 51–53, 57; resident homes 79, 104; retirement 171–72, *174*; runaway 19–20; sexual assault 1, 5, 81, 127, 130–32, *133*, 134–5, 167, 169, 170, 176; sexual assault trials 1, 12, 15, 141–2, 144, 146, 148–50, 152; 156–57, 159–160, 161–65, 166–68, 177; travels 18, 19–20, 20–21, 23, 24–25, 36, 38–40, 42, 48–49, 56, 111; vaudeville acts tours 67; work ethic 102, 103
Pantages, Carmen 71, 78, 79, 80, 125, 150, 159, *160*, 161, *162*, *166*, 171, 178
Pantages, Lloyd 6, 79, 80, *82*, 124, 150, 159, *160*, *166*, 170

Pantages (Mendenhall), Lois 55, 58, 78, 108, 124–5, 159, *160*, 161, *162*, *166*, 167, 170, 173, *174*, 177–78; and alcohol 124l divorce preparations 83; hospitalization 124; manslaughter 83, 102, 124; manslaughter trial 127, 141, 154, 156, 158
Pantages, Mrs. Rodney *166*
Pantages, Rodney 6, 17–18, 78–79, 118, 150, 159, 163, *166*, 170–71
Pantages Greek style 70
Pantages Theater circuit 2, 66, 78, 80, 101, 105–06, 118–119, 144
Paramount film studios 85, 88, *120*, 153
Paris 21
Parrish, Michael 169
Passion of Joan of Arc 146
Pathé 119
Payne Fund Studies 5, 10
Petersburg (Alaska) 38
La Petite Theater 61
Philadelphia (Pennsylvania) 75
Philadelphia Gear Works 84
Philippines 48
Pickford, Mary 123
Polk's Directory 65, 69
Portland 34, 35, 36, 51
Portland (Oregon) 105
Portland Pantages Theater 121
Postwar Immigrant America 9
Potato Famine 112
Presbyterian Church 126
Prevost, Zey 90, 97
The Prince from Hollywood 129, 149
Pringle, Dr. Earl 135–37, *138*, 144
Pringle, Eunice Alice: ambition 135; birth 129; civil lawsuit 157; early life 129; Kennedy conspiracy 12, 167; Pantages conviction 1; as protagonist in press narrative 14, 136–37, *138*, 139; relationship with Dunaev 130; sexual assault case 3, 131–32, 135, 143–45, 146–49, 150, 155–56, 159, 161, 164–65, 167–69, 172–73, 176
Pringle, Irene 136–37, *138*, 144, 146, 163
Priteca, B. Marcus: 7, 68–71, 104, 177
Procter, Ben 128
Proctor, F.F. 119
Prohibition 86, 89
Prostitution 52
Protestants 112–13, 126
Publick Occurrences 3
Publix Theater company 120
Puget Sound (Washington) 35, 59
Pulitzer, Joseph 28, 43–44, 47–48
Pullen, Harriet "Ma" 39

Queen Kelly 117

Rainbow's End: The Crash of 1929 151
Rappe, Virginia 4, 89, 90, 92–93, 94–95, 96, 97, 98, 100, 143

Ravel, Maurice 54
Recojidas prison 46
RKO film studios 2, 105, 116–20, 124, 168
Rockefeller, John D. 5
Rockwell, Kathleen Eloise ("Klondike Kate") 34, 50–53, 54, 55, 56, 58–59, 78, 80, 155–56, 173, 177; and alcohol 51, 55; breach of promise lawsuit 58–59; financial assistance to Pantages 57, 80; *Flame Dance* 54; movie theater 56, 61
Roebling brothers 20–21
Rogers, Harry 171
Rokumoto, Juro 124, 145
Rokumoto, Karuko 125, 127
Roosevelt, President Franklin D. 114–15, 176
Roosevelt, Theodore (Teddy) 61
Rosie the Riveter 86
Russia 126
Russian Revolution of 1917 75
Ryan, Katherine (Kate) 52, 58

Saint Demetrios Greek Orthodox Church 79
St. Francis Hotel 89
St. Michael (Alaska) 35
Saloutos, Theodore 7, 19
Salt Lake City (Utah) 66, 104, 105, 171
Salt Lake City Pantages Theater 120
San Diego (California) 105, 169, 172–73, 175
San Diego Pantages Theater 121
San Francisco (California) 4, 7, 24–25, 34, 35, 37, 40, 59, 60, 77, 87, 89, 96, 100, 105, 177; boxing matches 27; City Receiving Hospital 30; Earthquake 66; as Las Vegas 87; theater scene 26
San Francisco Chronicle 11, 13, 74, 149, 157, 161
San Francisco Examiner 12–13, 27, 28–30, 31, 33, 43, 91, 92–94, 95, 96, 97, 98; famous personalities on staff 29, 30; *see also* Hearst, William Randolph
San Francisco Pantages Theater 69, 83, 120
San Quentin (California) 1, 127, 150, 154, 172
San Simeon (California) 32, 104
Sanai (Egypt) 20, 21
Santa Ana (California) 110
Santa Anita Racetrack 171
Saskatoon (Canada) 66
Saturday Evening Post 73
Screen Writers Guild 96
Seattle (Washington) 24, 34, 35, 37, 38, 51, 56, 57, 59–60, 64, 66, 69, 78, 79, 104, 105, 108, 168, 171, 177; Concordia Club 61; Denny Hill Regrade 65; Electric Car Line 66; ethnic makeup 59; growth 59, 63–64; motion picture theaters 65, 69; "Movie Town, U.S.A." 61; Plymouth Congregational Church 66; railroads 59; "Tender-

loin" district 64; theater scene 61; saloons 61; worker crews 59
Seattle Pantages Theater **67** 70, 84
Seattle Post-Intelligencer 38
Seattle Times 11, 36, 38, 55, 58, 135, 177
Securities & Exchange Commission 114, 176
Semnacher, Alfred 89, 90
Sex in the Movies 86
Sexual mores, United States 86
Shakespeare, William 44, 53
Sherman, Lowell 88–90
Shuler, Rev. Robert "Fighting Bob" 92, 102, 103, 125, 127; *Eunice Pringle* 127; *Millionaires and Hired Girls* 127
Skagway (Alaska) 37, 38–40, 48
Sklar, Robert 86
Skouras, Spyros 7
Sloan, Sally Chandler 63
Smith, "Mysterious" Billy 26–27
Southern California 80, 104, 172
Southern Methodist Church 125–26
Southern Pacific Railroad 30
Spain 43, 44, 45, 46, 47, 48
Spanish-American War 47, 76
Spokane (Washington) 50, 104, 105
Spokane Pantages Theater 121
Steuer, Max 142
Steward, Chief Deputy D.A. Robert P 142, 150
Stock Market crash 1; *see also* New York Stock Exchange
The Story of the Films 116
Strong, Benjamin 122
Suez Canal 18, 20–21
Sunday, Billy 125, 175
Sunset Boulevard (Los Angeles) 124
Suratt, Valeska 87; *see also* vamp actors
Swanson, Gloria 117, 168

Tabloidization of news 12
Tacoma (Washington) 105
Tacoma Pantages Theater 121
Tappan, Superior Court Judge Clair S. 162
Tarrach, Dean Arthur 110
Taube, Mae 90, 94
Taylor, William Desmond 98, 115
Tennessee 126
Texas 57, 58
Thanksgiving 165–66
Thermopolis (Wyoming) 96
Toronto (Canada) 106
Trinity Methodist Church 126
Twentieth Century Film Studios 7

Ueda, Reed 9
United Artists film studios 117
United States Congress 44, 47
United States Embassy, Havana, Cuba 46, 48
United States House of Representatives 77

United States Supreme Court 6
University of Southern California 129, 135
Uplifters Club 129

Valentino, Rudolph 87
Vamp actors 10, 87; *see also* Bara, Theda
Vamp films 86
Vancouver Pantages Theater 71
Vancouver (Canada) 105
Variety (Daily) 105, 106, 107, 108, 118, 119, 151, 153–54, 170, 171
Vaude-film 60, 153
Vaudeville 53–54, 80, 111, 153; and bigotry 54; democratic art-form 53; development in the U.S. 53; ethnicities in 53–54; gender diversity 53–54; global reach 53; as popular culture 53; and railroads 53; and telegraph 53
Vaudeville Managers' Protective Association (Vaudeville Managers Association) 108
Venice Beach (California) 103
Verdi's *Aida* 21
Vertical integration, movie industry 6
Victoria (Canada) 56, 105
Vitascope Hall 63

Walker, Robert 86
Wall Street 114, 116, 121–3, 143, 151, 152; *see also* New York Stock Exchange
Washington 84
Washington, D.C. 34, 106
Washington Post 177
Watsonville (California) 88
Weyler y Nicolau, Gen. Valeriano 44, 45
White ethnicity 4, 76
White House 44, 47
White Pass Trail (Alaska) 36, 38, 39, 48
White Pine County (Nevada) 75
Whiteness of a Different Color 76
Wilde, Oscar 15
Wilson, President Woodrow 75
Winnipeg (Canada) 7, 105
Wise, Frederick T. 164
Wolf, Marvin J. 169
Woman's Vigilant Committee 95–96
Women's Rights 86; right to vote 86
Wood, Mayor W.D. 37–38
World War I 78, 86, 141
Worthingon, Marcy 169
Wrangell (Alaska) 38

y Cisneros, Evangelina Cosio 45–46, 47, 48
Yellow Journalism 47
YMCA 126
Yukon River (Canada) 36, 51, 52, 69
Yukon (Canada) 32–33, 36, 40–41, 49, 56, 59, 177

Zeus, Greek God of 15–16
Zukor, Adolph 85

www.ingramcontent.com/pod-product-compliance
Ingram Content Group UK Ltd.
Pitfield, Milton Keynes, MK11 3LW, UK
UKHW041954140426
5217IPUK00015B/789